CHOCTAW BY BLOOD

ENROLLMENT CARDS

1898-1914

VOLUME XVI

TRANSCRIBED BY

JEFF BOWEN

NATIVE STUDY
Gallipolis, Ohio
USA

Originally published:
Baltimore, Maryland
2017

Reprinted by:

Native Study LLC
Gallipolis, OH
www.nativestudy.com

Library of Congress Control Number: 2020911767

ISBN: 978-1-64968-019-8

Made in the United States of America.

This series is dedicated to
Mike Marchi,
who keeps my spirits up.

Other Books and Series by Jeff Bowen

1901-1907 Native American Census Seneca, Eastern Shawnee, Miami, Modoc, Ottawa, Peoria, Quapaw, and Wyandotte Indians (Under Seneca School, Indian Territory)

1932 Census of The Standing Rock Sioux Reservation with Births And Deaths 1924-1932

Census of The Blackfeet, Montana, 1897- 1901 Expanded Edition

Eastern Cherokee by Blood, 1906-1910, Volumes I thru XIII

Choctaw of Mississippi Indian Census 1929-1932 with Births and Deaths 1924-1931   Volume I

Choctaw of Mississippi Indian Census 1933, 1934 & 1937, Supplemental Rolls to 1934 & 1935 with Births and Deaths 1932-1938, and Marriages 1936-1938   Volume II

Eastern Cherokee Census Cherokee, North Carolina 1930-1939 Census 1930-1931 with Births And Deaths 1924-1931 Taken By Agent L. W. Page   Volume I

Eastern Cherokee Census Cherokee, North Carolina 1930-1939 Census 1932-1933 with Births And Deaths 1930-1932 Taken By Agent R. L. Spalsbury   Volume II

Eastern Cherokee Census Cherokee, North Carolina 1930-1939 Census 1934-1937 with Births and Deaths 1925-1938 and Marriages 1936 & 1938 Taken by Agents R. L. Spalsbury And Harold W. Foght Volume III

Seminole of Florida Indian Census, 1930-1940 with Birth and Death Records, 1930-1938

Texas Cherokees 1820-1839 A Document For Litigation 1921

Choctaw By Blood Enrollment Cards 1898-1914 Volumes I thru XV

Visit our website at **www.nativestudy.com** to learn more about these and other books and series by Jeff Bowen

CREEK CENSUS.

SECOND NOTICE.

Members of the Dawes Commission will be present at the following times and places for the purpose of enrolling Creek citizens, as required by Act of Congress of June 10, 1896:

At Muskogee, Nov. 8 to 30, 1897, inclusive.
At Wagoner, Nov. 8 to 13, " inclusive.
At Eufaula, Nov. 8 to 13, " inclusive.
At Sapulpa, Nov. 15 to 20, " inclusive.
At Wetumpka, Nov. 15 to 20, " inclusive.
At Okmulgee, Nov. 22 to 30, " inclusive.

All persons who have not heretofore enrolled before the Dawes Commission should appear and enroll. Parents and guardians can enroll their families and wards.

TAMS BIXBY,
FRANK C. ARMSTRONG,
A. S. McKENNON,
THOS. B. NEEDLES,
Commissioners.

The above illustration is similar in nature to what was found throughout Indian Territory for different tribes as far as postings on bulletin boards, public centers, or wherever they could be read so people would be notified of where and when they needed to be for enrollment with the Dawes Commission.

This is a picture of the Dawes Commission at Camp Jones in Stonewall, Indian Territory on September 8, 1898.

The images below are of two of the original cards given on the microfilm. The cards given in this book have been formatted to fit on one page and still give all the information found on the original cards.

Introduction

This series of Choctaw Enrollment Cards for the Five Civilized Tribes 1898-1914 has been transcribed from National Archive Film M-1186 Rolls 39-46.

The series contains more than 6100 Choctaw enrollment cards. All of the cards list age, sex and degree of blood, the parties' Dawes Roll Numbers, and date of enrollment by the Secretary of Interior for each person. The contents also give the enrollee's parents' names as well as miscellaneous notes pertaining to the enrollee's circumstances, when needed. Most entries indicate whether or not a spouse is an Intermarried White, with the initials I.W.

Enrollment wasn't as simple a process as most would think just by going through these pages. The relationships between the Five Tribes and the Dawes Commission were weak at best. There were political battles going on between the tribes and the U.S. Government as it was, but the struggles didn't stop there. Each tribe had its own political factions pulling it from every direction. On top of everything else, people from every corner of the United States were trying to figure how to get in on the spoils (Money and Land Allotment) by means of political favor. Kent Carter, author of *The Dawes Commission*, describes the continuous effort required to enroll the different tribes and the pressure the Commission incurred from people all over the country who tried to insinuate themselves into the equation:

"In May 1896 the Dawes Commission Returned To Indian Territory for its third visit, establishing its headquarters at Vinita in the Cherokee Nation. It now had to process applications for citizenship in addition to negotiating allotment agreements; these circumstances make the narrative of events more confusing because the commission attempted the two tasks concurrently. The commissioners resumed making their usual speeches to tribal officials and public gatherings to promote negotiations, but now they inevitably had to respond to questions about how the application process for citizenship would work. They also began receiving letters from people all over the United States asking how they could 'get on the rolls' so they could 'get Indian land'."[1]

For the actual process of Choctaw enrollment, "A commission was appointed in each county of the Choctaw Nation under an act of September 18 to make separate rolls of citizens by blood, by intermarriage, and freedmen; it was to deliver them to recently elected Chief Green McCurtain by October 20, but he rejected them even before they were completed because of charges that people were being left off for political reasons. On October 30, the National Council authorized establishment of a five-member

---

[1] *The Dawes Commission* by Kent Carter, page 15, para. 1

commission to revise the rolls within ten days and then directed McCurtain to turn them over to the Dawes Commission on November 11, 1896. The Choctaws hired the law firm of Stuart, Gordon, and Hailey, of South McAlester to represent the tribe at all proceedings held by the Dawes Commission,"[2] another indication that throughout the Commission's efforts there was always controversy between the tribes and the negotiators.

When completed, this multi-volume series will contain thousands of names, all of them accounted for in the indexes carefully prepared by the author. Hopefully this work will help many researchers find their ancestors and satisfy the questions that so many have had about their Native American heritage.

Jeff Bowen
Gallipolis, Ohio
NativeStudy.com

---

[2] *The Dawes Commission* by Kent Carter, page 16, para. 5

Choctaw By Blood Enrollment Cards 1898-1914

RESIDENCE:	Tobucksy	COUNTY.			
POST OFFICE:	McAlester, I.T.				

Choctaw Nation

Choctaw Roll (Not Including Freedmen)

CARD No.

FIELD No. **4501**

Dawes' Roll No.	NAME	Relationship to Person First Named	AGE	SEX	BLOOD	TRIBAL ENROLLMENT		
						Year	County	No.
14430	1 Waldron, Eddie 8	First Named	5	M	1/8			
14431	2 Williams, Alonzo D 5	Bro	1½	"	1/8			
	3							
	4							
	5							
	6							
	7	ENROLLMENT OF NOS. 1 and 2 HEREON APPROVED BY THE SECRETARY OF INTERIOR Apr 2, 1903						
	8							
	9							
	10							
	11							
	12							
	13							
	14							
	15							
	16							
	17							

TRIBAL ENROLLMENT OF PARENTS

	Name of Father	Year	County	Name of Mother	Year	County
1	George Waldron	Dead	Non Citz	Joanna Williams	Dead	Tobucksy
2	L. X. Williams		" "	" "	"	"
3						
4						
5						
6						
7	Further action in connection with allotment					
8	to No.1 and 2 suspended under protest					
9	of Choctaw and Chickasaw Nations Jan 23, 1904					
10	Protest overruled by Department March 31-04 No.1 admitted by Dawes Com, Case No 506 No appeal					
11	Mother of Nos 1&2 " " " " " " " "					
12	No.2 Affidavit of birth to be					
13	supplied. Filed Oct. 27/99					
14						
15				Date of Application for Enrollment	Sept 4/99	
16						
17						

1

Choctaw By Blood Enrollment Cards 1898-1914

| | RESIDENCE: Sans Bois COUNTY. | | POST OFFICE: Whitefield, I.T. | Choctaw Nation | | Choctaw Roll (Not Including Freedmen) | CARD NO. FIELD NO. 4502 | | |

Dawes' Roll No.	NAME		Relationship to Person	AGE	SEX	BLOOD	TRIBAL ENROLLMENT		
							Year	County	No.
12498	1 Surratt, Cooper	39	First Named	36	M	1/2	1896	Sans Bois	11108
	2								
	3								
	4								
	5								
	6								
	7								
	8								
	9								
	10								
	11								
	12								
	13								
	14								
	15	ENROLLMENT OF NOS. 1 HEREON APPROVED BY THE SECRETARY OF INTERIOR MAR 6 1903							
	16								
	17								

TRIBAL ENROLLMENT OF PARENTS

	Name of Father	Year	County	Name of Mother	Year	County
1	Henry Surratt		Non Citz	Lucy Surratt	Dead	Sans Bois
2						
3						
4						
5						
6						
7						
8						
9						
10						
11						
12						
13						
14						
15				DATE OF APPLICATION FOR ENROLLMENT.	Sept 4/99	
16						
17						

2

Choctaw By Blood Enrollment Cards 1898-1914

RESIDENCE:	Tobucksy	COUNTY.								
POST OFFICE:	Scipio, I.T.		Choctaw Nation				Choctaw Roll (Not Including Freedmen)		CARD No. FIELD No. 4503	

Dawes' Roll No.	NAME		Relationship to Person First Named	AGE	SEX	BLOOD	TRIBAL ENROLLMENT		
							Year	County	No.
DEAD.	1 Aduddell, Anna	DEAD.		21	F	1/2	1896	Tobucksy	4011
12499	2 Aduddell, Carl	4	Son	7mo	M	1/4			
I.W. 1134	3 " John L	28	Husband	28	M	I.W.			
	4 No. 1 HEREON DISMISSED UNDER								
	5 ORDER OF THE COMMISSION TO THE FIVE								
	CIVILIZED TRIBES OF MARCH 31, 1905.								
	6								
	7								
	8		ENROLLMENT	HEREON					
	9		OF NOS. 3						
	10		APPROVED BY THE SECRETARY OF INTERIOR NOV 16 1904						
	11								
	12								
	13		ENROLLMENT						
	14	OF NOS. 2	HEREON						
	15	APPROVED BY THE SECRETARY OF INTERIOR MAR 6 1903							
	16								
	17								

TRIBAL ENROLLMENT OF PARENTS

	Name of Father	Year	County	Name of Mother	Year	County
1	Ben Frazier	Dead	Chick Roll	Emily Frazier	Dead	Jackson
2	Jno L. Aduddell		white man	No 1		
3	Geo. Aduddell		Non-Citz	Susan Aduddell		Non-Citz
4						
5						
6	No 1 on 1896 roll as Annie Frazier					
7	No 2- Affidavit of birth to be					
8	supplied:- Filed Nov 2/99					
9	Husband: Jno L. Aduddell on Card No D 428					
10	No.1 Died October 10 1899. Evidence of death filed					
11	No.3 transferred from Choctaw card #D-428 Oct 31, 1904: See decision of Oct. 15, 1904.					
12						
13						
14					#182	
15				Date of Application for Enrollment.	Sept 4/99	
16						
17						

3

Choctaw By Blood Enrollment Cards 1898-1914

RESIDENCE: Sans Bois   COUNTY. **Choctaw Nation**   **Choctaw Roll**   CARD NO.
POST OFFICE: Whitefield, I.T.   *(Not Including Freedmen)*   FIELD NO. **4504**

Dawes' Roll No.	NAME		Relationship to Person	AGE	SEX	BLOOD	TRIBAL ENROLLMENT		
							Year	County	No.
12500	1 Woolridge, Nicholas	28	First Named	25	M	1/2	1896	Sans Bois	12703
12501	2 " Adeline	22	Wife	19	F	1/2	1896	" "	12706
12502	3 " Siney	16	Sister ~~Bro~~	13	"	1/2	1896	" "	12704
12503	4 " Martha	14	Sister	11	"	1/2	1896	" "	12705
12504	5 " William	11	Bro	8	M	1/2	1896	" "	12707
12505	6 " Agnes	3	Dau	1/2	F	1/2			
12506	7 " Flora Lizzie	1	Dau	4mo	F	1/2			
	8								
	9								
	10								
	11								
	12								
	13								
	14								
	15	ENROLLMENT OF NOS. 1 2 3 4 5 6-7 HEREON APPROVED BY THE SECRETARY OF INTERIOR Mar 6 1903							
	16								
	17								

TRIBAL ENROLLMENT OF PARENTS

	Name of Father	Year	County	Name of Mother	Year	County
1	Mose Woolridge	Dead	Sans Bois	Lizzie Woolridge	Dead	Sans Bois
2	Peter Garland	"	" " "	Margaret Perry		" "
3	Mose Woolridge	"	" " "	Lizzie Woolridge	Dead	" "
4	" "	"	" " "	" "		" " "
5	" "	"	" " "	" "		" " "
6	No1			No2		
7	No1			No2		
8						
9			No2 on 1896 roll as Adaline Woolridge			
10			No5 on 1896 roll as Willie Woolridge			
11			No6: Enrolled Feby 20, 1900			
12			No7 born July 29, 1901 Enrolled Dec 10, 1901		#1 to 5
13			For child of Nos 1&2 see NB (March 3 1905) #1355		Date of Application for Enrollment.
14						
15						Sept 4/99
16						
17						

4

Choctaw By Blood Enrollment Cards 1898-1914

RESIDENCE: Tobucksy COUNTY.
POST OFFICE: South McAlester, I.T. **Choctaw Nation**

Dawes' Roll No.		NAME		Relationship to Person	AGE	SEX	BLOOD	TRIBAL ENROLLMENT		
								Year	County	No.
12507	1	Boatwright, James H	33	First Named	30	M	1/8	1896	Tobucksy	936
I.W. 444	2	" Zena	33	Wife	30	F	IW	1896	"	14309
12508	3	" Ida M	11	Dau	8	"	1/16	1896	"	937
12509	4	" Ada I	8	"	5	"	1/16	1896	"	938
	5									
	6									
	7									
	8									
	9									
	10									
	11									
	12									
	13									
	14									
	15									
	16									
	17									

ENROLLMENT
OF NOS. 2 HEREON
APPROVED BY THE SECRETARY
OF INTERIOR SEP 12 1903

ENROLLMENT
OF NOS. 1, 3 & 4 HEREON
APPROVED BY THE SECRETARY
OF INTERIOR MAR 6 1903

TRIBAL ENROLLMENT OF PARENTS

	Name of Father	Year	County	Name of Mother	Year	County
1	Elias Boatwright	Dead	Non Citz	Ruthie Moseley		Tobucksy
2	Josh Goddard		" "	Martha Goddard		Non Citz
3	No1			No2		
4	No1			No2		
5						
6						
7	No1 on 1896 roll as James Boatwright					
8	No4 " 1896 " " Ela J "					
9	No2- Admitted by Dawes Com, Case No 907 as Zema Boatright					
10						
11	No.1 is the guardian of John H. Lacy on Choc Card 3728.					
12						
13						
14						
15				Date of Application for Enrollment.	Sept 4/99	
16						
17	Okra, I.T. 10/24/02					

P.O. [Illegible] IT 4/9/03

Choctaw By Blood Enrollment Cards 1898-1914

RESIDENCE: Tobucksy COUNTY. **Choctaw Nation**   **Choctaw Roll** CARD NO.
POST OFFICE: South McAlester, I.T. (Not Including Freedmen) FIELD No. 4506

Dawes' Roll No.	NAME	Relationship to Person First Named	AGE	SEX	BLOOD	TRIBAL ENROLLMENT		
						Year	County	No.
DEAD.	1 Mosby, Ruthy ~~DEAD.~~	Named	55	F	1/4	1896	San____is	8433
	2							
	3							
	4							
	5							
	6							
	7							
	NO. 1 HEREON DISMISSED UNDER ORDER OF THE COMMISSION TO THE FIVE CIVILIZED TRIBES OF MARCH 31, 1905.							
	10							
	11							
	12							
	13							
	14							
	15							
	16							
	17							

TRIBAL ENROLLMENT OF PARENTS

	Name of Father	Year	County	Name of Mother	Year	County
1	Allen Stanton	Dead		Susie Stanton	Dead	
2						
3						
4						
5		On 1896 roll as Ruth A Mosby				
6		No 1 died May 24, 1900. Proof of death filed Oct. 28, 1902.				
7						
8						
9						
10						
11						
12						
13						
14				Date of Application for Enrollment.		
15				Sept 4/99		
16						
17						

Choctaw By Blood Enrollment Cards 1898-1914

RESIDENCE: Tobucksy COUNTY. **Choctaw Nation** **Choctaw Roll** CARD NO.
POST OFFICE: South M<u>c</u>Alester, I.T. *(Not Including Freedmen)* FIELD NO. 4507

Dawes' Roll No.	NAME	Relationship to Person	AGE	SEX	BLOOD	TRIBAL ENROLLMENT		
						Year	County	No.
12510	1 Boatwright, David W [23]	First Named	20	M	1/8	1896	Tobucksy	893
	2							
	3							
	4							
	5							
	6							
	7							
	8							
	9							
	10							
	11							
	12							
	13							
	14							
	15							
	16							
	17							

ENROLLMENT
OF NOS. 1 HEREON
APPROVED BY THE SECRETARY
OF INTERIOR MAR 6 1903

TRIBAL ENROLLMENT OF PARENTS

	Name of Father	Year	County	Name of Mother	Year	County
1	Elias Boatwright	Dead	Non Citz	Ruthy Mosby		Sans Bois
2						
3						
4						
5						
6						
7	On 1896 roll as W<u>m</u> Boatwright					
8						
9						
10						
11						
12						
13						Date of Application for Enrollment.
14						Sept 4/99
15						
16						
17						

Choctaw By Blood Enrollment Cards 1898-1914

RESIDENCE: Tobucksy   COUNTY. **Choctaw Nation**   Choctaw Roll   CARD No.
POST OFFICE: Holleman, I.T.   (Not Including Freedmen)   FIELD No. **4508**

Dawes' Roll No.	NAME	Relationship to Person First Named	AGE	SEX	BLOOD	TRIBAL ENROLLMENT Year	County	No.
14432	1 Boatwright, Thomas J⁴⁰	Named	37	M	1/8	1896	Tobucksy	947
I.W. 445	2 " Alice M ²⁷	Wife	23	F	IW	1896	"	14306
14433	3 " Ruthie L ¹⁵	Dau	12	"	1/16	1896	"	948
14434	4 " Thomas D ¹³	Son	10	M	1/16	1896	"	949
14435	5 " Lonnie E ¹³	"	10	"	1/16	1896	"	950
14436	6 " Edith ⁵	Dau	2	F	1/16			
14437	7 " James Granville¹	Son	1wk	M	1/16			
	8 No6 Affidavit of birth to							
	9 be supplied:- Filed Oct 27/99							
	10 Nos 3-4-5 Evidence of							
	marriage filed herewith							
	11							
	12 No.7 Born Sept 23, 1902 enrolled Sept 30, 1902							
	13 ENROLLMENT							
	14 OF NOS. 1 3 4 5 6 and 7 HEREON							
	APPROVED BY THE SECRETARY							
	15 OF INTERIOR Apr 11 1903							
	16 Was No1 also admitted in 1896? yes							
	17 See original papers in Case No. 892							

TRIBAL ENROLLMENT OF PARENTS

	Name of Father	Year	County	Name of Mother	Year	County
1	Elias Boatwright	Dead	Non Citz	Ruthy Mosby		Tobucksy
2	Granville Albert		" "	Mary J Albert		Non Citz
3	No1			Eliz Boatwright	Dead	" "
4	No1			" "		" " "
5	No1			" "		" " "
6	No1			No2		
7	No1			No2		
8						
9						
10	No.1 on 1896 roll as T J. Boatwright			ENROLLMENT		
11	No3 " 1896 " " Ruth L "			OF NOS. ~2~ HEREON		
12	No4 " 1896 " " Tom D "			APPROVED BY THE SECRETARY		
	No5 " 1896 " " Lona "			OF INTERIOR Sep 12 1903		
13	Nos 1-2-3-4-5 were admitted by Dawes Com					
14	Case No. 892 No appeal					
15	No.2 admitted as Alice M Boatwright			Date of Application for Enrollment. Sept 4/99		
16	No3 " Ruthie L "					
	No4 " Thomas "			➤ 1 to 6		
17	No5 " Laura "					

For child of No.3 see NB (Apr 26 '06) Card #96
   "   "   "   "   "   " (Mar 3 '05) " #347

Choctaw By Blood Enrollment Cards 1898-1914

RESIDENCE:	Tobucksy	COUNTY.							
POST OFFICE:	Scipio I.T.								

Choctaw Nation

Choctaw Roll *(Not Including Freedmen)*

CARD NO. FIELD NO. 4509

Dawes' Roll No.	NAME	Relationship to Person First Named	AGE	SEX	BLOOD	TRIBAL ENROLLMENT		
						Year	County	No.
12511	1 Wheat, Agnes 26	Named	23	F	Full	1893	Gaines	109
	2							
	3							
	4							
	5							
	6							
	7							
	8							
	9							
	10							
	11							
	12							
	13							
	14							
	15							
	16							
	17							

ENROLLMENT
OF NOS. 1 HEREON
APPROVED BY THE SECRETARY
OF INTERIOR MAR 6 1903

TRIBAL ENROLLMENT OF PARENTS

	Name of Father	Year	County	Name of Mother	Year	County
1	John Carr	Dead	Gaines	Louisa Carr	Dead	Gainesa
2						
3						
4						
5						
6						
7	On 1893 Pay Roll, Page 11, No 109, Gaines					
8	Co as Agnes Carr					
9						
10						
11						
12						
13						
14					Date of Application for Enrollment.	
15					Sept 4/99	
16						
17						

Choctaw By Blood Enrollment Cards 1898-1914

| RESIDENCE: Tobucksy | COUNTY. | CARD No. |
| POST OFFICE: Krebbs, I.T. | **Choctaw Nation** | **Choctaw Roll** (Not Including Freedmen) | FIELD No. **4510** |

Dawes' Roll No.	NAME	Relationship to Person	AGE	SEX	BLOOD	TRIBAL ENROLLMENT		
						Year	County	No.
I.W. 1221	1 Hodges, Nancy A 30	First Named	29	F	IW			
15482	2 " Elisha 6	Son	3	M	1/2			
	3							
	4							
	5							
	6	ENROLLMENT						
	7	OF NOS. ~~ 2 ~~ HEREON APPROVED BY THE SECRETARY						
	8	OF INTERIOR May 9 1904						
	9							
	10	ENROLLMENT						
	11	OF NOS. ~~ 1 ~ HEREON APPROVED BY THE SECRETARY						
	12	OF INTERIOR Dec 13 1904						
	13							
	14							
	15							
	16							
	17							

TRIBAL ENROLLMENT OF PARENTS

	Name of Father	Year	County	Name of Mother	Year	County
1	Jas Phillips		Non Citz	Sarah Phillips	Dead	Non Citz
2	Lee Hodges		Gains[sic]	No1		
3						
4						
5						
6						
7						
8	No1 & 2 Admitted by Dawes Com Case No			Appeal dismissed		
9	432					
10	No1 formerly wife of Lee Hodges, a recognized Choctaw by blood whose whereabouts are unknown.					
11						
12						
13					Date of Application for Enrollment.	
14						
15					Sept 4/99	
16	Cade OK 6/25/08					
17	Boswell I.T. 12/2/02 2/29/04					

P.O. Caddo I.T.   11/11/03

Choctaw By Blood Enrollment Cards 1898-1914

| RESIDENCE: Tobucksy | COUNTY. | **Choctaw Nation** | Choctaw Roll | CARD NO. |
| POST OFFICE: Celestine, I.T. | | | (Not Including Freedmen) | FIELD NO. **4511** |

Dawes' Roll No.	NAME		Relationship to Person	AGE	SEX	BLOOD	TRIBAL ENROLLMENT		
							Year	County	No.
I.W. 1018	1 Hoff, Lizzie	25	First Named	22	F	IW			
	2								
	3								
	4								
	5								
	6 Take no further action relative to								
	7 enrollment of No1 Protest of								
	8 Atty for Choctaw and								
	9 Chickasaw Nation Jan 23 '04								
	10								
	11 ENROLLMENT								
	12 OF NOS. ~ 1 ~ HEREON APPROVED BY THE SECRETARY								
	13 OF INTERIOR Oct 21 1904								
	14								
	15								
	16								
	17								

TRIBAL ENROLLMENT OF PARENTS

	Name of Father	Year	County	Name of Mother	Year	County
1	Henry Troutt		Non Citz	Jennie Troutt	Dead	Non Citz
2						
3						
4						
5						
6	See her testimony as to separation					
7						
8	Address Henry Troutt, South McAlester					
9	I.T. when certificate of marriage is returned					
10	No.1 claims through marriage to Charles Beams 7-4677					
11						
12	No1 is mother of Robert Joseph Hoff on Choctaw Card D1008					
13	For children of No1 see NB (Apr 26 '06) #1119					
14					Date of Application for Enrollment.	
15					Sept 4/99	
16						
17						

11

Choctaw By Blood Enrollment Cards 1898-1914

RESIDENCE: Tobucksy COUNTY. **Choctaw Nation** **Choctaw Roll** *(Not Including Freedmen)* CARD NO.
POST OFFICE: South McAlester, I.T. FIELD NO. 4512

Dawes' Roll No.	NAME	Relationship to Person	AGE	SEX	BLOOD	TRIBAL ENROLLMENT		
						Year	County	No.
I.W. 1427	1 Goddard, Mary 48	First Named	40	F	I.W.	1896	Tobucksy	14568
	2 " Arizona	Dau	19	"			D	
	3 " Annie	"	17	"			D	
	4 " James F	Son	11	M			D	
	5 " Ophelia D	Dau	4	F			D	
	6 See Loula West petition C 13							
	7							
	8 ENROLLMENT OF NOS							
	9 APPROVED BY THE SECRETARY OF INTERIOR Jun 12 1905							
	10							
	11 No1 formerly wife of Gabriel							
	12 Grubbs, a recognized citizen							
	13 by blood of the Choctaw Nation, who died in about the year 1877							
	14							
	15							
	16							
	17 See petition #C-13							

TRIBAL ENROLLMENT OF PARENTS

	Name of Father	Year	County	Name of Mother	Year	County
1	Jno. Ingram	Dead	White man		Dead	white woman
2	Joshua Goddard	" "		No1		
3	" "	" "		No1		
4	" "	" "		No1		
5	" "	" "		No1		

6 2,3,4,5 Denied Citizenship by the Choctaw and Chickasaw Citizenship Court Nov. 29'04 117M
7 Nos 2 to 5 incl denied in 96 Case #270
8 Nos 2 to 5 incl now in C.C.C.C. Case #117
9 2 to 5 incl Admitted by U.S. Court, Central Dist, Aug 27/97 Case Nº48
10 Nº4 admitted as James Franklin Goddard
11 Nº5 " " Ophelia Pocahontas "
12 As to residence, see testimony of
13 Joshua.
14 Parents of above children are both white
15 Nº1 on 1896 roll as Mary Goddard
16 Nº1 admitted as an intermarried citizen by Dawes Commission in 1896 Case #270 no appeal

2 to 5 incl Judgement[sic] of U.S. Ct admitting Nos 2 to 5 incl vacated and set aside by Decree of C.C.C.C. 12/17/02
Action approved by Secretary of Interior Mar 1, 1907
Notice of Departmental action forwarded attorneys for Choctaw and Chickasaw Nations Apr 3 1907
Notice of departmental action forwarded attorney for applicant Apr 3 1907
Notice of departmental action mailed applicant Sept 4/99
Date of Application for Enrollment Sept 4/99

Choctaw By Blood Enrollment Cards 1898-1914

Dawes' Roll No.	NAME		Relationship to Person	AGE	SEX	BLOOD	TRIBAL ENROLLMENT		
							Year	County	No.
12512	1 Smith, Willie V. L.	5	First Named	2	M	1/32			
12513	2 " Jesse M	4	Bro	7mo	"	1/32			
12514	3 " Hill T.	26	Fath.	23	"	1/16	1896	Sans Bois	11094
I.W. 1135	4 " Myrtle	24	Mother	24	F	I.W.			15015
	5								
	6								
	7								
	8								
	9								
	10	ENROLLMENT OF NOS. ~~~~4~~~~ HEREON APPROVED BY THE SECRETARY							
	11	OF INTERIOR NOV 16 1904							
	12								
	13								
	14								
	15	ENROLLMENT OF NOS. 1 2 & 3 HEREON APPROVED BY THE SECRETARY							
	16								
	17	OF INTERIOR MAR 6 1903							

TRIBAL ENROLLMENT OF PARENTS

	Name of Father	Year	County	Name of Mother	Year	County
1	Hill T. Smith		Tobucksy	Myrtle Smith		white woman
2	" " "		"	" "		" "
3	H. R. Smith		"	E. J. Smith		Tobucksy
4	Saml. Stubblefield		non-citizen	Orphie Stubblefield		Non-Citz
5						
6	Nos 3 and 4 separated in 1898 and were subsequently divorced					
7						
8	Mother on Card No D429. Evidence of marriage attached thereto					
9						
10	Affidavits of birth to be supplied:- Filed Oct 27/99					
11	No.4 transferred from Choctaw card #D-429, Oct. 31, 1904; See decision of Oct. 15, 1904					
12	No.3 Admitted by Choc. Council #28 apprd. Oct 26-86 as Hill Smith 9/14/99					
13	For child of No.3 see NB (Mar 3, 1905) #487					
14						
15				Date of Application for Enrollment.	Sept 4/99	
16					1 to 3	
17	No.4 P.O. Blanco, I.T. 9/1/04					

No4 PO Canadian 1908

13

Choctaw By Blood Enrollment Cards 1898-1914

RESIDENCE: Tobucksy COUNTY.
POST OFFICE: Mc.Alester, I.T.

Choctaw Nation

Choctaw Roll
(Not Including Freedmen)

CARD NO.
FIELD NO. 4514

Dawes' Roll No.	NAME	Relationship to Person First Named	AGE	SEX	BLOOD	TRIBAL ENROLLMENT Year	County	No.
12515	1 Ansley, Gilbert 25	Named	22	M	1/8	1896	Tobucksy	103
12516	2 " Henry Ray 1	Son	1mo	M	1/16			
I.W.679	3 " Dollie May 21	Wife	21	F	IW			
	4							
	5							
	6							
	7							
	8							
	9							
	10							
	11	ENROLLMENT OF NOS. 3 HEREON APPROVED BY THE SECRETARY						
	12	OF INTERIOR MAR 26 1904						
	13							
	14	ENROLLMENT OF NOS. 1 and 2 HEREON APPROVED BY THE SECRETARY						
	15							
	16	OF INTERIOR MAR 6 1903						
	17							

TRIBAL ENROLLMENT OF PARENTS

	Name of Father	Year	County	Name of Mother	Year	County
1	William Ansley		Tobucksy	Anternet Ansley	Dead	Non Citz
2	No.1			Dollie May Ansley		
3	Frank Gorseline		noncitizen	Mary Gorseline		noncitizen
4						
5						
6	As to marriage of parents see enrollment					
7	of William Ansley.					
8	No.1 is now the husband of Dollie May Ansley					
9	on Choctaw card #D.607 Jany 12, 1901					
10	No.2 Born September 7, 1901 and Enrolled October 16, 1901.					
11	No3 Transferred from Choctaw card D607 January 19,z 1904. See					
12	decision of January 2, 1904					
13	For child of Nos 1 and 3 see NP (Mar 3 '05) #348					
14						
15					Date of Application for Enrollment.	
16					Sept 5/99	
17						

14

RESIDENCE: **Tobucksy**   COUNTY. **Choctaw Nation**   **Choctaw Roll** *(Not Including Freedmen)*   CARD No. FIELD No. **4515**

POST OFFICE: **McAlester, I.T.**

Dawes' Roll No.	NAME	Relationship to Person First Named	AGE	SEX	BLOOD	TRIBAL ENROLLMENT		
						Year	County	No.
I.T. 843	1 Richards, Edwin T (33)		31	M	I.W.	1896	Tobucksy	149711
12517	2 " Irena A (27)	Wife	24	F	1/8	1896	"	10776
12518	3 " Clifton L (7)	Son	4	M	1/16	1896	"	10777
12519	4 " Oscar Horton (2)	"	2w.	"	1/16			
	5							
	6 CITIZENSHIP CERTIFICATE							
	7 ISSUED FOR NO. 2-3-4							
	APR 27 1903							
	8							
~CITIZENSHIP CERTIFICATE~								
~ISSUED FOR NO ~~~One~~~								
JUL 23 1904								
	10							
	11 ENROLLMENT							
	12 OF NOS. One HEREON							
	APPROVED BY THE SECRETARY							
	13 OF INTERIOR MAY 21 1904							
	14							
	15 ENROLLMENT							
	16 OF NOS. 2, 3 and 4 HEREON							
	APPROVED BY THE SECRETARY							
	17 OF INTERIOR MAR 6 1903							

TRIBAL ENROLLMENT OF PARENTS

	Name of Father	Year	County	Name of Mother	Year	County
1	P.A. Richards		Non Citz	Caroline L. Richards		Non Citz
2	William Ansley		Tobucksy	Anternet Ansley	Dead	" "
3	No.1			No.2		
4	No.1			No.2		
5						
6						
7	No.3 On 1896 roll as Clifton R. Richards					
8	No.2 As to proof of marriage of parents, see enrollment of William Ansley					
9	No.4 Enrolled February 5, 1906					
10	Affidavits of Nos 1 and 2 as to residence of No.2 at the					
11	time of her marriage to No.1 filed May 18, 1903.					
12						
13						
14						
15						Sept 5/99
16						
17						

Choctaw By Blood Enrollment Cards 1898-1914

RESIDENCE:	Tobucksy	COUNTY.	**Choctaw Nation**		**Choctaw Roll**	CARD NO.		
POST OFFICE:	Alderson, I.T.				*(Not Including Freedmen)*	FIELD NO. **4516**		

Dawes' Roll No.	NAME	Relationship to Person First Named	AGE	SEX	BLOOD	TRIBAL ENROLLMENT		
						Year	County	No.
Dead	1 Drake, Thomas M	Named	72	M	IW			
15483	2 " George W 18	Son	15	"	1/4	1896	Tobucksy	3316
15484	3 Crow Mable 16	Dau	13	F	1/4	1896	"	3317
15485	4 Drake John W 14	Son	11	M	1/4	1896	"	3318
15486	5 Crow, Andrew Dow 1	Gr Son	10mo	M	1/8			
	6							
	7							
	8	ENROLLMENT						
	9	OF NOS. 2-3-4-5 HEREON						
	10	APPROVED BY THE SECRETARY OF INTERIOR May 9 1904						
	11							
	12	No1 dismissed, see decision						
	13	of Commission March 2, 1904						
	14	For child of No3 see NB (Apr 26 06) Card #282						
	15	" " " No2 " " (Mar 3-05) " #1315						
	16							
	17							

TRIBAL ENROLLMENT OF PARENTS						
Name of Father	Year	County	Name of Mother	Year	County
1 Simeon Drake	Dead	Non Citz	Patience Drake	Dead	Non Citz
2 No. 1			Rufina Drake	"	Choctaw
3 No. 1			" "	"	"
4 No. 1			No. 1		
5 Andrew J Crow		Non-Citizen	No 3		
6					
7 Admitted by Dawes Com, Case No 300			appeal dismissed Cr 3172		
8 No2 admitted as Geo W Drake					
9 No3 " " Mable "					
10 No1 died Mar 2, 1902. Proof of death filed Dec 30-02					
11 No2 on 1896 roll as Geo W Drake					
12 No4 " 1896 " " Jno W "					
13 N°3 is now the wife of Andrew J Crow a non-citizen:					
14 Evidence of marriage requested Aug. 4, 1902				#1 to 4 inc
15 No.5 Born Oct 6, 1901; enrolled Aug 4, 1902				Date of Application for Enrollment.
16 See decision of March 2, 1904				Sept 5/99
17 No2 Box 26 Dow. I.T. 2/5/04 Haileyville I.T.				
No3 Craig I.T. 12/22/02				

No3 Chickasha I.T. 11/11/03

Choctaw By Blood Enrollment Cards 1898-1914

RESIDENCE:	**Sans Bois**	COUNTY.							
POST OFFICE:	**Russellville, I.T.**								

Choctaw Nation

Choctaw Roll
(Not Including Freedmen)

CARD NO.
FIELD NO. **4517**

Dawes' Roll No.	NAME	Relationship to Person First Named	AGE	SEX	BLOOD	TRIBAL ENROLLMENT Year	County	No.
12520	1 Folsom, Jefferson D 41	Named	38	M	3/4	1896	Sans Bois	3822
I.W. 929	2 " Tabitha ㊳	Wife	35	F	IW	1896	" "	14506
12521	3 " Davis L 16	Son	13	M	3/8	1896	" "	3823
12522	4 " Mattie 13	Dau	10	F	3/8	1896	" "	3826
12523	5 " Alice 10	"	7	"	3/8	1896	" "	3824
12524	6 " Jessie M 8	"	5	"	3/8	1896	" "	3825
12525	7 " Eunice 6	"	3	"	3/8			
	8							
	9							
	10	ENROLLMENT						
	11	OF NOS. 2 HEREON APPROVED BY THE SECRETARY						
	12	OF INTERIOR Aug 3 1904						
	13							
	14							
	15	ENROLLMENT						
	16	OF NOS. 1,3,4,5,6 and 7 HEREON APPROVED BY THE SECRETARY						
	17	OF INTERIOR Mar 6 1903						

TRIBAL ENROLLMENT OF PARENTS

Name of Father	Year	County	Name of Mother	Year	County
1 John Folsom	Dead	Blue	Manette Folsom	Dead	Blue
2 Geo. Beard		Non Citz		"	Non Citz
3 No.1			No2		
4 No1			No2		
5 No1			No2		
6 No1			No2		
7 No1			No2		
8					
9					
10					
11	No1 on 1896 roll as Jeff D. Folsum				
12	No3 " 1896 " " Davis Folsom				
13	No4 " 1896 " " Mattie Folsum				
14	No5 " 1896 " " Alice "				
15	No6 " 1896 " " Jessie May "		Date of application for enrollment Sept 5/99		
16	No7 Affidavit of birth to be supplied Recd Dec 18/99 Irregular and returned for correction Recd & filed Jan 17, 1900		Date of Application for Enrollment.		
17					

17

RESIDENCE: Tobucksy   COUNTY. **Choctaw Nation**   **Choctaw Roll** (Not Including Freedmen)   CARD NO.
POST OFFICE: Carbit, I.T.   FIELD NO. **4518**

Dawes' Roll No.	NAME Carbon I.T.	Relationship to Person Named	AGE	SEX	BLOOD	TRIBAL ENROLLMENT Year	County	No.
✓ *	1 Biddy, Samuel	First Named	46	M	1/16			
✓ *	2 " Elizabeth	Wife	45	F	I.W.			
✓ *	3 " Foley	Son	10	M	1/32			
✓ *	4 " Pearley	Dau	5	F	1/32			
	5							
	6 Denied Citizenship by the Choctaw and Chickasaw Citizenship Court Feb 4'04							
	7							
	8							
	9							
	10							
	11							
	12							
	13							
	14							
	15							
	16							
	17							

TRIBAL ENROLLMENT OF PARENTS

Name of Father	Year	County	Name of Mother	Year	County
1 Daniel Biddy	Dead	Non Citz	Lucy Biddy	Dead	Choctaw
2 J.D. Moore	"	"	Catherine Moore	"	Non Citz
3 No 1			No 2		
4 No 1			No 2		
5					
6	Nos 1 to 4 incl denied by Dawes Com in 96 Choc Cit Case #598				
7	Admitted by U.S. Court, Central				
8	Dist, Aug 24/97 Case No 94 As to residence see testimony of No1				
9	Judgment of U.S. Court C.D. admitting Nos 1 to 4 incl vacated and				
10	set aside by Decree of Choctaw – Chickasaw Citizenship Court Dec 17 '02				
11	No⁵ 1 to 4 incl denied by Choctaw – Chickasaw Court Feb 1 '04				
12	Case #13M				
13					
14				Date of Application for Enrollment.	
15				Sept 5/99	
16					
17					

18

Choctaw By Blood Enrollment Cards 1898-1914

RESIDENCE: Tobucksy   COUNTY. **Choctaw Nation**   **Choctaw Roll** CARD NO.
POST OFFICE: Simpson, I.T.   *(Not Including Freedmen)*   FIELD NO. **4519**

Dawes' Roll No.	NAME		Relationship to Person First Named	AGE	SEX	BLOOD	Year	County	No.
Dead	1	Cephus, Wilson		26	M	Full	1896	Tobucksy	2379
12526	2	" Jemima ²⁷	Wife	24	F	"	1896	"	2380
12527	3	" Sampson ⁷	Son	4	M	"	1896	"	2381
12528	4	Moore, Angeline ¹⁵	S.D.	12	F	"	1893	Kiamitia	91
12529	5	Wesley Standley ²⁰	S.Son	17	M	"	1896	Gaines	12954
	6								
	7	No __1__ hereon							
	8	dismissed under							
	9	order of the Commission to the Five							
	10	Civilized Tribes of							
	11	March 31, 1905.							
	12								
	13								
	14	ENROLLMENT HEREON							
	15	OF NOS. 2,3,4 and 5 APPROVED BY THE SECRETARY OF INTERIOR Mar 6 1903							
	16								
	17								

TRIBAL ENROLLMENT OF PARENTS

	Name of Father	Year	County	Name of Mother	Year	County
1	Willie Cephus	Dead	Tobucksy		Dead	Tobucksy
2		"			"	
3	No1			No2		
4	Moore	Dead	Tobucksy	No2		
5	Thomp Wesley	"	Gaines	" 2		Tobucksy
6						
7						
8						
9						
10						
11	No.4 on 1893 Pay Roll, Page 120, No. 91					
12	Kiamitia Co, as Anjaline Moore					
13	No1 died Dec. 1901. Proof of death filed Dec 23, 1902 For child of No.4, see NB (Apr 26, 1906) Card No.4					#1 to 4
14					Date of Application for Enrollment	
15				Date of application for enrollment Sept 5/99		
16						
17	Krebs, I.T. 12/23/02					

19

Choctaw By Blood Enrollment Cards 1898-1914

RESIDENCE:	Gaines	COUNTY.							
POST OFFICE:	Bower, I.T.	**Choctaw Nation**		**Choctaw Roll** *(Not Including Freedmen)*		CARD NO. FIELD NO. **4520**			

Dawes' Roll No.	NAME	Relationship to Person Named	AGE	SEX	BLOOD	TRIBAL ENROLLMENT		
						Year	County	No.
LW.4019	1 Featherston, Henry B ³⁷	First Named	34	M	IW	1896	Gaines	14518
12530	2 Long Letitia C ³³	Wife	30	F	5/16	1896	"	3985
	3							
	4							
	5	Take no further action relative to enrollment of No.						
	6	Protest of Attys for Choctaw and Chickasaw Nations						
	7	Jan 23 /04						
	8							
	9	ENROLLMENT OF NOS. ~ 1 ~~ HEREON APPROVED BY THE SECRETARY OF INTERIOR OCT 21 1904						
	10							
	11							
	12							
	13	ENROLLMENT OF NOS. 2 HEREON APPROVED BY THE SECRETARY OF INTERIOR MAR 6 1903						
	14							
	15							
	16							
	17							

TRIBAL ENROLLMENT OF PARENTS

	Name of Father	Year	County	Name of Mother	Year	County
1	Chas H Featherston	Dead	Non Citz	Nancy Y Featherston		Non Citz
2	Edmond F Krebbs	"	Gaines	Permalia Krebbs	Dead	Skullyville
3						
4						
5						
6						
7						
8						
9	No1 admitted by Dawes Com. Case No					
10	467 as H.B. Featherstone No.2 also admitted in same case.					
11	No1 on 1896 roll as Henry B. Featherstone					
12	No2 " 1896 " " Lutitia C "					
13	Nº1&2 are divorced. Evidence of divorce to be supplied.					
14	Nº2 is now the wife of J.S. Long on Choctaw card #D238. Evidence					Date of Application for Enrollment
15	of marriage filed Oct. 9, 1902.					
16	No1 is now husband of Viola Krebs on Choctaw card #4531					Sept 5/99
	Evidence of marriage filed Dec 11, 1902					
	Evidence of divorce between Nºˢ 1 and 2 filed Dec. 24, 1902					
17	Pauls Valley I.T. 10/23/02					

Choctaw By Blood Enrollment Cards 1898-1914

RESIDENCE:		COUNTY.					CARD NO.
POST OFFICE: So McAlester		**Choctaw Nation**			Choctaw Roll *(Not Including Freedmen)*		FIELD NO. 4521

Dawes' Roll No.	NAME	Relationship to Person First Named	AGE	SEX	BLOOD	TRIBAL ENROLLMENT		
						Year	County	No.
1	Mickle, Joanna	Named	64	F				
2								
3								
4								
5								
6								
7								
8								
9								
10								
11								
12								
13								
14								
15								
16								
17								

TRIBAL ENROLLMENT OF PARENTS

	Name of Father	Year	County	Name of Mother	Year	County
1	Peter McSweeney	Dd	Jackson Cit	Joanna McSweeney	Dd	
2						
3						
4						
5						
6						

No1 Denied in 96 Case #400

Judgment of U.S. C. admitting No1 vacated and set aside by Decree of C.C C.C. Decr 17 '02

No1 now in C.C.C.C. Case #37

Admitted by U.S. Court at So McAlester
Aug 25-97, Court Case #240. As to residence see
her testimony.
No1 is mother of Nicholas J. Mickle on Choctaw
card #5232 and William Mickle on Choctaw
card #5233

Date of Application for Enrollment.
9/5/99

(watermark: No1 DENIED CITIZENSHIP BY THE CHOCTAW AND CHICKASAW CITIZENSHIP COURT Nov 28 '04)

21

RESIDENCE:		COUNTY.								
POST OFFICE: Enterprise		**Choctaw Nation**				**Choctaw Roll** *(Not Including Freedmen)*		CARD No.		
								FIELD No.		

Dawes' Roll No.	NAME	Relationship to Person First Named	AGE	SEX	BLOOD	TRIBAL ENROLLMENT		
						Year	County	No.
12531	1 King, William ⁴⁸	First Named	45	M	3/8	1896	Sans Bois	7444
12532	2 ~~Patsy~~ DIED PRIOR TO SEPTEMBER 25, 1902	Wife	60	F	3/4	1896	" "	7445
12533	3 Morrell, Sophia ¹¹	Ward	8	"	1/2	1896	" "	8434
	4							
	5							
	6							
	7							
	8							
	9							
	10							
	11							
	12							
	13							
	14							
	15	ENROLLMENT OF NOS. 1, 2 and 3 HEREON APPROVED BY THE SECRETARY OF INTERIOR MAR 6 1903						
	16							
	17							

TRIBAL ENROLLMENT OF PARENTS

	Name of Father	Year	County	Name of Mother	Year	County
1	Jeff King	Dd.	Skullyville	Martha Folsom		San[sic] Bois
2	~~Jim Goings~~	"	~~Jackson~~			~~Jackson~~
3	Pishachubbe		Sans Bois	Melvina		Sans Bois
4						
5						
6						
7						
8	No. 2 died March 9, 1901. Enrollment cancelled by Department July 8, 1904					
9						
10						
11						
12						
13						
14						
15					Date of Application for Enrollment.	
16					Sept 5, 1899	
17						

Choctaw By Blood Enrollment Cards 1898-1914

RESIDENCE:
POST OFFICE: So McAlester, I.T. COUNTY. **Choctaw Nation** **Choctaw Roll** (Not Including Freedmen) CARD No.
FIELD No. 4523

Dawes' Roll No.	NAME	Relationship to Person First Named	AGE	SEX	BLOOD	TRIBAL ENROLLMENT Year	County	No.
12534	1 Wheat, Alice ²²		19	F	1/2	1896	San[sic] Bois	9
12535	2 " Rebecca S ⁶	Dau	1½	F	1/4			
12536	3 " Rena ²	Dau	7mo	F	1/4			
	4							
	5							
	6							
	7							
	8							
	9							
	10							
	11							
	12							
	13							
	14							
	15	ENROLLMENT OF NOS. 1 2 and 3 HEREON						
	16	APPROVED BY THE SECRETARY						
	17	OF INTERIOR MAR 6 1903						

TRIBAL ENROLLMENT OF PARENTS

	Name of Father	Year	County	Name of Mother	Year	County
1	Semon Alexander	Dd.	San[sic] Bois	Sena Alexander		San[sic] Bois
2	Sish Wheat		Non cit.	No.1		
3	" "		" "	No.1		
4						
5						
6						
7						
8						
9						
10				No.1 on roll as ^ Alexander. Alice		
11				No3 Enrolled Aug 17, 1901		
12	For child of No1 see NB (Apr 26 1906) Card No. 135					
13	" " " " " " (Mar 3, 1905) " " 1431					
14						
15						
16					#1&2	
17	P.O. Quinton I.T. 5/4/05			Date of Application for Enrollment.	9/5/99	

Choctaw By Blood Enrollment Cards 1898-1914

RESIDENCE:
POST OFFICE: San[sic] Bois, I.T. COUNTY. **Choctaw Nation** **Choctaw Roll** *(Not Including Freedmen)* CARD NO.
FIELD NO. 4524

Dawes' Roll No.	NAME		Relationship to Person	AGE	SEX	BLOOD	TRIBAL ENROLLMENT		
							Year	County	No.
12537	1 Coley, David	23	First Named	20	M	Full	1896	San Bois	2066
12538	2 " Lovina	21	Wife	18	F	"	1896	" "	2076
12539	3 " Joseph Ed.	2	Son	1mo	M	"			
12540	4 " Dora May	1	Dau	3mo	F	"			
	5								
	6								
	7								
	8								
	9								
	10								
	11								
	12								
	13								
	14								
	15	ENROLLMENT OF NOS. 1, 2, 3 and 4 HEREON							
	16	APPROVED BY THE SECRETARY							
	17	OF INTERIOR MAR 6 1903							

TRIBAL ENROLLMENT OF PARENTS

	Name of Father	Year	County	Name of Mother	Year	County
1	Joe Coley	Dd.	San Bois	Sophia Coley		San Bois
2	Israel Cooper		" "	Sallie Cooper	Dd.	" "
3	No.1			No.2		
4	No1			No2		
5						
6						
7						
8						
9	For child of Nos 1&2 see NB (March 3, 1905) #1375					
10						
11				Lovina		
12				No.2 on roll as ∧ Cooper		
13			No.3 Enrolled May 24, 1900			
			No4 born July 28, 1902: enrolled Dec. 11 1902			
14						
15						
16				#1&2 inc		
17				Date of Application for Enrollment 9/5/99		

Choctaw By Blood Enrollment Cards 1898-1914

RESIDENCE:
POST OFFICE: Hartshorne, I.T.

COUNTY.
Choctaw Nation

Choctaw Roll
(Not Including Freedmen)

CARD NO.
FIELD NO. 4525

Dawes' Roll No.	NAME		Relationship to Person	AGE	SEX	BLOOD	TRIBAL ENROLLMENT		
							Year	County	No.
12541	₁ Folsom, Ellie	33	First Named	30	F	Full	1896	Tobucksy	9192
	₂								
	₃								
	₄								
	₅								
	₆								
	₇								
	₈								
	₉								
	₁₀								
	₁₁								
	₁₂								
	₁₃								
	₁₄								
	₁₅	ENROLLMENT OF NOS. 1 HEREON							
	₁₆	APPROVED BY THE SECRETARY							
	₁₇	OF INTERIOR MAR 6 1903							

TRIBAL ENROLLMENT OF PARENTS

	Name of Father	Year	County	Name of Mother	Year	County
₁	Amzi Folsom	Dd.	San[sic] Bois	Elaham	Dd.	Tobucksy
₂						
₃						
₄						
₅						
₆	No1 Died prior to September 25, 1902; not entitled to land or money. See Indian Office Letter					
₇	May 11 1905 (Land 25852-1905					
₈						
₉						
₁₀						
₁₁				on roll as Ellie F. McNally.		
₁₂						
₁₃						
₁₄						
₁₅						
₁₆						
₁₇					Date of Application for Enrollment.	9/5/99

Choctaw By Blood Enrollment Cards 1898-1914

RESIDENCE:	COUNTY.			CARD NO.
POST OFFICE: Alderson, I.T.	**Choctaw Nation**	**Choctaw Roll** (Not Including Freedmen)		FIELD NO. 4526

Dawes' Roll No.	NAME	Relationship to Person First Named	AGE	SEX	BLOOD	TRIBAL ENROLLMENT		
						Year	County	No.
CHICKASAW. 1	Colbert, Ely		31	F	full			
CHICKASAW. 2	" Emily	Dau	10	F	"			
3								
4								
5								
6								
7								
8								
9								
10								
11								
12								
13								
14								
15								
16								
17						CHICKASAW.		

Cancelled See Chic 1554

TRIBAL ENROLLMENT OF PARENTS

	Name of Father	Year	County	Name of Mother	Year	County
1	Silas Colbert	Dd.	Gaines	Julia Colbert	Dd.	San[sic] Bois
2	Nels Thompson		Sugar Loaf	No. 1		
3						
4						
5						
6						
7						
8						
9						
10				No.1 on roll as Aly Colbert – P.R. Gaines Co.		
11				Page 8 #79		
12				No.2 – Page 8 - #79.		
13						
14						
15						
16						
17				Date of Application for Enrollment.	9/5/99	

CANCELLED

Choctaw By Blood Enrollment Cards 1898-1914

RESIDENCE:		COUNTY.							CARD NO.	
POST OFFICE: So McAlester, I.T.		**Choctaw Nation**				Choctaw Roll (Not Including Freedmen)			FIELD NO. 4527	

Dawes' Roll No.	NAME	Relationship to Person First Named	AGE	SEX	BLOOD	TRIBAL ENROLLMENT		
						Year	County	No.
12542	1 Boatwright, Edward R²⁴	Named	21	M	1/8	1896	Tobucksy	935
	2							
	3							
	4							
	5							
	6							
	7							
	8							
	9							
	10							
	11							
	12							
	13							
	14							
	15							
	16							
	17							

ENROLLMENT
MAR 6 1905

TRIBAL ENROLLMENT OF PARENTS

Name of Father	Year	County	Name of Mother	Year	County
1 Elias Boatwright	Dd	Non Cit.	Ruthy Moore		Tobucksy
2					
3					
4					
5					
6					
7					
8					
9			on roll as Ed R. Boatwright		
10					
11					
12					
13					
14					
15					
16				Date of Application for Enrollment.	9/5/99
17					

27

Choctaw By Blood Enrollment Cards 1898-1914

RESIDENCE:		COUNTY.					CARD NO.	
POST OFFICE: Bower, I.T.		**Choctaw Nation**		**Choctaw Roll** *(Not Including Freedmen)*			FIELD NO. **4528**	

Dawes' Roll No.	NAME		Relationship to Person	AGE	SEX	BLOOD	TRIBAL ENROLLMENT		
							Year	County	No.
15487	₁ Tilly Ada A	20	First Named	17	F	1/8			
15488	₂ Standley, Mabel	13	Sis	10	F	1/8			
15489	₃ " Inez	21	"	18	F	1/8			
	4								
	5								
	6								
	7								
	8								
	9								
	10								
	11								
	12								
	13								
	14								
	15	ENROLLMENT OF NOS. 1 – 2 – 3 HEREON APPROVED BY THE SECRETARY OF INTERIOR May 9 1904							
	16								
	17								

TRIBAL ENROLLMENT OF PARENTS

	Name of Father	Year	County	Name of Mother	Year	County
₁	B. F. Standley	Dd	Gaines	Sylvia Robinson		Gaines
2	" " "	"		" "		
3	" " "	"		" "		
4						
5						
6						
7						
8						
9						
10						
11				Admitted by Dawes Comm #822 No appeal		
12				No1 as Adir O Standley		
13	For child of No2 see NB (Mar 3-1905) Card #1187			" 2 " May B "		
				" 3 " Ernest "		
14				See Enrollment of Ida Norman		
15						
16				Date of Application for Enrollment.		
17	No2 P.O. Hugo I.T. 4/20/05					9/5/99

Choctaw By Blood Enrollment Cards 1898-1914

RESIDENCE: Purcell I.T. Oct 14 '03 COUNTY.
POST OFFICE: So McAlester, I.T.

Choctaw Nation

Choctaw Roll
(Not Including Freedmen)

CARD NO.
FIELD NO. **4529**

Dawes' Roll No.	NAME	Relationship to Person First Named	AGE	SEX	BLOOD	TRIBAL ENROLLMENT		
						Year	County	No.
12543	1 Mattix, Harriet 66 ✓	First Named	63	F	1/8	1896	Tobucksy	8562
void	2 Parnell, Ewing	Gr.Son	4	M	1/16	1896	"	10245
15490	3 Hoyt, Emma ✓ 32	Dau	29	F	1/16	1896	"	5373
	4							
	5							
	6							
	7							
	8 ENROLLMENT OF NOS. ~~~ 3 ~~~ HEREON							
	9 APPROVED BY THE SECRETARY OF INTERIOR May 9 1904							
	10							
	11 No2 transferred to Choctaw card							
	12 5768 with mother April 13, 1904							
	13							
	14							
	15 ENROLLMENT OF NOS. 1 HEREON							
	16 APPROVED BY THE SECRETARY OF INTERIOR Mar 6 1903							
	17							

TRIBAL ENROLLMENT OF PARENTS

	Name of Father	Year	County	Name of Mother	Year	County
1	Jacob Folsom	Dd	Blue	Elzira Nail	Dd	Blue
2	Jesse Parnell		Non Cit	Serena Parnell		Tobucksy
3	Milo A Hoyt	dead	Cher Cit	No.1		
4						
5						
6						

7 No.2 Decision prepared (Put No2 with mother when Decision approved).
8 See testimony of mother of No.2 of April 24, 1902 as to final enrollment as Choctaw
9 Sept 29/99. Serena Parnell, daughter of No1 and Serena Parnell on 1894
   her son Hoyt Parnell by Jesse Parnell are on Cherokee Strip Payment
10 card No D 465, it being claimed that Serena is on Roll as Czarina Parnell
11 1880 Cherokee Roll. Should not No2 be placed Hoyt Parnell on 1894
   on same card with mother? And is it not roll with her.
12 probable that Nos 1-3 are also on Cherokee Roll
13 of 1880 No2 on roll as Huin Parnell
14 No3 on 1894 Cherokee Strip payment roll; page 44; No 974
   Canadian district
15 No.1 is Choctaw by blood and on none of the Cherokee rolls.
16 No3 Elects as a Choctaw Nov. 22, 1903
17

Date of Application for Enrollment.
9/5/99

29

Choctaw By Blood Enrollment Cards 1898-1914

RESIDENCE:		COUNTY.					CARD NO.		
POST OFFICE: Duncan, I.T.		**Choctaw Nation**				**Choctaw Roll** (Not Including Freedmen)		FIELD NO. 4530	

Dawes' Roll No.	NAME	Relationship to Person	AGE	SEX	BLOOD	TRIBAL ENROLLMENT		
						Year	County	No.
12544	1 Plato, Charles 25	First Named	22	M	1/2	1896	Atoka	10543
I.W. 1020	2 " Alton Aladin 56	Father	53	M	I.W.			
	3							
	4							
	5	ENROLLMENT						
	6	OF NOS. ~~~ 2 ~~~ HEREON APPROVED BY THE SECRETARY						
	7	OF INTERIOR OCT 21 1904						
	8							
	9							
	10							
	11							
	12							
	13	ENROLLMENT						
	14	OF NOS. 1 HEREON APPROVED BY THE SECRETARY						
	15	OF INTERIOR MAR 6 1903						
	16							
	17 See Petition No W 56							

TRIBAL ENROLLMENT OF PARENTS

	Name of Father	Year	County	Name of Mother	Year	County
1	Alton Plato		Atoka	Lavina Plato		Atoka
2	Joshua W Plato	D'd	non citiz	Harriet C Plato		non citiz
3						
4						
5						
6						
7						
8						
9	Also on 1896 roll as Charles Platoe					
10	Page 271, No 10636, Chick. Dist.					
11	No2 Married Levenia Nail, a Choctaw woman in 1875. She died in 1881					
12	" " Cynthia P College a white " " 1883 " " " 1896					
	" " Geneva Thurlow a white " " Apr 1898					
13	" is father of Lurind Moss Choc card #405. Also father of Wilmoth					
14	Helen Plato on Choc card #R751					
15	on roll as Charley Plato					
16	No2- admitted by Dawes Com Choctaw Case #592. No appeal.					
	No2 transferred from Choctaw D #80- See Decision of Sept 9, 1904					
17	For children of No2 see NB (Apr 26-06) No 1136		Date of Application for Enrollment	9/5/99		

30

Choctaw By Blood Enrollment Cards 1898-1914

RESIDENCE: Gaines COUNTY. **Choctaw Nation** **Choctaw Roll** CARD No.
POST OFFICE: Bower, I.T. *(Not Including Freedmen)* FIELD No. 4531

Dawes' Roll No.	NAME	Relationship to Person	AGE	SEX	BLOOD	TRIBAL ENROLLMENT		
						Year	County	No.
I.W. 1021	1 Featherston Viola 31	First Named	29	F	IW	1896	Gaines	14718
2								
3								
4								
5	ENROLLMENT							
6	OF NOS. ~~~ 1 ~~~ HEREON APPROVED BY THE SECRETARY							
7	OF INTERIOR OCT 21 1904							
8								
9								
10								
11								
12								
13								
14								
15								
16								
17								

TRIBAL ENROLLMENT OF PARENTS

	Name of Father	Year	County	Name of Mother	Year	County
1	Adams		Non Citz	Jane Adams		Non Citz
2						
3						
4						
5						
6						
7						
8	Admitted by Dawes Com, Case No 1204					
9	No1 is now wife of Henry B Featherstone[sic] on Choctaw card #4520					
10	Evidence of marriage filed Dec 11, 1902					
11						
12	No.1 was formerly wife of James F Krebs, deceased, who is identified					
13	upon the 1893 Leased District Roll, Choctaw Nation					
14						
15				Date of Application for Enrollment.	Sept 5/99	
16						
17	Pauls Valley I.T. 10/23/02					

31

Choctaw By Blood Enrollment Cards 1898-1914

RESIDENCE:	Sugar Loaf	COUNTY.							

RESIDENCE: Sugar Loaf COUNTY. **Choctaw Nation** Choctaw Roll (Not Including Freedmen) CARD NO. FIELD NO. **4532**

POST OFFICE: ~~Poteau~~ I.T.

Dawes' Roll No.	NAME	Relationship to Person First Named	AGE	SEX	BLOOD	Year	County	No.
✓	1 ~~Braun, George H~~	Named	36	M	I.W.			
✓ *	2 " ~~Daisy D~~	Wife	23	F	1/32			
✓	3 " ~~George H Jr~~	Son	1	M	1/64			
	4							
	5 No 2 Denied Citizenship by the Choctaw and Chickasaw Citizenship Court Mar. 28 '04							
	6							
	7							
No1	8 Dismissed May 7, 1904							
	9							
No3	10 Dismissed May 27, 1904							
	11							
	12							
	13							
	14							
	15							
	16							
	17							

TRIBAL ENROLLMENT OF PARENTS

Name of Father	Year	County	Name of Mother	Year	County
1 ~~Herman Braun~~		~~Non Citz~~	~~Maria Braun~~	~~Dead~~	~~Non Citz~~
2 ~~John N. Moore~~	~~Dead~~	~~Choctaw~~	~~Victoria Moore~~		~~Intermarried~~
3 ~~No.1~~			~~No.2~~		
4					
5					
6					
7	No2 denied in 96 Case #355				
8	No2 admitted by U.S. Court, Central				
9	Dist, Aug 24/97, as Daisy Deen ~~Moore~~				
10	No.3 born Nov. 28, 1900; Enrolled Jany 20th 1902				
11	Judgement[sic] of U.S. Court admitting No2 vacated and set aside by Decree of Choctaw Chickasaw Citizenship Court Dec 17'02				
12	No appeal to C.C.C.C. (She ought to be in C.C.C.C. 50				
13	~~No2 denied by C.C.C.C. Case #50 March 28th 04~~				
14				Date of Application for Enrollment.	Sept 5/99
15					
16					
17	1-14-02 PO Carterville I.T.				

32

Choctaw By Blood Enrollment Cards 1898-1914

<table>
<tr><td>RESIDENCE:
POST OFFICE: So McAlester, I.T.</td><td>COUNTY.</td><td colspan="2">Choctaw Nation</td><td colspan="2">Choctaw Roll
(Not Including Freedmen)</td><td>CARD No.
FIELD No. 4533</td></tr>
</table>

Dawes' Roll No.	NAME	Relationship to Person First Named	AGE	SEX	BLOOD	TRIBAL ENROLLMENT		
						Year	County	No.
I.W. 446	1 Buck, Francis E 42	Named	39	M	I.W.	1896	Tobucksy	14308
12545	2 " Sophia A. 31	Wife	28	F	3/4	1896	Tobucksy	926
12546	3 " Charles A. 32	Son	12	M	3/8	"	"	927
	4							
	5							
	6							
	7							
	8							
	9							
	10							
	11 ENROLLMENT OF NOS. 1 HEREON							
	12 APPROVED BY THE SECRETARY OF INTERIOR Sep 12 1903							
	13							
	14							
	15 ENROLLMENT OF NOS. 2 and 3 HEREON							
	16 APPROVED BY THE SECRETARY							
	17 OF INTERIOR Mar 6 1903							

TRIBAL ENROLLMENT OF PARENTS

Name of Father	Year	County	Name of Mother	Year	County
1 E. W. Buck		Non Cit	Eliz. Buck		Non Cit
2 S. A. Cochneame	Dd	Blue		Dd	Blue
3 No.1			No.2		
4					
5					
6					
7					
8					
9					
10					
11			No.1 admitted by Dawes Com. #881 No appeal		
12			" 2 on roll as Sopha Buck.		
13					
14					
15					
16					
17				Date of Application for Enrollment. 9/5/99	

Choctaw By Blood Enrollment Cards 1898-1914

RESIDENCE:	Tobucksy	COUNTY.							
POST OFFICE:	Stuart, I.T.	Choctaw Nation			Choctaw Roll (Not Including Freedmen)		CARD NO. FIELD NO. 4534		

Dawes' Roll No.	NAME		Relationship to Person	AGE	SEX	BLOOD	TRIBAL ENROLLMENT		
							Year	County	No.
12547	1 Taylor, Talitha	33	First Named	30	F	1/32	1896	Tobucksy	10768
12548	2 Rozel Lucy	15	Dau	12	F	1/64	"	"	10769
12549	3 " Harvey	13	Son	10	M	1/64	"	"	10770
12550	4 " Edward	11	"	8	M	1/64	"	"	10771
12551	5 " Lizzie	9	Dau	6	F	1/64	"	"	10772
12552	6 " Susan	6	"	3	F	1/64	"	"	10773
14323	7 " John Newton	2	Son	1mo	M	1/64			

ENROLLMENT OF NOS. 7 HEREON APPROVED BY THE SECRETARY OF INTERIOR MAY 20 1903

ENROLLMENT OF NOS. 1,2,3,4,5,6 HEREON APPROVED BY THE SECRETARY OF INTERIOR MAR 6 1903

TRIBAL ENROLLMENT OF PARENTS

	Name of Father	Year	County	Name of Mother	Year	County
1	Wm Stanton	Dd.	Tobucksy	Liza A Kirk	Dd.	Tobucksy
2	Newton Rozel		Non cit	No. 1		
3	" "			" 1		
4	" "			" 1		
5	" "			" 1		
6	" "			" 1		
7	" "			No. 1		

No1 on roll as Taletha Rozel
As to marriage see testimony of
For child of No.1 see NB (Apr 26-06) No. 566   Benj. Grubbs.
No.7 Enrolled Feby 8th, 1901

N⁰1 is now wife of J. T. Taylor. Evidence of marriage filed Dec 30, 1902
For child of No.1 see NB (March 3 1905) Card #324
" children " " 2 " " " " " #325

#1 to 6 inc

Date of Application for Enrollment 9/5/99

34

Choctaw By Blood Enrollment Cards 1898-1914

RESIDENCE:									
POST OFFICE: Savanna, I.T.	COUNTY. **Choctaw Nation**					**Choctaw Roll** (Not Including Freedmen)		CARD NO. FIELD NO. 4535	

Dawes' Roll No.	NAME	Relationship to Person First Named	AGE	SEX	BLOOD	TRIBAL ENROLLMENT Year	County	No.
I.W. 761	1 Harper, Isham W 28	First Named	25	M	I.W.			
12553	2				1/16	1896	Tobucksy	10761
	3							
	4							
	5							
	6							
	7							
	8							
	9							
	10							
	11	ENROLLMENT OF NOS. ~~~~ 1 ~~~~~HEREON APPROVED BY THE SECRETARY OF INTERIOR MAY -7 1904						
	12							
	13							
	14	ENROLLMENT OF NOS. 2 HEREON APPROVED BY THE SECRETARY OF INTERIOR MAR 6 1903						
	15							
	16					DECISION PREPARED		
	17							

TRIBAL ENROLLMENT OF PARENTS

	Name of Father	Year	County	Name of Mother	Year	County
1	Geo. Harper	Dd	Non cit.	Mary J Harper	Dd.	Tobucksy
2	Ryan	"	Tobucksy	Lena Dawson		"
3						
4						
5						
6						
7	No1 See Decision o March 2 '04					
8	Evidence of marriage between Nos 1 and 2 filed Nov 26-1902					
9						
10						
11				No2 on roll as Maggie E. Ryan		
12				as to remarriage see his testimony		
13						
14						
15					Date of Application for Enrollment.	
16						
17	Kiowa I.T.					9/5/99

RESIDENCE: POST OFFICE: Pontotoc, I.T.	COUNTY, Choctaw Nation		Choctaw Roll (Not Including Freedmen)	CARD NO. FIELD NO. 4536			

Dawes' Roll No.	NAME	Relationship to Person First Named	AGE	SEX	BLOOD	TRIBAL ENROLLMENT		
						Year	County	No.
12554	1 Jefferson, Sweeny ³¹		28	M	full	1896	Gaines	6602
	2							
	3							
	4							
	5							
	6							
	7							
	8							
	9							
	10							
	11							
	12							
	13							
	14							
	15	ENROLLMENT OF NOS. 1 HEREON						
	16	APPROVED BY THE SECRETARY OF INTERIOR MAR 6 1903						
	17							

TRIBAL ENROLLMENT OF PARENTS

Name of Father	Year	County	Name of Mother	Year	County
1 Wich. Jefferson		Sans Bois	Ellis Jefferson	Dd.	Sans Bois
2					
3					
4					
5					
6					
7	Nº1 is now the husband of Rosa Anderson on Choctaw Card #5374, Nov. 12, 1902				
8	For child of No.1 see NB (March 3, 1905) #1045				
9					
10					
11					
12					
13					
14					
15					
16				Date of Application for Enrollment.	9/5/99
17					

Choctaw By Blood Enrollment Cards 1898-1914

RESIDENCE:
POST OFFICE: Wayne, I.T.   COUNTY. **Choctaw Nation**   **Choctaw Roll** (Not Including Freedmen)   CARD NO.
FIELD NO. 4537

Dawes' Roll No.	NAME	Relationship to Person	AGE	SEX	BLOOD	TRIBAL ENROLLMENT		
						Year	County	No.
12555	1 Rogers, Mary E ⁶⁸	First Named	65	F	1/8	1896	Tobucksy	10778
12556	2 " John M ²⁵	Son	22	M	1/16	"	"	10774
	3							
	4							
	5							
	6							
	7							
	8							
	9							
	10							
	11							
	12							
	13							
	14							
	15	ENROLLMENT OF NOS. 1 and 2 HEREON APPROVED BY THE SECRETARY OF INTERIOR MAR 6 1903						
	16							
	17							

TRIBAL ENROLLMENT OF PARENTS

	Name of Father	Year	County	Name of Mother	Year	County
1	Samuel Garland	Dd.	Red River	Mary Garland	Dd.	Red River
2	John P. Rogers	"	Atoka	No 1		
3						
4						
5						
6						
7						
8						
9						
10				No1 on roll as Mary E Roggers		
11				No2 " " " John M Rodgers		
12						
13						
14						
15						
16						
17	Paoli I.T. 10/23/02			Date of Application for Enrollment 9/5/99		

37

Choctaw By Blood Enrollment Cards 1898-1914

RESIDENCE:
POST OFFICE: Wayne, I.T.   COUNTY. **Choctaw Nation**   **Choctaw Roll** (Not Including Freedmen)   CARD NO. FIELD NO. **4538**

Dawes' Roll No.	NAME	Relationship to Person Named	AGE	SEX	BLOOD	TRIBAL ENROLLMENT Year	County	No.
I.W. 1262	1 Stealey, Charles L 30	First Named	27	M	I.W.	1896	Tobucksy	15033
14945	2 " Lloyd G. B. 8	Son	5	M	1/16	1896	"	11279
14946	3 " Lorenzo P 6	"	3	M	1/16	1896	"	11280
14947	4 " Knoxa K 4	Dau	15m	F	1/16			
	5							
	6							
	7							
	8							
	9							
	10							
	11							
	12							

ENROLLMENT
OF NOS. ~~ 1 ~~ HEREON
APPROVED BY THE SECRETARY
OF INTERIOR Dec 30 1904

13 See testimony of No1 as to his status as an intermarried
14 citizen Sept 25, 1902, taken at Muskogee I.T. Nov. 18, 1902,
also election made for enrollment of himself and children as Choctaws
15 No1 formerly husband of Leona Stealey (nee Rogers)
16 1893 Atoka, No 891, and 1896 Tobucksy No 11278, now deceased.
17

TRIBAL ENROLLMENT OF PARENTS

	Name of Father	Year	County	Name of Mother	Year	County
1	R. L. Stealey	Dd	non cit	L. E. Stealey	Dd	non cit
2	No1			Leona Stealey	"	Tobucksy
3	" 1			" "		
4	" 1			" "		

7 Nos 1,2 and 3 admitted by Dawes Commission in 1896 as Cherokees: Cherokee case #5442: no appeal
8 Nos 1,2 and 3 admitted by Dawes Commission in 1896 as Choctaws: Choctaw case #1391: no appeal
9 No application for the enrollment of any of the persons on this card has been made as
citizens of the Cherokee Nation Nov. 18, 1902
10 P.O. address, Purcell, Ind. Ter. May 29, 1902
11 No4 born June 6, 1893   No1 admitted by Dawes Com #1391
12 " 1 as C. Lloyd Stealey
13 " 2 " Goodwin B "
14 " 3 " Lorenzo P "
15 " 2 on 96 roll as Lloyd G.B. Stealey
16 " 3 " " " " Lorenzo P "
17 " 1 " " " " Chas. L "

ENROLLMENT
OF NOS. 2 3 and 4 HEREON
APPROVED BY THE SECRETARY
OF INTERIOR Oct 15 1903

Date of Application for Enrollment 9/5/99

38

Choctaw By Blood Enrollment Cards 1898-1914

RESIDENCE:
POST OFFICE: So McAlester, I.T.
COUNTY.
Choctaw Nation
Choctaw Roll
(Not Including Freedmen)
CARD No.
FIELD No. 4539

Dawes' Roll No.	NAME	Relationship to Person First Named	AGE	SEX	BLOOD	TRIBAL ENROLLMENT		
						Year	County	No.
DEAD.	1 Allen, Joshua J DEAD.	Named	36	M	full	1896	Tobucksy	101
I.W. 522	2 " Anna P 31	Wife	28	F	I.W.	"	"	14253
	3							
	4							
	5							
	6 No. 1 HEREON DISMISSED UNDER							
	7 ORDER OF THE COMMISSION TO THE FIVE CIVILIZED TRIBES OF MARCH 31, 1905.							
	8							
	9 ENROLLMENT							
	10 OF NOS. ~~ 2 ~~~~ HEREON							
	11 APPROVED BY THE SECRETARY OF INTERIOR DEC 24 1903							
	12							
	13							
	14							
	15							
	16							
	17							

TRIBAL ENROLLMENT OF PARENTS

	Name of Father	Year	County	Name of Mother	Year	County
1	John Allen	Dd.	Blue	Janessy Allen	Dd.	Blue
2	H. S. McQuarter		Non cit.	Rainy McQuarter		Non cit
3						
4						
5						
6						
7						
8						
9						
10				No 2 admitted by Dawes Comm.		
11				as Anna Allen #4761 No appeal		
12	N^o1 Died April 20 1902; proof of death filed Aug 7, 1902					
13						
14						
15						
16				Date of Application for Enrollment.		
17						9/5/99

39

Choctaw By Blood Enrollment Cards 1898-1914

RESIDENCE: COUNTY. **Choctaw Nation**   **Choctaw Ro**
POST OFFICE: Brooklyn, N.Y.   *(Not Including Freedm*

Dawes' Roll No.	NAME	Relationship to Person	AGE	SEX	BLOOD	TRIBAL ENROLLMENT		
						Year	County	No.
15491	1 Allen, Emmerson A ³⁶	First Named	33	M	full	1896	Tobucksy	402
	2							
	3							
	4							
	5							
	6	ENROLLMENT						
	7	OF NOS. ~~~ 1 ~~~ HEREON APPROVED BY THE SECRETARY						
	8	OF INTERIOR May 9 1904						
	9							
	10							
	11							
	12							
	13							
	14							
	15							
	16							
	17							

TRIBAL ENROLLMENT OF PARENTS

	Name of Father	Year	County	Name of Mother	Year	County
1	John Allen	Dd	Blue	Janessy Allen	Dd	Blue
2						
3						
4						
5						
6						
7						
8						
9						
10						
11				on roll as Emmerson E. Allen		
12						
13	Sept 29/99. Note that post office is					
14	Brooklyn, N.Y. No note as to this on memorandum issued 9/5/99					
15	No 1 in 1894 sentenced for life to penitentiary, Brooklyn, N.Y					
16	Sentence remitted for ten years and released March 1901					
17	P.O. Caddo I.T. 5/12/03			Date of Application for Enrollment		9/5/99

40

Choctaw By Blood Enrollment Cards 1898-1914

RESIDENCE:	COUNTY.								

POST OFFICE: So McAlester, I.T. **Choctaw Nation** **Choctaw Roll** (Not Including Freedmen) CARD NO. FIELD NO. 4541

Dawes' Roll No.	NAME	Relationship to Person	AGE	SEX	BLOOD	TRIBAL ENROLLMENT		
						Year	County	No.
I.W. 844	1 McKasson, Thadeus S ⑥⓪	First Named	57	M	I.W.			
12557	2 " Mary J 38	Wife	35	F	1/8	1896	Tobucksy	9193
12558	3 " John L 21	Son	18	M	1/16	"	"	9194
12559	4 " Mary E 15	Dau	12	F	1/16	"	"	9195
12560	5 " James C 12	Son	9	M	1/16	"	"	9196
12561	6 " Laura I 10	Dau	7	F	1/16	"	"	9197
12562	7 " Thadeus E 8	Son	5	M	1/16	"	"	9198
12563	8 " Emuel[sic] O 6	"	3	M	1/16			
	9							
	10							
	11	ENROLLMENT						
	12	OF NOS. 1 HEREON						
		APPROVED BY THE SECRETARY						
	13	OF INTERIOR MAY 21 1904						
	14							
	15	ENROLLMENT						
	16	OF NOS. 2,3,4,5,6,7-8 HEREON APPROVED BY THE SECRETARY						
	17	OF INTERIOR MAT 6 1903						

TRIBAL ENROLLMENT OF PARENTS

	Name of Father	Year	County	Name of Mother	Year	County
1	Jno L McKosson[sic]	Dd	non cit	Isabel McKasson		non cit
2	Elias Boatwright	"	Tobucksy	Ruthy Boatwright		Tobucksy
3	No. 1			No.2		
4	" 1			" 2		
5	" 1			" 2		
6	" 1			" 2		
7	" 1			" 2		
8	" 1			" 2		new born
9						
10	Evidence of marriage between Nos 1 and 2 filed Jany 3 1903			No.3 on Roll as Jno L.		
11	Affidavit of Nº1 as to residence of his wife of date			" 5 " " Jas C		
12	of his marriage to her, filed May 18, 1903			" 6 " " Laura J.		
13	For child of No.4 see NB (Apr 26-06) No. 543					
14						
15						
16					Date of Application for Enrollment.	
17					9/5/99	

41

Choctaw By Blood Enrollment Cards 1898-1914

RESIDENCE:		COUNTY.					Choctaw Roll		CARD NO.
POST OFFICE: Savanna I.T.		Choctaw Nation					(Not Including Freedmen)		FIELD NO. 4542

Dawes' Roll No.	NAME		Relationship to Person	AGE	SEX	BLOOD	TRIBAL ENROLLMENT		
							Year	County	No.
12564	1 Grubbs, Benj F	46	First Named	43	M	1/4	1896	Tobucksy	4691
I.W. 447	2 " Eliza C	44	Wife	40	F	I.W.	"	"	14567
See 5355	3 " John		Son	23	M	1/8	"	"	4692
12565	4 " Eli	23	"	20	M	1/8	"	"	4693
12566	5 " Mary V	21	Dau	18	F	1/8	"	"	14694[sic]
12567	6 " Robert	19	Son	16	M	1/8	"	"	4695
12568	7 " William	17	"	14	M	1/8	"	"	4696
12569	8 " Addie M	14	Dau	11	F	1/8	"	"	4697
12570	9 " Benj jr	10	Son	10	M	1/8	"	"	4698
12571	10 " Frank	8	"	5	M	1/8	"	"	4699
12572	11 " Minnie	4	Dau	1	F	1/8	"	"	
12573	12 Johnston Arthur	18	Neph	15	M	1/8	"	"	6638
12574	13 " John	14	"	11	M	1/8	"	"	6639
	14								
	15								
	16								
	17								

ENROLLMENT
OF NOS. 1,4,5,6,7,8,9,10,11,12-13 HEREON
APPROVED BY THE SECRETARY
OF INTERIOR MAR 6 1903

TRIBAL ENROLLMENT OF PARENTS

	Name of Father	Year	County	Name of Mother	Year	County
1	Curtis Grubbs	Dd	Non Cit	Betsy Grubbs		Blue
2	W. C. Burke	"	" "	Mary Burke		Non Cit
3	No. 1			No. 2		
4	" 1			" 2		
5	" 1			" 2		
6	" 1			" 2		
7	" 1			" 2		
8	" 1			" 2		
9	" 1			" 2		
10	" 1			" 2		
11	" 1			" 2		new born
12	J. S. Johnson[sic]	Dd	Tobucksy	Mary J Johnson[sic]	Dd	Tobucksy
13	"			" " "		

ENROLLMENT HEREON
OF NOS. 2
APPROVED BY THE SECRETARY
OF INTERIOR SEP 12 1903

14 For child of No4 see NB (Apr 26-06) Card #471

No 1 on roll as Benjamin Grubbs
" 4 " " " Elie "

15 No. 3 transferred to Choctaw card #5355

As to marriage of 1 and 2 see testimony of

16 with his wife   Dec. 7, 1900

No.1 and also of Forbis S Grubbs

Date of Application for Enrollment.   9/5/99

17   For child of No 8 see NB (Mar 3 '05) #326

" " " " 4 " " " " #327

No 1 P.O. S McAlester I [illegible]

42

Choctaw By Blood Enrollment Cards 1898-1914

RESIDENCE:	COUNTY.					CARD No.
POST OFFICE: Enterprise, I.T.	**Choctaw Nation**			Choctaw Roll (Not Including Freedmen)		FIELD No. **4543**

Dawes' Roll No.	NAME	Relationship to Person	AGE	SEX	BLOOD	TRIBAL ENROLLMENT		
						Year	County	No.
12575	1 Harris, Blanche Adeline 20	First Named	17	F	1/8	1896	San[sic] Bois	9011
12576	2 " Samuel 5	Son	1	M	1/16			
12577	3 " Joseph 3	Son	5mo	M	1/16			
12578	4 " Willey 2	Son	9mo	M	1/16			
	5							
	6							
	7							
	8							
	9							
	10							
	11							
	12							
	13							
	14							
	15 ENROLLMENT							
	16 OF NOS. 1,2,3 and 4 HEREON APPROVED BY THE SECRETARY							
	17 OF INTERIOR Mar 6 1903							

TRIBAL ENROLLMENT OF PARENTS

	Name of Father	Year	County	Name of Mother	Year	County
1	Joe McIntosh		San[sic] Bois	Katie McIntosh		San[sic] Bois
2	M. S. Harris		Choc. Frd	No.1		
3	Martin Harris		" "	No.1		
4	" "		" "	No.1		
5						
6						
7						
8						
9						
10						
11			No 1 is the wife of Martin Harris on			
12			Choctaw freedmen card 236. Feby 6, 1900.			
13	Error: The above named Martin Harris is on Choctaw freedman card #1108 See testimony of July 9, 1903					Not on roll as Blanch McIntosh
14			No1 full name is Blanche Adeline Harris.			
15						
16			No.3 enrolled Feby 20, 1900			#1&2
17	No.4 born Feby 6th, 1901: Enrolled Oct. 11, 1901				Date of Application for Enrollment.	9/5/99

43

Choctaw By Blood Enrollment Cards 1898-1914

RESIDENCE:		COUNTY.	**Choctaw Nation**				**Choctaw Roll** *(Not Including Freedmen)*		CARD NO.	
POST OFFICE:	So McAlester, I.T.								FIELD NO. **4544**	

Dawes' Roll No.	NAME		Relationship to Person First Named	AGE	SEX	BLOOD	TRIBAL ENROLLMENT		
							Year	County	No.
12579	1 Grubbs, Forbis L	44	Named	41	M	1/4	1896	Tobucksy	4687
I.W.523	2 " Carrie	26	Wife	23	F	I.W.	"	"	14566
12580	3 " Vernon L	6	Son	3	M	1/8	"	"	4688
12581	4 " Osborn L	4	"	7ᵐ	M	1/8			
12582	5 " Leroy	1	Son	1	M	1/8			
	6								
	7								
	8								
	9	ENROLLMENT							
	10	OF NOS. ~~~ 2 ~~~ HEREON APPROVED BY THE SECRETARY							
	11	OF INTERIOR Dec 24 1903							
	12								
	13								
	14								
	15	ENROLLMENT OF NOS. 1,3,4 and 5 HEREON							
	16	APPROVED BY THE SECRETARY							
	17	OF INTERIOR Mar 6 1903							

TRIBAL ENROLLMENT OF PARENTS

	Name of Father	Year	County	Name of Mother	Year	County
1	Curtis Grubbs	Dd	Non Cit	Eliz Grubbs		Blue
2	Aleck Murphy		" "	Murphy		Non Cit
3	No.1			No.2		
4	" 1			" 2		
5	Nº1			Nº2		
6						
7						
8						
9						
10				No.1 on roll as Forbis Grubbs		
11				" 3 " " " Lethaniel "		
12	Evidence of marriage of Nº1 to Nº2 received and filed Aug. 13, 1902					
13	Nº5 Born Aug 24, 1901; enrolled Aug. 13, 1902.					
14						
15						
16				Date of Application for Enrollment.		#1 to 4
17						9/5/99

44

Choctaw By Blood Enrollment Cards 1898-1914

POST OFFICE: Savanna, I.T.   **Choctaw Nation**   Choctaw Roll
(Not Including Freedmen)

Dawes' Roll No.	NAME		Relationship to Person First Named	AGE	SEX	BLOOD	TRIBAL ENROLLMENT		
							Year	County	No.
12583	1 Artice, Mary	27	First Named	24	F	1/2	1896	Tobucksy	138
12584	2 Sumter, Emma	23	Sis	20	F	1/2	"	"	139
12585	3 Albright, Servie	16	Bro	13	M	1/2	"	"	140
	4								
	5								
	6								
	7								
	8								
	9								
	10								
	11								
	12								
	13								
	14								
	15	ENROLLMENT OF NOS. 1, 2 - 3 HEREON APPROVED BY THE SECRETARY OF INTERIOR MAR 6 1903							
	16								
	17								

TRIBAL ENROLLMENT OF PARENTS

	Name of Father		Year	County	Name of Mother		Year	County
1	Frank Albright		Dd	Tobucksy	Sarah Albright		Dd	Tobucksy
2	"	"			"	"		
3	"	"			"	"		
4								
5								
6	No2 is now wife of J.M. Sumter: evidence of marriage							
7								
8								
9				No.1 on roll as Mary Artiste				
10				" 3 " " " Louis Albright				
11								
12	For children of No.2 see NB (Mar 3 '05) #328							
13								
14								
15								
16							Date of Application for Enrollment.	
17	No.2 P.O. Atoka I.T. 11/20/02							9/5/99

Choctaw By Blood Enrollment Cards 1898-1914

RESIDENCE:
POST OFFICE: Savanna, I.T.　COUNTY. **Choctaw Nation**　**Choctaw Roll** *(Not Including Freedmen)*　CARD NO.　FIELD NO. **4546**

Dawes' Roll No.	NAME		Relationship to Person First Named	AGE	SEX	BLOOD	TRIBAL ENROLLMENT		
							Year	County	No.
I.W. 448	1 Davis, James S	52	First Named	50	M	I.W.	1896	Tobucksy	14463
12586	2 " Annie	51	Wife	48	F	1/8	1896	"	3308
12587	3 " Jas G	21	Son	18	M	1/16	1896	"	3311
12588	4 " Geo T	19	"	16	M	1/16	1896	"	3312
12589	5 " Lillie G	13	Dau	10	F	1/16	1896	"	3313
12590	6 " Joseph L	7	Son	4	M	1/16	1896	"	3314
	7								
	8								

ENROLLMENT
OF NOS. 1 HEREON
APPROVED BY THE SECRETARY
OF INTERIOR Sep 12 1903

ENROLLMENT
OF NOS. 2,3,4,5 and 6 HEREON
APPROVED BY THE SECRETARY
OF INTERIOR Mar 6 1903

TRIBAL ENROLLMENT OF PARENTS

	Name of Father	Year	County	Name of Mother	Year	County
1	Will Davis	Dd	Non Cit	Gillie Davis	Dd	Non Cit
2	Goings	"		Sophia Goings		Skullyville
3	No.1			No.2		
4	" 1			" 2		
5	" 1			" 2		
6	" 1			" 2		

For child of No.4 See NB (Apr 26-06) Card #591

No.1 Admitted by Dawes Com #308 as Jas S Davis. No appeal.
No.3 on roll as Jas S Davis
" 4 " " " Geo T Davis

Date of Application for Enrollment.

P.O. Spiro I.T. 12/24/02　9/5/99

46

Choctaw By Blood Enrollment Cards 1898-1914

RESIDENCE:
POST OFFICE: Legal I.T.

COUNTY. **Choctaw Nation**

Choctaw Roll
(Not Including Freedmen)

CARD NO.
FIELD NO. **4547**

Dawes' Roll No.	NAME	Relationship to Person First Named	AGE	SEX	BLOOD	TRIBAL ENROLLMENT Year	County	No.
IW 573	1 Cunningham Alfred H 44	First Named	41	M	IW	1896	Tobucksy	14397
12591	2 " Martha J 31	Wife	28	F	1/16	"	"	2351
12592	3 " Alfred H Jr 15	Son	12	M	1/32	"	"	2352
12593	4 " James W 12	"	9	"	1/32	"	"	3253
12594	5 " Augustus 9	"	6	"	1/32	"	"	2354
12595	6 " Walter 7	"	4	"	1/32	"	"	2355
12596	7 " John W 5	"	2	"	1/32			
12597	8 " Hazel Ellen 3	Dau	3mo	F	1/32			
	9							
	10							

11 ENROLLMENT
OF NOS. ~ 1 ~ HEREON
12 APPROVED BY THE SECRETARY
13 OF INTERIOR Feb 8 1904

14

15 ENROLLMENT
OF NOS. 2,3,4,5,6,7-8 HEREON
APPROVED BY THE SECRETARY
OF INTERIOR Mar 6 1903
17

TRIBAL ENROLLMENT OF PARENTS

	Name of Father	Year	County	Name of Mother	Year	County
1	Jno Cunningham	Dd	Non Cit	Nicey Lane		Non Cit
2	Jim Johnston	"	Tobucksy	Mary Johnston	Dd	Tobucksy
3	No1			No2		
4	" 1			" 2		
5	" 1			" 2		
6	" 1			" 2		
7	No1			No2		new born
8	No1			No2		
9						
10	Affidavit of No1 as to his residence at			No1 on roll as Alfred Cunningham		
11	the time of his marriage to No2 filed May 28, 1903			" 2 " " " Martha "		
12				" 3 " " " Alfred "		
13				" 4 " " " James "		
14	For child of Nos 1&2 see NB (Apr 26-06) card # 186					
15	" " " " " " (Mar 3 '05) " #329				#1 to 7 inc	
16					Date of Application for Enrollment.	
17				No 8 Enrolled 6/5/1900	9/5/99	

47

Choctaw By Blood Enrollment Cards 1898-1914

RESIDENCE:		COUNTY.					CARD No.	
POST OFFICE: McAlester, I.T.		Choctaw Nation			Choctaw Roll (Not Including Freedmen)		FIELD No. 4548	

Dawes' Roll No.	NAME	Relationship to Person Named	AGE	SEX	BLOOD	TRIBAL ENROLLMENT		
						Year	County	No.
IW449	1 Tanehill, Joseph D 36	First Named	32	M	IW	1896	Tobucksy	15100
12598	2 " Mintie 24	Wife	21	F	1/4	"	"	12008
DEAD ✓	3 " Irvin C 6 DEAD	Son	3	M	1/8			
12499	4 " Edgar P 5	"	1½	M	1/8			
12600	5 " Francis Ward 3	"	2mo	M	1/8			
	6							
	7 No. 3 Hereon Dismissed under order							
	8 of the Commission to the Five Civilized							
	9 Tribes of March 31, 1905.							
	10							
	11 ENROLLMENT OF NOS. 1 HEREON							
	12 APPROVED BY THE SECRETARY OF INTERIOR Sep. 12 1903							
	13							
	14 ENROLLMENT OF NOS. 2, 4, 5 HEREON							
	15 APPROVED BY THE SECRETARY OF INTERIOR Mar 6, 1903							
	16							
	17							

TRIBAL ENROLLMENT OF PARENTS

	Name of Father	Year	County	Name of Mother	Year	County
1	David Tanehill	Dd	Non Cit	Mary Tanehill	Dd	Non Cit
2	Ward Folsom	"	Skullyville	Eliz Folsom		Tobucksy
3	No1			No2		
4	" 1			" 2		
5	No1			No2		
6						
7						
8						
9				No.2 on roll as Minty Tamehee		
10				" 1 admitted by Dawes Com #469 as no appeal		
11				J.D. Tannyhill - on 96 roll as Joe D Tannehill		
12				as to marriage of parents of No.1 see enrollment of Elizabeth G. Folsom		
13						
14				No5 Enrolled May 24, 1900		
15				No3 Died April 12, 1900: Proof of death filed Dec 23, 1902		
16				For child of Nos 1&2 see N.B. (Mar 3'05) #330		
17				Date of Application for Enrollment, 9/5/99		

Choctaw By Blood Enrollment Cards 1898-1914

| RESIDENCE: | | COUNTY. | Choctaw Nation | | | | Choctaw Roll | CARD NO. | |
| POST OFFICE: Scipio, I.T. | | | | | | | (Not Including Freedmen) | FIELD NO. 4549 | |

Dawes' Roll No.	NAME		Relationship to Person	AGE	SEX	BLOOD	TRIBAL ENROLLMENT		
							Year	County	No.
12601	1 Anderson, David	27	First Named	24	M	full	1896	Tobucksy	105
12602	2 " Siney	21	Wife	18	F	"	"	"	106
12603	3 " Hampton W	6	Son	3	M	"	"	"	107
12604	4 " Houston Jasper	1	Son	1/2	M	"			
	5								
	6								
	7								
	8								
	9								
	10								
	11								
	12								
	13								
	14	ENROLLMENT OF NOS. 1,2,3 and 4 HEREON							
	15	APPROVED BY THE SECRETARY							
	16	OF INTERIOR MAR 6 1903							
	17								

TRIBAL ENROLLMENT OF PARENTS

Name of Father	Year	County	Name of Mother	Year	County
1 Andle Anderson		Tobucksy	Anderson	Dd	Tobucksy
2 David J Byington		"	Ella Byington	"	"
3 No.1			No.2		
4 No.1			No.2		
5					
6					
7					
8 No.4 Born June 7, 1901: Enrolled Nov. 12, 1901.					
9					
10					
11					
12					
13					
14					
15				#1 to 3	
16				Date of Application for Enrollment	
17				9/5/99	

49

Choctaw By Blood Enrollment Cards 1898-1914

RESIDENCE:
POST OFFICE: Celestine, I.T.   COUNTY. **Choctaw Nation**   **Choctaw Roll** *(Not Including Freedmen)*   CARD NO.
FIELD NO. **4550**

Dawes' Roll No.	NAME		Relationship to Person Named	AGE	SEX	BLOOD	TRIBAL ENROLLMENT		
							Year	County	No.
12605	1 Holloway, Frank A	56	First Named	53	M	1/4	1896	Tobucksy	5335
IW1022	2 " Alice	39	Wife	37	F	IW	"	"	
12606	3 " Rebecca	12	Dau	9	F	1/8	"	"	5336
12607	4 " Fannie	8	"	5	F	1/8			5337
12608	5 " William	4	Son	1	M	full	1896	Tobucksy	
12609	6 Colbert, Sam	13	Ward	10	M	1/8			2385
12610	7 Holloway Ivy Amelia	2	Dau	6mo	F				
	8								
	9								
	10								
	11	ENROLLMENT							
	12	OF NOS. ~2~ HEREON APPROVED BY THE SECRETARY							
	13	OF INTERIOR Oct 21, 1904							
	14								
	15	ENROLLMENT							
	16	OF NOS. 1,3,4,5,6-7 HEREON APPROVED BY THE SECRETARY							
	17	OF INTERIOR Mar. 6, 1903							

TRIBAL ENROLLMENT OF PARENTS

	Name of Father	Year	County	Name of Mother	Year	County
1	Wm Holloway	Dd	Tobucksy	Rebecca Holloway	Dd	Tobucksy
2	Martin Jno	"	Non cit	Mary Martin	"	Non Cit
3	No1			No2		
4	" 1			" 2		
5	" 1			" 2		
6	Reuben Colbert	Dd	Gaines			Tobucksy
7	No1			No2		
8						
9						
10						
11						
12						
13			Evidence of marriage to be supplied			
14			No3 on roll as Beckie Holloway			
15			No7 Enrolled July 30 1901			
16			Evidence of marriage of Nos 1 and 2 filed Aug 24, 1901			
17	P.O. Savanna IT 1/20/05		For child of Nos 1&2 see NB (Mar 3'05) #331 #1 to 6			

Date of Application for Enrollment   9/5/99

50

Choctaw By Blood Enrollment Cards 1898-1914

RESIDENCE:
POST OFFICE: So MᶜAlester, I.T.   COUNTY. **Choctaw Nation**   **Choctaw Roll** (Not Including Freedmen)   CARD NO. FIELD NO. **4551**

Dawes' Roll No.	NAME	Relationship to Person First Named	AGE	SEX	BLOOD	TRIBAL ENROLLMENT		
						Year	County	No.
✓ 1	Hardin, Mary C ＊		47	F	1/8			
✓ 2	Bryant, David C ＊		20	M	1/16			
✓ 3	" Samuel W ＊		19	"	1/16			
✓ 4	" Fannie L ＊		13	F	1/16			
5								
6								
7								
8								
9								
10								
11								
12								
13								
14								
15								
16								
17								

TRIBAL ENROLLMENT OF PARENTS

	Name of Father	Year	County	Name of Mother	Year	County
1	David Powers	Dd		Tabitha Powers	Dd	
2	S.A. Bryant	"	Non Cit	No 1		
3	"		" "	" 1		
4	"		" "	" 1		
5						
6						
7						
8	Nos 1 to 4 incl denied in 96 Case #1122					
9	Judgement[sic] of U.S. Court admitting Nos 1 to 4 incl vacated and set aside by Decree of CCCC Decʳ 17-02					
10	Nos 1 to 4 incl now in CCCC case #86			Admitted by U.S Court at So MᶜAlester		
11				Sept. 8-97 Case No 41		
12				No 1 as Mrs. M. C. Bryant		
13				" 4 " Fannie Lee "		
				as to residence see testimony of No1		
14						
15						
16				See C 106		
17	Olney I.T. 12/19/02			See 7-3647 for record	Date of Application for Enrollment	9/5/99

P.O. Bradley, Okla 12/22/08

Choctaw By Blood Enrollment Cards 1898-1914

RESIDENCE: COUNTY. **Choctaw Nation** **Choctaw Roll** CARD NO.
POST OFFICE: So McAlester, I.T.   *(Not Including Freedmen)* FIELD NO. **4552**

Dawes' Roll No.	NAME	Relationship to Person	AGE	SEX	BLOOD	TRIBAL ENROLLMENT		
						Year	County	No.
✓✓ 1	Bryant, John T	First Named	25	M	1/8			
DP 2	" Myrtle L	Dau	1½	F	1/16			
DP 3	" Jerel William	Son	3mo	M	1/16			
DP 4	" Annie Lee	Dau	2mo	F	1/16			
5								
6	No1 Denied Citizenship by the Choctaw and							
7	Chickasaw Citizenship Court Case #86 April 18 '04							
8								
Nos 2,3&4 Dismissed May 27-1904								
10								
11								
12								
Nos 2,3 and 4 Dismissed Case #86 April 18. 1904								
14								
15								
16								
17	For record see 7-3646. See C. 106							

TRIBAL ENROLLMENT OF PARENTS

	Name of Father	Year	County	Name of Mother	Year	County
1	S. A. Bryant	Dd	Tobucksy	M. C. Bryant		Tobucksy
2	No1			Dora Bryant		D-No-438
3	No1			" "		" " "
4	No1			" "		" " "
5						
6						
7						
8						
9						
10	No1 denied in 96 Case #1122					
	Judgement[sic] of U.S. Ct admitting No1 vacated and set aside by Decree of CCCC Decr 17 '02					
11	Nos 1 to 4 incl now in CCCC Case #86					
12	Admitted by U.S. Court at So McA. Sep 8-97, Case #42					
	As to residence see his testimony					
13	As to remarriage see testimony					
14	Wife on D-438					
15	No3 Enrolled Oct. 18th 1900					
16	No4 Born Feby 25, 1902, enrolled May 8 1902					
17					Date of Application for Enrollment.	9/5/99

52

Choctaw By Blood Enrollment Cards 1898-1914

RESIDENCE:									
POST OFFICE: Stonewall, I.T.	COUNTY. **Choctaw Nation**				**Choctaw Roll** (Not Including Freedmen)			CARD NO. FIELD NO. **4553**	

Dawes' Roll No.	NAME	Relationship to Person	AGE	SEX	BLOOD	TRIBAL ENROLLMENT		
						Year	County	No.
12611	1 Babb, Belzora 16	First Named	13	F	1/4	1896	Chick Dist	3149
12612	2 Correll[sic] Ella 13	Sis	10	F	1/4	"	" "	3150
12613	3 Babb Ocial 1	Son	3mo	M	1/8			
	4							
	5							
	6							
	7							
	8							
	9							
	10							
	11	ENROLLMENT OF NOS. 1-2-3 APPROVED BY THE SECRETARY OF INTERIOR Mar 5 1903 HEREON						
	12							
	13							
	14							
	15							
	16							
	17							

TRIBAL ENROLLMENT OF PARENTS

	Name of Father	Year	County	Name of Mother	Year	County
1	John Correll		Chic cit	Eliza Correll		Blue
2	" "					
3	Garland Babb		non citizen	No.1		
4						
5						
6						
7						
8						
9						
10				No1 on roll as Belizora Carrol		
11				" 2 " " " Ella "		
12	No1 is now wife of G.L. Babb, a noncitizen: evidence of marriage					
13	filed December 20, 1902					
14	No3 Born August 30, 1902. Enrolled December 22, 1902					
15	For child of No1 see NB (Apr 26-06) Card #517					
16	" " " " " " (Mar 3-05) " #708					
17	P.O. Ada, I.T. 12/16/02				Date of Application for Enrollment #1 & 2 9/5/99	

53

Choctaw By Blood Enrollment Cards 1898-1914

RESIDENCE: COUNTY. **Choctaw Nation** **Choctaw Roll** CARD NO.
POST OFFICE: So McAlester, I.T. *(Not Including Freedmen)* FIELD NO. **4554**

Dawes' Roll No.	NAME	Relationship to Person	AGE	SEX	BLOOD	TRIBAL ENROLLMENT		
						Year	County	No.
IW524	1 Folsom, Elizabeth G 61	First Named	58	F	I.W.	1896	Tobucksy	14522
	2							
	3							
	4							
	5							
	6							
	7							
	8							
	9							
	10							
	11							
	12							
	13							
	14							
	15							
	16							
	17							

ENROLLMENT
OF NOS. ~~1~~ HEREON
APPROVED BY THE SECRETARY
OF INTERIOR Dec. 24, 1903

TRIBAL ENROLLMENT OF PARENTS

Name of Father	Year	County	Name of Mother	Year	County
1 Peter Mickle		Non cit	Frances Hunt		non cit
2					
3					
4					
5					
6					
7					
8					
9					
10		As to marriage see her testimony and that			
11		of Wm Folsom			
12					
13	Mother of Peter W Folsom 7-4558 on final roll #12631 approved March 6 '03				
14					
15					
16					
17 Dec 23-02 P.O. Fox I.T.			Date of Application for Enrollment. 9/5/99		

54

Choctaw By Blood Enrollment Cards 1898-1914

RESIDENCE:
POST OFFICE: Savanna, I.T. COUNTY. **Choctaw Nation** **Choctaw Roll** *(Not Including Freedmen)* CARD No. FIELD No. **4555**

Dawes' Roll No.	NAME	Relationship to Person First Named	AGE	SEX	BLOOD	TRIBAL ENROLLMENT Year	County	No.
12614	1 Folsom, Wᵐ S ⁴⁸	First Named	45	M	1/2	1896	Tobucksy	4041
12615	2 " Ophelia P ⁴¹	Wife	39	F	1/4	"	"	4042
12616	3 " Aurora A ²⁵	Dau	22	"	3/8	"	"	4043
12617	4 Jones, Zenobia V ²⁴	"	21	"	3/8	"	"	4044
12618	5 Folsom, Chlora A ²²	"	19	"	3/8	"	"	4045
12619	6 " William W ²⁰	Son	17	M	3/8	"	"	4046
12620	7 " Alexander H ¹⁵	"	12	"	3/8	"	"	4048
12621	8 " Rodolph D ¹²	"	9	"	3/8	"	"	4049
12622	9 " Odus W ⁷	"	4	"	3/8	"	"	4050
12623	10 " Lillie P ¹⁸	Dau	15	F	3/8	"	"	4047
12624	11 " Edgar R ⁵	Son	2	M	3/8	as to marriage see enrollment of		
12625	12 " George R ³	Son	5mo	M	3/8	No4 is now wife of H.G. Jones noncitizen		
12626	13 " Oura P ¹	Dau	3mo	F	3/8	evidence of marriage requested Oct 2, 1902		
12627	14 Jones, Ester Gray ¹	Gr. Dau	10das	F	3/16	Rec &filed Oct 13, 1902		

Father of No14 is A.G. Jones non citizen
Mother of No14 is No4

15 No12 Enrolled May 24, 1900
" 13 Born April 10-1902: Enrolled July 2ⁿᵈ 1902 No14 Born Sept 22 1902 enrolled Oct 2 1902
16 For child of No5 see NB (Apr 26-06) Card #795
17 " " No6 " " (Mar 3-05) " #1261

TRIBAL ENROLLMENT OF PARENTS

	Name of Father	Year	County	Name of Mother	Year	County
1	Ward Folsom	Dd	Skullyville	Eliza Folsom	Dd	Skullyville
2	And. J. Stanton	"	"	Eliz. G. Stanton	"	Tobucksy
3	No1			No2		
4	" 1			" 2		
5	" 1			" 2		
6	" 1			" 2		
7	" 1			" 2		
8	" 1			" 2		
9	" 1			" 2		
10	" 1			" 2		
11	" 1			" 2	New born	
12	No1			No2		
13	No1			No2		

ENROLLMENT OF NOS 1234567891011121314HEREON APPROVED BY THE SECRETARY OF INTERIOR Mar 6, 1903

No1 on roll as Wᵐ S Fulsom
14 " 2 " " " Ophelia "   No6 on roll as W Fulsom
15 " 3 " " " Anrora "   " 7 " " " Alexander H "
16 " 4 " " " Zenobia "   " 8 " " " Rodolph "
" 5 " " " Chlora "   " 9 " " " Odus W "
17   " 10 " " " Lillie P "

Date of Application for Enrollment 9/5/99 #1 to 11

No6 is husband of No1 on Card No 6049

55

RESIDENCE:		COUNTY.	**Choctaw Nation**				**Choctaw Roll**	CARD NO.	
POST OFFICE:	So McAlester, I.T.						*(Not Including Freedmen)*	FIELD NO. 4556	

Dawes' Roll No.	NAME	Relationship to Person	AGE	SEX	BLOOD	TRIBAL ENROLLMENT		
						Year	County	No.
12628	₁ Stanton, Rudolph J ³¹	First Named	28	M	1/8	1896	Tobucksy	11264
12629	₂ " Clyde E ⁶	Son	3	"	1/16	1896	"	11265
	3							
	4							
	5							
	6							
	7							
	8							
	9							
	10							
	11							
	12							
	13							
	14	ENROLLMENT OF NOS 1-2 HEREON						
	15	APPROVED BY THE SECRETARY OF INTERIOR MAR 6 1903						
	16							
	17							

TRIBAL ENROLLMENT OF PARENTS

	Name of Father	Year	County	Name of Mother	Year	County
₁	Andrew Stanton	Dd	Skullyville	Eliza. Stanton		Tobucksy
₂	No.1		Non cit[sic]	Kitty Stanton	Dd	
3						
4						
5						
6						
7						
8						
9				No.1 on roll as Rudolph Stenton		
10				" 2 " " " Clyde "		
11				As to marriage see enrollment of Elizabeth G. Folsom		
12						
13						
14						
15						
16				Date of Application for Enrollment.	9/5/99	
17						

Choctaw By Blood Enrollment Cards 1898-1914

RESIDENCE:		COUNTY. **Choctaw Nation**				**Choctaw Roll** *(Not Including Freedmen)*	CARD NO.	
POST OFFICE: Muskogee, I.T.							FIELD NO. **4557**	

Dawes' Roll No.	NAME		Relationship to Person First Named	AGE	SEX	BLOOD	TRIBAL ENROLLMENT		
							Year	County	No.
12630	1 Garland, Simpson	50	First Named	47	M	1/2	1896	Atoka	4979
	2								
	3								
	4								
	5								
	6								
	7								
	8								
	9								
	10								
	11								
	12								
	13								
	14	ENROLLMENT OF NOS. 1 HEREON APPROVED BY THE SECRETARY OF INTERIOR MAR 6 1903							
	15								
	16								
	17								

TRIBAL ENROLLMENT OF PARENTS

	Name of Father	Year	County	Name of Mother	Year	County
1	Lewis Garland	Dd	Towson	Aurilla Folsom	Dd	Blue
2						
3						
4						
5						
6						
7	On 1896 roll Sampson F. Garland					
8	On page 35, #349 - 93 P.R. San[sic] Bois Co as Sim Garland					
9	No.1 is father of Louis, Libbie M., David M., and Floyd H Garland and husband of Tookah Garland on Creek Indian card Field No 15861 - Oct 29, 1902					
10						
11						
12						
13						
14						
15						
16						
17						9/5/99

Choctaw By Blood Enrollment Cards 1898-1914

RESIDENCE: _____ COUNTY.
POST OFFICE: So McAlester, I.T.

Choctaw Nation

Choctaw Roll *(Not Including Freedmen)*

CARD NO.
FIELD NO. 4558

Dawes' Roll No.	NAME	Relationship to Person	AGE	SEX	BLOOD	TRIBAL ENROLLMENT		
						Year	County	No.
12631	1 Folsom, Peter W ²³	First Named	20	M	1/4	1896	Tobucksy	4005
	2							
	3							
	4							
	5							
	6							
	7							
	8							
	9							
	10							
	11							
	12							
	13							
	14							
	15							
	16							
	17							

ENROLLMENT
OF NOS. 1 HEREON
APPROVED BY THE SECRETARY
OF INTERIOR MAR 6 1903

TRIBAL ENROLLMENT OF PARENTS

	Name of Father	Year	County	Name of Mother	Year	County
1	Ward Folsom	Dd	Skullyville	Eliza Folsom		Tobucksy
2						
3						
4						
5						
6						
7						
8						
9		On roll as Peter Folsom.				
10		As to parents[sic] marriage see enrollment of mother				
11		Elizabeth G. Folsom.				
12						
13						
14						
15						
16						
17	Fox , I.T. 11/8/02				Date of Application for Enrollment	9/5/99

58

Choctaw By Blood Enrollment Cards 1898-1914

RESIDENCE: Gaines	COUNTY.	**Choctaw Nation**		**Choctaw Roll** *(Not Including Freedmen)*		
POST OFFICE: Hartshorn[sic]						

Dawes' Roll No.	NAME	Relationship to Person First Named	AGE	SEX	BLOOD	TRIBAL ENROLLMENT		
						Year	County	No.
12632	1 Hampton Nancy 57	Named	54	F	1/2	1896	Gaines	5277
12633	2 " Lillie E 19	Dau	16	"	Fb.	1896	Do	5279
12634	3 " Oscar 7	Nephew	4	M	1/2	1896	Do	5280
	4							
	5							
	6							
	7							
	8							
	9							
	10							
	11							
	12							
	13							
	14	ENROLLMENT OF NOS. 1 2 3 HEREON APPROVED BY THE SECRETARY OF INTERIOR MAR 6 1903						
	15							
	16							
	17							

TRIBAL ENROLLMENT OF PARENTS

	Name of Father	Year	County	Name of Mother	Year	County
1	C D Irvin	Dead	Non Citizen	Sallie Irvin	Dead	Choctaw
2	Wade N Hampton	"	Choctaw	No 1		
3	Non-Citizen		---	Elizabeth Loman	Dead	Choctaw
4						
5						
6						
7						
8			No 2 on Choctaw rolls as Lillie E Hampton			
9						
10						
11			No 3 is duplicate of Willie Loman Choctaw card #1029 approved roll #2735 Enrollment cancelled under Departmental Authority			
12			of October 24, 1904 (I T D. #10760-1904) D C. #41180-1904			
13						
14						
15	No 2 P O Ada, I T 9/10/06					
16	For child of No2 see NB (Apr 26-06) Card # 521				Date of Application for Enrollment.	Sept 5/1899
17	P O Coalgate, Okla 3/17/08					

59

RESIDENCE: Gaines   COUNTY. **Choctaw Nation**   Choctaw Roll   CARD NO.
POST OFFICE: Hartshorn[sic]   *(Not Including Freedmen)*   FIELD NO. 4560

Dawes' Roll No.	NAME	Relationship to Person First Named	AGE	SEX	BLOOD	TRIBAL ENROLLMENT Year	County	No.
12635	1 Christian Emma ⁴¹	First Named	38	f	1/2	1896	Gaines	2286
12636	2 " Mona A ⁷	D	4	f	1/4	1896	Gaines	2287
12637	3 " Delilah F ⁶	D	2	f	1/4		Do	
12638	4 Willis Perry M ²⁰	Son	17	M	3/8	1896	Do	12950
12639	5 " Clarence L ¹⁹	"	16	"	3/8	1896	Do	12951
12640	6 " Florence ¹⁷	D	14	f	3/8	1896	Do	12952
12641	7 Ford Wᵐ A ¹⁶	D	13	M	1/4	1896	Do	3987
12642	8 Carpenter Daisy D ¹³	D	10	f	1/4	1896	"	2288
12643	9 Christian, Elmer Lee ³	Son	2mo	M	1/4			
12644	10 " Emma Levy²	Dau	7mo	F	1/4			
	11							
	12							
	13							
	14							
	15							
	16							
	17							

ENROLLMENT
OF NOS. 1,2,3,4,5,6,7,8,9-10 HEREON
APPROVED BY THE SECRETARY
OF INTERIOR MAR 6 1903

TRIBAL ENROLLMENT OF PARENTS

Name of Father	Year	County	Name of Mother	Year	County
1 C D Irvin	Dead	Non-Citizen	Sallie Irvin	Dead	Choctaw
2 S J Christian		Do Do	No 1		"
3 Do		" "	No 1		"
4 Wᵐ Willis	Dead	Choctaw	No 1		"
5 Wᵐ Willis	"	Do	No 1		"
6 Wᵐ Willis	"	Do	No 1		"
7 Wᵐ Ford	"	Non Citizen	No 1		"
8 Wᵐ Carpenter	"	Do Do	No 1		"
9 Sidney J Christian		Non Citz	No 1		
10 " " "		" "	No 1		
11					
12		No7 on roll Wᵐ A Ford			
13		No 10 Enrolled August 31 1901.			
14			Date of Application for Enrollment.	For Nos 1 to 8 Inclusive
15				9/5 - 1899
16			No9 enrolled Oct 27/99	
17				

Choctaw By Blood Enrollment Cards 1898-1914

| RESIDENCE: Tobucksy | COUNTY. | **Choctaw Nation** | **Choctaw Roll** | CARD NO. |
| POST OFFICE: So. McAlester | | | *(Not Including Freedmen)* | FIELD NO. 4561 |

Dawes' Roll No.	NAME	Relationship to Person	AGE	SEX	BLOOD	TRIBAL ENROLLMENT		
						Year	County	No.
12645	1 Witcher Fannie 29	First Named	26	f	1/16	1896	Tobucksy	13026
	2							
	3							
	4							
	5							
	6							
	7							
	8							
	9							
	10							
	11							
	12							
	13							
	14	ENROLLMENT						
	15	OF NOS. 1 HEREON APPROVED BY THE SECRETARY						
	16	OF INTERIOR MAR 6 1903						
	17							

TRIBAL ENROLLMENT OF PARENTS

	Name of Father	Year	County	Name of Mother	Year	County
1	Andrew J Stanton	Dead	Choctaw	Elizabeth G Folsom	IW	Tobucksy
2						
3						
4						
5						
6						
7			As to marriage of parents see enrollment			
8			of mother Elizabeth G Folsom			
9						
10						
11						
12						
13						
14						
15				Date of Application for Enrollment.	9 - 5 - 99	
16						
17						

RESIDENCE: Tobucksy COUNTY. **Choctaw Nation** **Choctaw Roll** CARD NO.
POST OFFICE: Krebs *(Not Including Freedmen)* FIELD NO. 4562

Dawes' Roll No.	NAME	Relationship to Person	AGE	SEX	BLOOD	TRIBAL ENROLLMENT		
						Year	County	No.
12646	1 Willis Joe 43	First Named	40	M	Fb	1896	Tobucksy	13035
12647	2 " Frank 19	Son	16	M	FB	1896	Do	13036
15587	3 Phillips Annie 8	Neice[sic]	5	f	1/2			
I.W. 1585	4 " George	Father of No.3	29	M	IW			
	5	ENROLLMENT						
	6	OF NOS. ~~~4~~~ HEREON APPROVED BY THE SECRETARY						
	7	OF INTERIOR NOV 26 190[?]						
	8	ENROLLMENT						
	9	OF NOS. ~3~ HEREON APPROVED BY THE SECRETARY						
	10	OF INTERIOR SEP 22 1904						
	11							
	12							
	13	ENROLLMENT						
	14	OF NOS. 1 - 2 HEREON APPROVED BY THE SECRETARY						
	15	OF INTERIOR MAR 6 1903						
	16							
	17	No4 GRANTED JUL 18 1906						

TRIBAL ENROLLMENT OF PARENTS

	Name of Father	Year	County	Name of Mother	Year	County
1	Willis	Dead	Tobucksy	Eliza Ann	Dead	Tobucksy
2	No 1		Do	Jane Willis	Dead	Do
3	Geo Phillips		Non Cit	Cillin Harrison		Gaines
4	[No information given]					
5						
6						
7	No.4 placed hereon under order of Commissioner to Five Civilized Tribes of June 23 1906					
8	holding application was made for his enrollment within the time provided by Act					
	of Congress of July 1, 1902 (32 Stat. 641)					
9	No.4 admitted by Dawes Commission in 1896 Choctaw case No. 683. No appeal.					
10	N°3 See affidavit of Ann Amos as to birth filed Dec 24, 1902					
11	Mother of N°3 is Cillin Harrison on Choctaw Card #D951. See her					
12	testimony Dec. 17, 1902. Cillin Harrison transferred to Choctaw card #2277					
13	March 19, 1904				Date of Application for Enrollment.	
14	Nos 1 and 2 admitted by act of Council of April 8, 1891					
15	N°3 Born Dec. 12, 1894, proof of birth filed July 21, 1904. Nos 1&2 enrolled Sept 4/99					
				No.3 " Sept 8/99		
16	No 4 was formerly married to Cillin Harrison Choctaw card #2277 Roll 15421					
17						

Choctaw By Blood Enrollment Cards 1898-1914

RESIDENCE:
POST OFFICE: Wilburton, I.T. COUNTY. **Choctaw Nation** **Choctaw Roll** *(Not Including Freedmen)* CARD NO. FIELD NO. 4563

Dawes' Roll No.	NAME		Relationship to Person First Named	AGE	SEX	BLOOD	TRIBAL ENROLLMENT		
							Year	County	No.
12648	1 Jones, Melvina	39	First Named	36	F	full	1893	Gaines	13
12649	2 " James	13	Bro	10	M	"	1896	Gaines	6606
	3								
	4								
	5								
	6								
	7								
	8								
	9								
	10								
	11								
	12								
	13								
	14								
	15								
	16								
	17								

ENROLLMENT
OF NOS. 1 - 2 HEREON
APPROVED BY THE SECRETARY
OF INTERIOR MAR 6 1903

TRIBAL ENROLLMENT OF PARENTS

	Name of Father	Year	County	Name of Mother	Year	County
1	Simon Jones	Dd	Gaines	Sissy Jones	Dd	Gaines
2	" "			" "		
3						
4						
5						
6						
7	No.1 on page 2- #13-93 P.R. Gaines Co. as Fanny Anderson.					
8						
9						
10	No1 also on 1896 roll as Melvinia[sic] Anderson page 3, No 93					
11						
12						
13						
14						
15						
16						
17	LeFlore I.T.				Date of Application for Enrollment.	9/5/99

Choctaw By Blood Enrollment Cards 1898-1914

RESIDENCE:
POST OFFICE: Enterprise, I.T.   COUNTY. **Choctaw Nation**   **Choctaw Roll** (Not Including Freedmen)   CARD NO.
FIELD NO. **4564**

Dawes' Roll No.	NAME	Relationship to Person	AGE	SEX	BLOOD	TRIBAL ENROLLMENT		
						Year	County	No.
DEAD	1 ~~Henry Edmond K~~ DEAD	First ~~Named~~	~~24~~	~~M~~	~~1/4~~	~~1896~~	~~San[sic] Bois~~	~~5065~~
I.W. 1023	2 Dyer Mary 22	Wife	19	F	I.W.			
12650	3 Henry Jesse P. 4	Son	14^{m}	M	1/8			
12651	4 " Briton 2	Son	2mo	M	1/8			
I.W. 1024	5 Dyer Thomas D 33	Husband of No.2	33	M	I.W.			
	6 No.1 hereon dismissed under order of							
	7 the Commission to the Five Civilized							
	8 Tribes of March 31, 1905.							
	9							
	10 ENROLLMENT							
	11 OF NOS. ~2 and 5~ HEREON APPROVED BY THE SECRETARY							
	12 OF INTERIOR Oct 21 1904							
	13							
	14 ENROLLMENT OF NOS. 3-4 HEREON							
	15 APPROVED BY THE SECRETARY OF INTERIOR Mar 6 1903							
	16							
	17							

TRIBAL ENROLLMENT OF PARENTS

	Name of Father	Year	County	Name of Mother	Year	County
1	~~Pat Henry~~		~~Creek Cit~~	~~Martha Henry~~	~~Dd~~	~~San[sic] Bois~~
2	A. A. Ellis		Non Cit	Cora B Ellis		Non Cit
3	No.1			No.2		
4	No.1			No.2		
5	Jas. L. Dyer		non citz	Susan F Dyer		non citz
6						
7	No.1 Died Decr 22nd 1900. Evidence of Death filed June 26th 1902					
8	No.4 Enrolled Oct 16th 1900					
9	~~No2 is the wife of Thomas D Dyer on Choctaw Card #D433 June 17 1902~~					
10	~~Evidence of birth of No3 filed June 17, 1902~~					
11	No2 Evidence of marriage to Thomas D Dyer Choctaw card #D433 filed June 26th 1902					
12	~~No5 transferred from Choctaw card #D.433. See decision of August 31, 1904.~~ Sept 15, 1904					
13	~~For child of Nos 2&5 see NB (Apr 26 06) #1111~~					
14	No.1 on roll as Edmond Henry					
15						
16						
17	~~P.O. Russelville[sic] May 1904~~			Date of Application for Enrollment.		9/5/99

Choctaw By Blood Enrollment Cards 1898-1914

RESIDENCE:		COUNTY.							
POST OFFICE: Paoli, I.T. 3/10/05		**Choctaw Nation**					Choctaw Roll *(Not Including Freedmen)*	CARD NO. FIELD NO. **4565**	

Dawes' Roll No.	NAME	Relationship to Person First Named	AGE	SEX	BLOOD	TRIBAL ENROLLMENT Year	County	No.
I.W. 845	1 Harkreader, Samuel B ⁽²⁸⁾	First Named	24	M	I,W.			
14824	2 " Lucy A ²⁶	Wife	23	F	3/16	1896	Chick Dist	4575
DEAD	3 " ~~Francis Lucile~~	~~Dau~~	~~2mos~~	~~F~~	~~3/32~~			
DEAD	4 " ~~Thomas Alton~~	~~Son~~	~~1mo~~	~~M~~	~~3/32~~			
	5							
	6 ENROLLMENT							
	7 OF NOS. 2 HEREON APPROVED BY THE SECRETARY							
	8 OF INTERIOR May 20 1903							
	9							
	10 ENROLLMENT							
	11 OF NOS. 1 HEREON APPROVED BY THE SECRETARY							
	12 OF INTERIOR May 21 1904							
	13							
	14							
	15 No. 3 and 4 hereon dismissed under order of the Commission to the Five							
	16 Civilized Tribes of March 31, 1905.							
	17							

	TRIBAL ENROLLMENT OF PARENTS						
	Name of Father	Year	County	Name of Mother	Year	County	
1	Jno I. Harkreader	Dd	Non Cit	Sarah Harkreader	Dd	Non Cit	
2	Robt. C Florence		Chick Dist	Mary J Florence		Chick Dist	
3	~~No.1~~			~~No.2~~			
4	~~No.1~~			~~No.2~~			
5							
6							
7							
8							
9	No.3 died March 11, 1901; proof of death filed Nov. 25, 1902						
10	No.4 died November 13, 1901; proof of death filed Nov. 25, 1902						
11							
12	For child of Nos 1&2 see NB (Mar 3 05) Card #332						
13	" " " " " " NB (Apr 26-06) " #391 See his testimony as to his residence						
14					No2 on 1896 roll as Lucy A Florence		
15	No.3 Enrolled May 24, 1900						
16	No.4 Enrolled July 25, 1901						
17	Woolsey I.T. 11/7/02				Date of Application for Enrollment 9/5/99		

65

Choctaw By Blood Enrollment Cards 1898-1914

RESIDENCE:
POST OFFICE: Krebs, I.T.

COUNTY. **Choctaw Nation**

Choctaw Roll *(Not Including Freedmen)*

CARD NO.
FIELD NO. 4566

Dawes' Roll No.	NAME		Relationship to Person	AGE	SEX	BLOOD	TRIBAL ENROLLMENT		
							Year	County	No.
12652	1 Moncrief, Cap R	31	First Named	28	M	1/4	1896	Tobucksy	8546
I.W. 450	2 " Annie	27	Wife	24	F	I.W.	"	"	14811
12653	3 " Ester	3	dau	6wks	"	1/8			
	4								
	5								
	6								
	7								
	8								
	9								
	10	ENROLLMENT							
	11	OF NOS. 2 HEREON APPROVED BY THE SECRETARY							
	12	OF INTERIOR SEP 12 1903							
	13	ENROLLMENT							
	14	OF NOS. 1 - 3 HEREON APPROVED BY THE SECRETARY							
	15	OF INTERIOR MAR 6 1903							
	16								
	17								

TRIBAL ENROLLMENT OF PARENTS

	Name of Father	Year	County	Name of Mother	Year	County
1	Geo Moncrief	Dd	Tobucksy	Moncrief	Dd	Tobucksy
2	Elijah Green		"	Kate Green		"
3	No1			No2		
4						
5						
6						
7						
8						
9						
10				As to marriage of parents of No.1,		
11				see testimony of S. E. Lewis		
12						
13						
14						
15						
16				No3 enrolled Dec 16/99		
17				Date of Application for Enrollment 9/5/99		

↘1 & 2

66

Choctaw By Blood Enrollment Cards 1898-1914

RESIDENCE: POST OFFICE: COUNTY. **Choctaw Nation**   **Choctaw Roll** *(Not Including Freedmen)*   CARD No.   FIELD No. **4567**

Dawes' Roll No.			Relationship to Person	AGE	SEX	BLOOD	TRIBAL ENROLLMENT		
							Year	County	No.
12654	1 Wi___ ___y	43	First Named	40	F	3/4	1896	Tobucksy	13027
12655	2 Jan___ ___	20	Son	17	M	7/8	1896	"	6646
12656	3 Jef___ ___ra	6	Du	3	F	7/8			
	4								
	5								
	6								
	7								
	8								
	9								
	10								
	11								
	12								
	13								
	14								
	15								
	16								
	17								

ENROLLMENT ___ HEREON ___ BY THE SECRETARY ___ MAR 6 1903

TRIBAL ENROLLMENT OF PARENTS

	Name of Father	Year	County	Name of Mother	Year	County
1	Sam Arth	Dd	Tobucksy	Aurenia Arth	Dd	Tobucksy
2	Wilson James	"	"	No.1		
3	Jos Jefferson		"	" 1		
4						
5						
6						
7						
8	No.2 also on 1896 Choctaw roll page 163, #6646 as Jacob Jones					
9						
10	Evidence of birth of Nº3 received and filed May 17, 1902					
11						
12				No.1 on roll as Maltsey Williams		
13				No.2 on page 100 #841-93-P.R. Tobucksy Co		
14						
15						
16				Date of Application for Enrollment.		
17				9/5/99		

Choctaw By Blood Enrollment Cards 1898-1914

RESIDENCE: COUNTY.   Choctaw Nation

POST OFFICE: McAlester, I.T.

Choctaw Roll
(Not Including Freedmen)

Dawes' Roll No.	NAME		Relationship to Person	AGE	SEX	BLOOD	TRIBAL ENROLLMENT		
							Year	County	No.
I.W. 1025	1 Catterton, Sarah E	34	First Named	31	F	IW.	1896	Gaines	14719
14438	2 Krebs, Edmund H	13	Son	10	M	1/4	1896	Gaines	7476
14439	3 " Minnie L	10	Dau	7	F	1/4	"	"	7477
14440	4 " Tisha V	7	"	4	F	1/4	"	"	7478
	5								
	6								
	7								
	8								

ENROLLMENT
OF NOS. 2 3 and 4 HEREON
APPROVED BY THE SECRETARY
OF INTERIOR APR 11 1903

ENROLLMENT
OF NOS. ~~~ 1 ~~~ HEREON
APPROVED BY THE SECRETARY
OF INTERIOR OCT 21 1904

9

10 Nov 13/99 No1 see if admitted by

11 Com as an intermarried citizen

12 or by blood. Married to white man since she was admitted

13 N^o1 was admitted by Dawes Commission in 1896 as

14 an intermarried citizen, citizenship case #1203, no appeal

15 For child of No1 see NB (Apr 26 '06) #1096

16

17

TRIBAL ENROLLMENT OF PARENTS

	Name of Father	Year	County	Name of Mother	Year	
1	Herman Burke		Gaines	Polly Burke		Ga
2	Joe Krebs	Dd	"	No. 1		
3	" "			" 1		
4	" "			" 1		
5						
6						
7						
8						
9			Admitted by Dawes Comm #1203.			
10			No.1 as Sarah E Krebs			
11			" 2 " Edmund "			
12			" 3 " Minnie Lee "			
13			" 4 " Lutishia Viola "			
14			" 4 on 96 Roll as Tishi V. Krebs			
			No1 on 1896 roll as Elizabeth D Krebs			

Date of Application for Enrollment.

9/5/9:

68

Choctaw By Blood Enrollment Cards 1898-1914

RESIDENCE:
POST OFFICE: Alderson, I.T.   COUNTY. **Choctaw Nation**   Choctaw Roll *(Not Including Freedmen)*   CARD NO. FIELD NO. 4569

Dawes' Roll No.	NAME	Relationship to Person	AGE	SEX	BLOOD	TRIBAL ENROLLMENT Year	County	No.
12657	1 Roberson, Reola ²⁵	First Named	22	F	1/4	1896	Gaines	10744
12658	2 " Elbert W ¹⁰	Son	7	M	1/8	1896	"	10745
12659	3 " Alfred W ⁶	"	3	"	1/8	1896	"	10746
12660	4 " Arthur L ⁴	"	1	"	1/8			
12661	5 " Gertie ²	Dau	3m	F	1/8			
I.W. 680	6 " James W ²⁸	Hus	28	M	I.W.			
	7							
	8	No6 transferred from Choctaw # 435 January 25, 1904. See decision						
	9	of January 7, 1904						
	10							
	11	ENROLLMENT OF NOS. 6						
	12	APPROVED BY THE SECRETARY HEREON						
	13	OF INTERIOR MAR 26 1904						
	14							
	15	ENROLLMENT OF NOS. 1 2 3 4-5 HEREON						
	16	APPROVED BY THE SECRETARY						
	17	OF INTERIOR MAR 6 1903						

TRIBAL ENROLLMENT OF PARENTS

	Name of Father	Year	County	Name of Mother	Year	County
1	Josh Hickman		Sugar Loaf	Sarah J Hickman		San[sic] Bois
2	Jas W Roberson		Tobucksy	No.1		
3	" " "		"	No.1		
4	" " "		"	No.1		
5	" " "		"	No.1		
6	J. R. Roberson		noncitizen	Sarah Roberson		non
7						
8			No1 on roll as Lula Robinson			
9			" 2 " " " Elbert "			
10			" 3 " " " Alfred "			
11			Evidence of parent's marriage to be supplied.			
12	J.W. Roberson, Husband of #1, and father of #2,3 and 4 on Choctaw D.435.					
13	No.5 Enrolled January 30. 1901					
14	For child of Nos 1 & 6 see NB (Apr 26-06) Card #769					
15	" " " " " " " (Mar 3-05) " #596					#1 to 4 inc
16						Date of Application for Enrollment.
17	PO Kiowa IT 4/1/05					Sept 5 - 99

Choctaw By Blood Enrollment Cards 1898-1914

| | RESIDENCE: POST OFFICE: McAlester, I.T. | COUNTY. Choctaw Nation | Choctaw Roll (Not Including Freedmen) | CARD No. FIELD No. 4570 |

Dawes' Roll No.	NAME		Relationship to Person First Named	AGE	SEX	BLOOD	TRIBAL ENROLLMENT		
							Year	County	No.
I.W. 451	1 Tennant, Lewis C	56	First Named	52	M	I.W.	1896	Tobucksy	15098
12662	2 " Emma H	47	Wife	44	F	1/4	"	"	12009
12663	3 " Carrie E	28	Dau	25	F	1/8	"	"	12010
12664	4 " Wm J R	16	Son	13	M	1/8	"	"	12012
12665	5 " Robert B	13	Son	10	"	1/8	"	"	12013
12666	6 " Mattie L	10	Dau	7	F	1/8	"	"	12014
	7								
	8								
	9								
	10								

ENROLLMENT OF NOS. 1 HEREON APPROVED BY THE SECRETARY OF INTERIOR SEP 12 1903

ENROLLMENT OF NOS. 2 3 4 5-6 HEREON APPROVED BY THE SECRETARY OF INTERIOR MAR 6 1903

TRIBAL ENROLLMENT OF PARENTS

	Name of Father	Year	County	Name of Mother	Year	County
1	Gilbert Tennant		Non Cit	Caroline Tennant		Non cit
2	E.J. McDuff		Tobucksy	Minerva McDuff	Dd	Tobucksy
3	No. 1			No. 2		
4	" 1			" 2		
5	" 1			" 2		
6	" 1			" 2		

No.1 Admitted by Dawes Comm #722 as Louis C. Tennant, No appeal.
No.4 on roll as Wm. J. R. Tennent[sic]
" 5 " " " Robt. B. "
For child of No.3 see NB (March 3,1905) Card #587

No4 Honolulu T.H. 7/14/06

Date of Application for Enrollment. 9/5/99

70

Choctaw By Blood Enrollment Cards 1898-1914

RESIDENCE:
POST OFFICE: So. McAlester, I.T. COUNTY. **Choctaw Nation** **Choctaw Roll** *(Not Including Freedmen)* CARD No.
FIELD No. 4571

Dawes' Roll No.	NAME		Relationship to Person First Named	AGE	SEX	BLOOD	TRIBAL ENROLLMENT		
							Year	County	No.
✓	1	Brazell, Edgar	Named	27	M	1/16			
DP	2	" Isabell	Wife	21	F	I.W.			
DP	3	" Georgia T	Dau	2ᵐ	F	1/32			
	4								
	5								
No2&3	6	DISMISSED MAY 27 1904							
	7								
	8								
	9								
	10								
	11								
	12								
	13								
	14								
	15								
	16								
	17								

TRIBAL ENROLLMENT OF PARENTS

	Name of Father	Year	County	Name of Mother	Year	County
1	J. H. Brazell		Non Cit	Jennie Brazell		Tobucksy
2	Wᵐ Bevridge		" "	Mary Bevridge		Non Cit
3	No.1			No.2		
4						
5						
6						
7	No1 denied in 96 Case #6					
8	Judgement[sic] of U.S. Ct admitting No1,2 vacated and set aside by Decree of C.C.C.C. Decʳ 17 '02					
9	No1 now in C.C.C.C. #63					
10				Admitted by U.S. Court at So. McA		
11				Aug 24-97 Case No. 96 - as to		
12				residence see his testimony.		
13						
14						
15						
16						
17				Date of Application for Enrollment.	9/5/99	

DENIED CITIZENSHIP BY THE CHOCTAW AND CHICKASAW CITIZENSHIP COURT Case 63 April 18-1904

Choctaw By Blood Enrollment Cards 1898-1914

RESIDENCE:		COUNTY.					CARD NO.
POST OFFICE: Enterprise, I.T.		**Choctaw Nation**				**Choctaw Roll** *(Not Including Freedmen)*	FIELD NO. 4572

Dawes' Roll No.	NAME		Relationship to Person	AGE	SEX	BLOOD	TRIBAL ENROLLMENT		
							Year	County	No.
I.W. 452	1 Baker, Sarah T	45	First Named	40	F	I.W.			
	2								
	3								
	4								
	5								
	6								
	7								
	8								
	9	ENROLLMENT OF NOS. 1 HEREON							
	10	APPROVED BY THE SECRETARY OF INTERIOR SEP 12 1903							
	11								
	12								
	13								
	14								
	15								
	16								
	17								

TRIBAL ENROLLMENT OF PARENTS

	Name of Father	Year	County	Name of Mother	Year	County
1	Dan Lofton	Dd	Non Cit	Sarah Lofton		Non Cit
2						
3						
4						
5						
6						
7						
8						
9						
10				Admitted by Dawes Com #198 No appeal.		
11			Husband and children on Choctaw card #R.424.			
12						
13						
14						
15						
16						
17				Date of Application for Enrollment		9/5/99

72

Choctaw By Blood Enrollment Cards 1898-1914

RESIDENCE:
POST OFFICE: So McAlester, I.T. COUNTY. **Choctaw Nation** Choctaw Roll (Not Including Freedmen) CARD NO. FIELD NO. 4573

Dawes' Roll No.	NAME	Relationship to Person First Named	AGE	SEX	BLOOD	TRIBAL ENROLLMENT		
						Year	County	No.
12667	1 Brock, Minnie L 25	First Named	22	F	1/32	1893	Sans Bois	972
14825	2 " August C 6	Son	3	M	1/64			
12668	3 " Juanita M 4	Dau	1	F	1/64			
12669	4 " Clifton Rex 2	Son	1mo	M	1/64			
	5							
	6							
	7							
	8							
	9							
	10							
	11							
	12							
	13							
	14							
	15							
	16							
	17							

ENROLLMENT OF NOS. 2 APPROVED BY THE SECRETARY OF INTERIOR MAY 20 1903 HEREON

ENROLLMENT OF NOS. 1 3 - 4 APPROVED BY THE SECRETARY OF INTERIOR MAR 6 1903 HEREON

TRIBAL ENROLLMENT OF PARENTS

	Name of Father	Year	County	Name of Mother	Year	County
1	Wm Harris	Dd	Skullyville	Callie Cowling		San[sic] Bois
2	W. E. Brock			No. 1		
3	" " "			" 1		
4	" " "			No.1		
5						
6						
7						
8						
9			On page 99 #972 - 93 - P.R. San[sic] Bois Co. as			
10			Minnie Lee Harris - As to parents[sic] marriage			
11			see testimony of Emma H. Tennant.			
			No.4 Enrolled November 27th, 1900			
12			No.2 Evidence of birth received and filed Dec. 24, 1902			
13			For child of No1 see NB (Apr 26-06) Card #744			
14			" " " (Mar 3 '05) " #333			
15						
16						
17					Date of Application for Enrollment. 9/5/99	

Choctaw By Blood Enrollment Cards 1898-1914

RESIDENCE:	COUNTY.	**Choctaw Nation**	**Choctaw Roll**	CARD NO.
POST OFFICE: Hartshorne, I.T.			*(Not Including Freedmen)*	FIELD NO. 4574

Dawes' Roll No.		NAME		Relationship to Person	AGE	SEX	BLOOD	TRIBAL ENROLLMENT		
								Year	County	No.
14826	1	Victor, John	30	First Named	27	M	1/8	1896	Tobucksy (orig)	851
	2									
	3									
	4	ENROLLMENT OF NOS. 1 HEREON								
	5	APPROVED BY THE SECRETARY OF INTERIOR MAY 20 1903								
	6									
	7									
	8									
	9									
	10									
	11									
	12									
	13									
	14									
	15									
	16									
	17									

TRIBAL ENROLLMENT OF PARENTS

	Name of Father	Year	County	Name of Mother	Year	County
1	Wm Victor		Skullyville	Phoebe Victor		Skullyville
2						
3						
4						
5						
6						
7						
8				Tobucksy County		
9				On original Choct of 1896 - on Page 177		
10				#851 - As to parents[sic] marriage see		
11				enrollment of Lutitia King.		
12				See testimony of S E Lewis Feb 9 '03		
13						
14						
15						
16						
17	Paoli I.T. 10/23/02				Date of Application for Enrollment	9/5/99

74

Choctaw By Blood Enrollment Cards 1898-1914

RESIDENCE: San[sic] Bois   COUNTY. **Choctaw Nation**   **Choctaw Roll** (Not Including Freedmen)   CARD NO.
POST OFFICE: Russellville   FIELD NO. **4575**

Dawes' Roll No.		NAME	Relationship to Person First Named	AGE	SEX	BLOOD	TRIBAL ENROLLMENT Year	County	No.
0	1	Bennight, Richard S	Named	32	M	1/8		San[sic] Bois	
0	2	" Anna	Wife	32	F	I.W.		"	
0	3	" Luther	Son	7	M	1/16		"	
0	4	" Winn	"	5	M	1/16		"	
0	5	" Dora J	Dau	3	F	1/16		"	
DP	6	" Tennie M	Dau	5mo	F	1/16			
	7								
	8	No. 6 - May 27 1904 DISMISSED							
	9								
	10								
	11								
	12								
	13								
	14								
	15								
	16								
	17								

TRIBAL ENROLLMENT OF PARENTS

	Name of Father	Year	County	Name of Mother	Year	County
1	James Bennight	IW	Gaines	Susan Bennight		Gaines
2	M. L. Hook		Non Citizen	Elizabeth Hook	Dead	Non Citizen
3	No1			No2		
4	No1			No2		
5	No1			No2		
6	No1			No2		
7						
8	Nos 1 to 5 incl denied in 96 Case #916					
9	Admitted by the U.S. Court at So McAlester Sept 11th 1897 Case #67. As to residence see testimony of No1.					
10	Judgement[sic] of U.S. Ct admitting Nos 1 to 5 incl vacated and set aside by Decree of C.C.C.C. Decr 17 '02					
11	Nos 1 to 5 incl now in C.C.C.C. Case #39					
12	DENIED CITIZENSHIP BY THE CHOCTAW AND					
13	1,2,3,4,5 CHICKASAW CITIZENSHIP COURT					
14	No6 Enrolled May 24, 1900 Case #39 April 18 '04					
15				Date of Application for Enrollment.	Sept 6th 1899	
16						
17		See C- 132.				

Choctaw By Blood Enrollment Cards 1898-1914

RESIDENCE: Kiamitia   COUNTY. **Choctaw Nation**   **Choctaw Roll** CARD NO.
POST OFFICE: Frogville   (Not Including Freedmen)   FIELD NO. **4576**

Dawes' Roll No.	NAME	Relationship to Person	AGE	SEX	BLOOD	TRIBAL ENROLLMENT		
						Year	County	No.
12670	1 Burney, John L 31	First Named	28	M	FB	1896	Kiamitia	1424
	2							
	3							
	4							
	5							
	6							
	7							
	8							
	9							
	10							
	11							
	12	ENROLLMENT						
	13	OF NOS. 1 HEREON APPROVED BY THE SECRETARY						
	14	OF INTERIOR Mar. 6, 1903						
	15							
	16							
	17	See letter of Sam L Oakes relative to funeral of No 1 filed herein						

TRIBAL ENROLLMENT OF PARENTS

Name of Father	Year	County	Name of Mother	Year	County
1 Wash Burney	Choctaw	Kiamitia	Listie Burney	Dead	Choctaw
2					
3					
4					
5					
6					
7					
8		On 1896 roll as John Lee Burney			
9					
10		Died July 10, 1901 Investigating			
11					
12					
13					
14					
15					
16				Date of Application for Enrollment.	
17				9-6-99	

Choctaw By Blood Enrollment Cards 1898-1914

RESIDENCE: Tobucksy   COUNTY. **Choctaw Nation**   **Choctaw Roll**   CARD NO.
POST OFFICE: MᶜAlester   *(Not Including Freedmen)* FIELD NO. **4577**

Dawes' Roll No.	NAME		Relationship to Person First Named	AGE	SEX	BLOOD	TRIBAL ENROLLMENT		
							Year	County	No.
I.W.453	₁ Lang, Henry	76	First Named	73	M	I.W.	1896	Tobucksy	14754
12671	₂ " Lina	45	Wife	42	F	1/2	1896	"	7857
12672	₃ " Annie M	15	D	12	F	1/4	1896	"	7858
12673	₄ " Benjamin	13	Son	10	M	1/4	1896	"	7859
DEAD	₅ " Lee R	11	Son	8	M	1/4	1896	"	7860
12674	₆ Folsom, Robt	16	Nephew	13	M	1/2	1893	PR "	500
	₇								
	₈								
	₉								
	₁₀ ENROLLMENT								
	₁₁ OF NOS. 1 HEREON APPROVED BY THE SECRETARY								
	₁₂ OF INTERIOR Sep 12, 1903								
	₁₃								
	₁₄ ENROLLMENT OF NOS. 2 3 4 - 6 HEREON		No.5 hereon dismissed under order of						
	₁₅ APPROVED BY THE SECRETARY OF INTERIOR Mar. 6, 1903		the Commission to the Five Civilized						
	₁₆		Tribes of March 31, 1905.						
	₁₇								

TRIBAL ENROLLMENT OF PARENTS

	Name of Father	Year	County	Name of Mother	Year	County
₁	Jos Lang		Non Citizen	Annie Lang		Non Citizen
₂	Sam'l Folsom	Dead	Blue			Blue
₃	No1			No2		
₄	No1			No2		
₅	No1			No2		
₆	Mitchell Folsom	Dead		Phoebe Chunn	Dead	Tobucksy
₇						
₈						
₉						
₁₀						
₁₁	No2 on 1896 roll as Sinie Lang					
₁₂	No5 Died Jan. 21, 1901: Proof of death filed Dec. 30, 1902					
₁₃	Evidence of divorce between No2 and her former husband Henry Scott, rec'd and filed Jan'y 6, 1902					
₁₄						
₁₅						
₁₆				Date of Application for Enrollment		9/6/99
₁₇						

Choctaw By Blood Enrollment Cards 1898-1914

RESIDENCE: Jacks Fork   COUNTY. **Choctaw Nation**   **Choctaw Roll**   CARD No.
POST OFFICE: Wilberton[sic]   *(Not Including Freedmen)*   FIELD No. 4578

Dawes' Roll No.	NAME	Relationship to Person	AGE	SEX	BLOOD	TRIBAL ENROLLMENT		
						Year	County	No.
12675	1 Whistler Robinson 26	First Named	23	M	FB	1896	Jacks Fork	14109
	2							
	3							
	4							
	5							
	6							
	7							
	8							
	9							
	10							
	11							
	12							
	13							
	14							
	15	ENROLLMENT OF NOS. 1 HEREON						
	16	APPROVED BY THE SECRETARY OF INTERIOR MAR 6 1903						
	17							

TRIBAL ENROLLMENT OF PARENTS

Name of Father	Year	County	Name of Mother	Year	County
1 Isaac Whistler	Dead	San[sic] Bois	Losinda	Dead	Choctaw
2					
3					
4					
5					
6 N°1 is now the husband of Dora Carnes on Choctaw card N°5426 Nov. 15, 1902.					
7 For child of No1 see NB (Apr. 26, 1906) Card No. 16					
8 " " " " " " (March 3 1905) " " 1109					
9					
10					
11					
12					
13					
14					
15					Date of Application for Enrollment.
16					
17 P.O. Connerville[sic] IT 2/20/06					9-6-99

Choctaw By Blood Enrollment Cards 1898-1914

RESIDENCE: Atoka COUNTY. **Choctaw Nation** | Choctaw Roll | CARD NO.
POST OFFICE: Brooken 4/19/05 | *(Not Including Freedmen)* | FIELD NO. **4579**

Dawes' Roll No.	NAME	Relationship to Person First Named	AGE	SEX	BLOOD	TRIBAL ENROLLMENT		
						Year	County	No.
I.W. 454	1 Westbrook, Andrew J 32	Named	28	M	I.W.	1896	Atoka	15190
12676	2 " Mattie 26	Wife	23	F	1/4	1896	"	13931
12677	3 " Edna 7	D	4	F	1/8	1896	"	13932
12678	4 " Joe 5	D	2	F	1/8			
12679	5 " Phena Ellen 1	Dau	4mo	F	1/8			
	6							
	7							
	8							
	9							
	10							
	11							
	12							
	13							
	14							
	15							
	16							
	17							

ENROLLMENT OF NOS. HEREON APPROVED BY THE SECRETARY OF INTERIOR

ENROLLMENT OF NOS. HEREON APPROVED BY THE SECRETARY OF INTERIOR

TRIBAL ENROLLMENT OF PARENTS

	Name of Father	Year	County	Name of Mother	Year	County
1	Wᵐ R Westbrook		Non Citizen	Annie Westbrook		Non Citizen
2	Jenette McDonald		Chickasaw Dist	Etha Wren		San[sic] Bois
3	No1			No2		
4	No1			No2		
5	No1			No2		
6						
7						
8	No1 on 1896 roll Jack Westbrook					
9	No3 " " " Etna "					
10	For child of Nos 1&2 see NB (March 3, 1905) #1177. As to Parents[sic] marriage , see enrollment					
11	of Etha Wren					
12	No5 enrolled Sept 16, 1901					
13	No4 Proof of birth received and filed Dec. 24, 1902				Date of Application for Enrollment.	#1 to 4 inc
14						
15					6-9-99	
16						
17	Quinton I.T. 12/27/02					

Choctaw By Blood Enrollment Cards 1898-1914

RESIDENCE: San[sic] Bois   COUNTY. **Choctaw Nation**   **Choctaw Roll** *(Not Including Freedmen)*   CARD NO.

POST OFFICE: Brooken   FIELD NO. 4580

Dawes' Roll No.	NAME	Relationship to Person First Named	AGE	SEX	BLOOD	TRIBAL ENROLLMENT Year	County	No.
12680	1 Walker Lindy ⁴⁴	First Named	41	f	FB	1896	San[sic] Bois	12691
12681	2 Folsom Sampson ¹⁹	Son	16	m	FB	1896	San[sic] Bois	3846
12682	3 Bacon Elizabeth ¹⁸	D	15	f	"	1896	" "	596
12683	4 Walker Eliza A ¹⁶	D	13	f	"	1893	PR " "	866
12684	5 " George W ¹²	Son	9	m	"	1896	" "	12692
12685	6 " Charles ⁹	Son	6	m	"	1896	" "	12693
	7							
	8							
	9							
	10							
	11							
	12							
	13							
	14							
	15							
	16							
	17							

ENROLLMENT
OF NOS. 1 2 3 4 5 - 6 HEREON
APPROVED BY THE SECRETARY
OF INTERIOR MAR 6 1903

TRIBAL ENROLLMENT OF PARENTS

	Name of Father	Year	County	Name of Mother	Year	County
1	Ben Washington	Dead	Choctaw			
2	Sam Folsom	"	Do	No1		
3	Solomon Bacon		Do	No1		
4	Wᵐ Walker		Do	No1		
5	" "		"	No1		
6	" "		"	No1		
7						
8						
9						
10						
11	No2 on roll 1896 Samuel Folsom					
12	No3 " " " Elizabeth Baker					
13	No4 " Payroll 1893 San[sic] Bois Co page 84 as Eliza Ann Walker					
14	No5 on roll 1896 Geo W. Walker					
15	Nos 4-5 and 6 in Creek card field No 2935					Date of Application for Enrollment.
16	No6 on Creek card field No 2935 as Chorts[sic] Walker Nos 4 5 and 6 will not appear on Creek final roll					
17	enroll all as Choctaws					6 ¼/9 ᵐ - 1899

For child of No4 see NB (Apr 26 06) Card No 623
" " " " 1 " " (Mar 3 05) " 864

80

Choctaw By Blood Enrollment Cards 1898-1914

RESIDENCE:	Tobucksy	COUNTY.	**Choctaw Nation**	**Choctaw Roll**	CARD NO.
POST OFFICE:	Indianola			(Not Including Freedmen)	FIELD NO. 4581

Dawes' Roll No.	NAME	Relationship to Person First Named	AGE	SEX	BLOOD	TRIBAL ENROLLMENT		
						Year	County	No.
X 1	Marrs Jane	Named	64	f	1/4			
2								
3								
4								
5								
6								
7								
8								
9								
10								
11								
12								
13								
14								
15								
16								
17								

TRIBAL ENROLLMENT OF PARENTS

	Name of Father	Year	County	Name of Mother	Year	County
1	Ruben Marlowe	Dead	Choctaw Citizen	Margaret Marlowe	Dead	Choctaw
2						
3						
4						
5						
6	No 1 denied in 96 Case #28					
7	Admitted by the US Court at So McAlester					
8	Aug 25, 1897 Case #88 As to residence see her testimony.					
9	Judgment of U.S. Ct admitting No 1 vacated and set aside by Decree of C.C.C. Dec 17 '02					
10	No 1 now in C.C.C. Case #109					
11	No 1 Denied by C.C.C. March 28 '04					
12						
13						
14						
15				Date of Application for Enrollment.	Sept 6th 1899	
16						
17						

RESIDENCE:	Tobucksy	COUNTY.			CARD NO.	
POST OFFICE:	Indianola	**Choctaw Nation**		**Choctaw Roll** (Not Including Freedmen)	FIELD NO. 4582	

Dawes' Roll No.	NAME	Relationship to Person First Named	AGE	SEX	BLOOD	TRIBAL ENROLLMENT		
						Year	County	No.
1	Smith Rebecca	First Named	35	f				
2	Harrison Reuben	Son	17	m	1/16			
3	Smith Jane	Dau	10	f	1/16			
4								
5								
6								
7								
8								
9								
10								
11								
12								
13								
14								
15								
16								
17								

TRIBAL ENROLLMENT OF PARENTS

	Name of Father	Year	County	Name of Mother	Year	County
1	J R Marrs	Dead	Non Citizen	Jane Marrs		Choctaw
2	Charles Harrison	Dead	" "	No 1		
3	G W Smith		" "	No 1		
4						
5						
6						
7						
8						
9						
10						
11	No 1 denied in 96 Case #28					
12	Admitted by the US Court at So McAlester Aug 25, 1897 Case #88.					
13	As to residence see testimony of No 1					
14	Judgment of U.S. Ct. admitting No 1, 2 & 3 vacated and set aside by Decree of C.C.C. Dec. 17 '02					
15	No 1, 2 & 3 now in C.C.C. Case #109					
16	No 1, 2 & 3 denied by C.C.C. March 28 '04			Date of Application for Enrollment.	Sept 6th 1899	
17						

82

Choctaw By Blood Enrollment Cards 1898-1914

RESIDENCE: Tobucksy   COUNTY.   **Choctaw Nation**   **Choctaw Roll** (Not Including Freedmen)   CARD NO.
POST OFFICE: McAlester   FIELD NO. 4583

Dawes' Roll No.	NAME	Relationship to Person First Named	AGE	SEX	BLOOD	TRIBAL ENROLLMENT Year	County	No.
✓ 1	Marrs Clara B	First Named	11	f	1/8			
Dis DP 2	" William R	Brother	9	m	1/8			
Dis DP 3	" Myrtle R	Sister	4	f	1/8			
4								
5								
6								
No 1 7								
8								
9								
10	No1 denied by C.C.C.C March 28 /04							
11	No2&3 dismissed " " "							
12								
13								
14	#2-3-							
15								
16								
17	For duplicate record see Choctaw D #706							

DENIED CITIZENSHIP BY THE CHOCTAW AND CHICKASAW CITIZENSHIP COURT Mar 28 04

DISMISSED JAN 26 1905

TRIBAL ENROLLMENT OF PARENTS

	Name of Father	Year	County	Name of Mother	Year	County
1	James Marrs		Non Citizen	Margaret Marrs		Choctaw
2	Do Do		" "	Do Do		
3	Do Do		" "	Do Do		
4						
5						
6						
7						
8	No1, 2&3 denied in 96 Case #28 Admitted by the US Court at So McAlester					
9	Aug 25-1897 Case #88					
10	Judgment of U.S. Ct admitting No1,2&3 vacated and set aside by Decree of C.C.C.C. Dec 17-02 No1 admitted as Clara Belle Marrs					
11	No2 " " W^m K [sic] Marrs					
12	No3 " " Rachel Marrs					
13	No1,2&3 now in C.C.C.C. Case #109 As to residence see testimony					
14	of James Marr[sic]					
15						
16				Date of Application for Enrollment. Sept 6th 1899		
17						

83

Choctaw By Blood Enrollment Cards 1898-1914

RESIDENCE:	Gaines	COUNTY.					CARD NO.
POST OFFICE:	Viraton[sic]	**Choctaw Nation**		**Choctaw Roll** *(Not Including Freedmen)*			FIELD NO. 4584

Dawes' Roll No.	NAME		Relationship to Person	AGE	SEX	BLOOD	TRIBAL ENROLLMENT		
							Year	County	No.
12686	1 Kemp Martin	24	First Named	21	M	FB	1893	Gaines	317
	2								
	3								
	4								
	5								
	6								
	7								
	8								
	9								
	10								
	11								
	12	ENROLLMENT							
	13	OF NOS. 1 HEREON APPROVED BY THE SECRETARY							
	14	OF INTERIOR MAR 6 1903							
	15								
	16								
	17								

TRIBAL ENROLLMENT OF PARENTS

	Name of Father	Year	County	Name of Mother	Year	County
1	Milton Kemp	Dead	Gaines	Amy Kemp		Gaines
2						
3						
4						
5						
6			On page 34, No 317 Pay roll Gaines Co 1893			
7			For child of No1 see NB (March 3 1905) #1333			
8						
9						
10						
11						
12						
13						
14						
15						
16				Date of Application for Enrollment.	Sept 6th 1899	
17						

Choctaw By Blood Enrollment Cards 1898-1914

RESIDENCE:		COUNTY.	**Choctaw Nation**				**Choctaw Roll** *(Not Including Freedmen)*		CARD NO.
POST OFFICE: Stuart, I.T.									FIELD NO. 4585

Dawes' Roll No.	NAME		Relationship to Person First Named	AGE	SEX	BLOOD	TRIBAL ENROLLMENT		
							Year	County	No.
I.W. 455	1 Quincy, Daisy	20	First Named	19	F	I.W.			
12687	2 " Fred Ross	2	Son	7wks	M	1/4			
12688	3 " Nanna Pearl	1	Dau	3wks	F	1/4			
	4								
	5								
	6								
	7								
	8								
	9								
	10	ENROLLMENT OF NOS. 1 HEREON APPROVED BY THE SECRETARY OF INTERIOR SEP 12 1903							
	11								
	12								
	13	ENROLLMENT OF NOS. 2 & 3 HEREON APPROVED BY THE SECRETARY OF INTERIOR MAR 6 1903							
	14								
	15								
	16								
	17								

TRIBAL ENROLLMENT OF PARENTS

	Name of Father	Year	County	Name of Mother	Year	County
1	J. M. Storie		Non Cit	Storie		Non Cit
2	Erwin Quincy	1896	Tobucksy	No.1		
3	" "	1896	"	No.1		
4						
5						
6						
7						
8				Husband on 314 - Jas. Ervin[sic] Quincy		
9				No.2 Enrolled March 4, 1901		
10	Nº3 Born Aug 3 1902: enrolled Aug 21, 1902 For child of No.1 see NB (March 3,1905) #1291					
11						
12						
13						
14						
15						
16						#1
17				DATE OF APPLICATION FOR ENROLLMENT. 9/5/99		

RESIDENCE: San[sic] Bois   COUNTY. **Choctaw Nation**   **Choctaw Roll** *(Not Including Freedmen)*   CARD NO.
POST OFFICE: Brooken, I.T.   FIELD NO. **4586**

Dawes' Roll No.	NAME		Relationship to Person First Named	AGE	SEX	BLOOD	TRIBAL ENROLLMENT		
							Year	County	No.
IW 1346	1 Autrey, Lock	32	Named	30	M	I.W.	1896	San[sic] Bois	14249
12689	2 " Anna B	14	Dau	11	F	1/16	"	" "	22
12690	3 " Goaly	12	"	9	F	1/16	"	" "	23
	4								
	5								
	6								
	7								
	8								
	9								
	10								
	11	ENROLLMENT							
	12	OF NOS. 1 HEREON APPROVED BY THE SECRETARY							
	13	OF INTERIOR MAR 14 1905							
	14	ENROLLMENT							
	15	OF NOS. 2, 3 HEREON APPROVED BY THE SECRETARY							
	16	OF INTERIOR MAR 6 1903							
	17								

TRIBAL ENROLLMENT OF PARENTS

	Name of Father	Year	County	Name of Mother	Year	County
1	John Autrey		Non Cit	Lucinda Autrey		Non Cit
2	No1			Ella Autrey	Dd	San[sic] Bois
3	" 1			" "		
4						
5						
6						
7	No.1 formerly husband of Ella Autrey (nee McDaniels)					
8	1893 Sans Bois, No.9 who died about 1896					
9						
10				On roll as L A Autrey		
11				As to marriage see his testimony and that of Simon Lewis		
12				No1 said to have married out		
13						
14						
15						
16				Date of Application for Enrollment. 9/6/99		
17	PO So McAlester IT 7/27/04					

Hartshorne IT 10/27/04

Choctaw By Blood Enrollment Cards 1898-1914

RESIDENCE: **Chick Nation** COUNTY. **Choctaw Nation** CARD No.
POST OFFICE: **Erin Springs, I.T.** **Choctaw Roll** (Not Including Freedmen) FIELD No. **4587**

Dawes' Roll No.	NAME		Relationship to Person First Named	AGE	SEX	BLOOD	TRIBAL ENROLLMENT		
							Year	County	No.
12691	1 Hazel, Seth J	28	First Named	25	M	1/32	1896	Chick Dist	6208
I.W. 456	2 " Nora	23	Wife	20	F	I.W.			
12692	3 " Jennie	3	Dau	5mo	F	1/64			
	4								
	5								
	6								
	7								
	8								
	9								
	10								
	11								
	12								
	13								
	14								
	15								
	16								
	17								

ENROLLMENT OF NOS. 2 HEREON APPROVED BY THE SECRETARY OF INTERIOR SEP 12 1903

ENROLLMENT OF NOS. 1-3 HEREON APPROVED BY THE SECRETARY OF INTERIOR MAR 6 1903

TRIBAL ENROLLMENT OF PARENTS

	Name of Father	Year	County	Name of Mother	Year	County
1	Jas. P. Hazel	Dd	Choc Roll	Jane Hazel	Dd	Non Cit
2	Jim Graham		Non Cit	Sallie Graham		" "
3	No.1			No.2		
4						
5						
6						
7						
8						
9	No1 on 1896 roll as Seth Hazel					
10	For child of Nos 1&2 see NB (Mar 3 '05) #334					
11						
12						
13						
14			No.3 Enrolled May 24, 1900			
15						
16						
17	PO Lindsay IT 1/20/05		No1 transferred from Choctaw Card #169	Date of Application for Enrollment 6/99		

87

Choctaw By Blood Enrollment Cards 1898-1914

RESIDENCE: Tobucksy COUNTY: **Choctaw Nation** **Choctaw Roll** (Not Including Freedmen) CARD NO.
POST OFFICE: Indianola, I.T. FIELD NO. **4588**

Dawes' Roll No.	NAME	Relationship to Person First Named	AGE	SEX	BLOOD	Year	County	No.
I.W. 1026	1 Hamilton, Hugh H 45	First Named	42	M	I.W.	1896	Tobucksy	2804 5
	2 " Julia A	Wife	32	F	1/8	and 9		
	3 " Della M	Dau	4	F	1/16			
Dis	4 " Thadeus	Son	7m	M	1/16			
12693	5 Dickerson, Rosa E 20	Dau	17	F	1/16	1896	Tobucksy	5349
12694	6 Walker, Ada 17	"	14	F	1/16	"	"	5350
12695	7 Hamilton, Douglas 15	Son	12	M	1/16	"	"	5351
12696	8 Dickerson, Bulah 2	Grand Dau	3m	F	1/32			
	9 Hamilton, Tandy	Son	4½yrs	M	1/16			
Dis	10 " Ruben H	Son	2wks	M	1/16			
12697	11 Walker, George 1	Gr Son	3wks	M	3/16			

Nos 2&3 Denied C.C.C. March
and 10 Dismissed

DISMISSED May 27 1904

Judgment of U.S. Ct admitting Nos 2and3 vacated and set aside by Decree of C.C.C.C. Dec 17 '02
13 No5 is now the wife of Jodie Dickerson a noncitizen Evidence of
marriage filed May 21,1901. No.6 is now the wife of William T Walker
14 No8 enrolled May 21,1901 on Choctaw card #4768, June 3,1902 7/1/01
15 Full maiden name of No5 was Rosa Eller Hamilton. See letter of Jodie L Dickerson filed
16 No10 Born March 18,1902: enrolled March 28,1902
Nos2,3,4,9 and 10 now in C.C.C.C. Case #109 Evidence of birth of No4 received and filed Feby 13, 1902.

TRIBAL ENROLLMENT OF PARENTS

Name of Father	Year	County	Name of Mother	Year	County
1 A.B. Hamilton	Dd	Non Cit	Sulitia Hamilton		Non Cit
2 J.R. Morris	" "		Jane Morris		Tobucksy
3 No 1			No 2		
4 " 1			" 2		
5 " 1			Arabelle Russell		Tobucksy
6 " 1			" "		
7 " 1			" "		
8 Jodie Dickerson		Non Citizen	No 5		
9 No 1			No 2		
10 No 1			No 2		
11 William T Walker	1896	Tobucksy	No 6		

ENROLLMENT OF NOS. 5 6 7 8-11 APPROVED BY THE SECRETARY OF INTERIOR Mar. 6, 1903

ENROLLMENT OF NOS. ~~~1~~~ HEREON APPROVED BY THE SECRETARY OF INTERIOR Oct 21, 1904

12 No1 admitted by Dawes Comm #1411. No appeal
13 " 2 " " U.S. Court So McA Aug 25-97 Case #88
14 " 2 " as Julia Hamilton
" 2 " " Delia May "
15 as to residence and birth of child see testimony of Hugh Hamilton
16 No9 Born April 8, 1897: Enrolled Feby 24, 1902
No11 Born Aug 20, 1902 enrolled Sept 9, 1902
17 For child of No6 see NB (Mar 3 '05) Card #335
" " " " 5 " " " " " #336

Date of Application for Enrollment. 9/6/99

88

Choctaw By Blood Enrollment Cards 1898-1914

		RESIDENCE: Tobucksy		COUNTY.					CARD NO.	

RESIDENCE: Tobucksy   COUNTY. **Choctaw Nation**   Choctaw Roll   CARD NO.
POST OFFICE: McAlester, I.T.   (Not Including Freedmen)   FIELD NO. 4589

Dawes' Roll No.	NAME	Relationship to Person First Named	AGE	SEX	BLOOD	TRIBAL ENROLLMENT		
						Year	County	No.
✓ ✗ 1	Marrs, Samuel	Named	28	M	1/16			
✓ ✗ 2	" Bertha	Dau	4	F	1/32			
✓ 3	" Archie L	Son	14ᵐ	M	1/32			
✓ 4	" Clarence J	"	8ᴹᴼ	M	1/32			
5								
6								
7	**DISMISSED** MAY 27 1904							
8								
9	Nos 1 and 2 denied by C.C.C.C. March 28 '04					No 1&2 denied in 96 Case #28		
10	No 4 dismissed							
11								
12								
13								
14								
15								
16								
17								

TRIBAL ENROLLMENT OF PARENTS

	Name of Father	Year	County	Name of Mother	Year	County
1	Robert Marrs		Non Cit	Jane Marrs		Tobucksy
2	No.1			Zoney "		Non Cit
3	" 1			" "		" "
4	No.1			" "		" "
5						
6	DENIED CITIZENSHIP BY THE CHOCTAW AND					
7	Nos 1,2 CHICKASAW CITIZENSHIP COURT					Mar 28 '04
8						
9						
10						
11	Admitted by U.S. Court at So M^cA Aug 25-97, Case 88. As to residence and birth of child see testimony No.1					
12	N⁰ 4 Born July 25, 1901; enrolled March 28, 1902 Evidence of birth of No.3 received and filed April 14, 1902					
13	Judgment of U.S. C't admitting Nos 1 and 2 vacated and set aside by Decree of C.C.C.C. Dec 17 '02					
14	Nos 1 and 2 now in C.C.C.C. Case #109					
15						
16						Date of Application for Enrollment.
17	Newberg I.T.					9/6/99

89

Choctaw By Blood Enrollment Cards 1898-1914

POST OFFICE: Featherston, I.T.   (Not Including Freedmen)   FIELD NO. 4590

Dawes' Roll No.	NAME	Relationship to Person First Named	AGE	SEX	BLOOD	TRIBAL ENROLLMENT Year	County	No.
	1 Burris, Molsey		41	F	full	1896	San[sic] Bois	687
12698	2 Carney, Albert 25	Son	22	M	"	"	" "	2092
12699	3 " Calvin 15	"	12	M	"	"	" "	688
12700	4 Burris, Lee 7	"	4	M	"	"	" "	689
15748	5 " Berthena 5	Dau	2	F	"			
	6							
	7							
	8	ENROLLMENT OF NOS. ~5~ HEREON APPROVED BY THE SECRETARY OF INTERIOR DEC -2 1904						
	9							
	10							
	11	ENROLLMENT OF NOS. 2, 3 - 4 HEREON APPROVED BY THE SECRETARY OF INTERIOR MAR 6 1903						
	12							
	13							
	14							
	15	No. 1 HEREON DISMISSED UNDER ORDER OF THE COMMISSION TO THE FIVE CIVILIZED TRIBES OF MARCH 31, 1905.						
	16							
	17							

TRIBAL ENROLLMENT OF PARENTS

	Name of Father	Year	County	Name of Mother	Year	County
1	Charlie Beams	Dd	San[sic] Bois	Wicey Beams	Dd	San[sic] Bois
2	Wilson Carney			No.1		
3	" "			" 1		
4	Sidney Burris			" 1		
5	" "			" 1		
6						
7						
8	Nº1 Died October 10 1901, proof of death filed					
9	Nº5 Born in November 1897. Affidavits as to birth					
10	No.2- Died prior to September 25, 1902 not entitled to land or money (see Indian Office letter October 3, 1910 I.D.C. #1572-1910					
11				No.3 on roll as Calvin Borris		
12						
13						
14						
15				Date of Application for Enrollment.		
16						
17						

RESIDENCE: Tobucksy   COUNTY. **Choctaw**
POST OFFICE: Indianola, I.T.   *(Not Including Freedmen)* FIELD NO. 4

Dawes' Roll No.	NAME		Relationship to Person First Named	AGE	SEX	BLOOD	TRIBAL ENROLLMENT		
							Year	County	No.
12701	1 Perkins	Lyman H 49	First Named	46	m	1/2	1896	Tobucksy	10332
I.W. 1027	2 "	Hattie A 41	Wife	38	f	IW	1896	"	1493[?]
12702	3 "	Cora 15	Dau	12	f	1/4	1896	"	10233
12703	4 "	Hugh H 13	Son	10	m	1/4	1896	"	10234
12704	5 "	Albert T 9	"	6	"	1/4	1896	"	10235
12705	6 "	Hattie A 7	D	4	f	1/4	1896	"	10236
12706	7 "	Dora M 6	D	3	f	1/4			
12707	8 "	Pearly Lee 2	Son	2mo	M	1/4	ENROLLMENT OF NOS. ~~~ 2 ~~~ HEREON APPROVED BY THE SECRETARY OF INTERIOR OCT 21 1904		
12709	9 "	William Alfred 1	Son	1½mo	M	1/4			
	10								
	11	ENROLLMENT OF NOS. 1 3 4 5 6 7 8-9 HEREON APPROVED BY THE SECRETARY							
	12	OF INTERIOR MAR 6 1903							
	13	No.2 denied by Dawes Commission							
	14	in 1896; Choctaw case #554, no appeal							
	15	Enrollment of No.2 cancelled by order of							
	16	Department March 4, 1907							
	17								

	TRIBAL ENROLLMENT OF PARENTS					
	Name of Father	Year	County	Name of Mother	Year	Cou
1	Geo Perkins	Dead	Choctaw	Jane F Perkins	Dead	Choctaw
2	Heny[sic] Stuart		Non Citizen	Susan Stuart		Non Citi
3	No1			No2		
4	No1			No2		
5	No1			No2		
6	No1			No2		
7	No1			No2		
8	No.1			No.2		
9	Nº1			Nº2		
10						
11	No2 restored to roll by Departmental authority of January 19 19					
12	As to marriage see testimony of					
13	No1 and Alex B Hamilton		For child of Nos 1&2 see NB (Mar 3-05)			
14	Evidence of birth of No 7 filed Feby 24, 1902 " " " No 3 " " " "					
	No3 on roll Cora B Perkins					
15	No8 Enrolled Aug 29th 1900 Nº9 Born March 18,1902 Enrolled May 3 1902					
16	No2 See Dawes Commission		Date of Application for Enrollment.	#1 to 7		
	Record 1896, Case 554					
17	No2 remarried under Choctaw law Aug 4th 1900		Sept 6th 1899			

Choctaw By Blood Enrollment Cards 1898-1914

RESIDENCE: Tobusky[sic]   COUNTY. **Choctaw Nation**   **Choctaw Roll**   CARD NO.
POST OFFICE: Thurman   (Not Including Freedmen)   FIELD NO. 4592

Dawes' Roll No.	NAME		Relationship to Person	AGE	SEX	BLOOD	TRIBAL ENROLLMENT		
							Year	County	No.
12709	1 Landis Clara A	26	First Named	23	f	1/4	1896	Tobusky[sic]	7866
12710	2 " W^m H	9	Son	6	m	1/8	1896	"	7867
12711	3 " Joseph E	5	"	2	m	1/8			
12712	4 " Syrena M	3	Dau	3mo	f	1/8			
12713	5 " Harry Edmon	1	Son	2mo	M	1/8			
12714	6 " Carrie Ann	1	Dau	2mo	F	1/8			
	7								
	8								
	9								
	10								
	11								
	12								
	13								
	14								
	15								
	16								
	17								

ENROLLMENT
OF NOS. 1 2 3 4 5 6 HEREON
APPROVED BY THE SECRETARY
OF INTERIOR   MAR 6 1903

TRIBAL ENROLLMENT OF PARENTS

	Name of Father	Year	County	Name of Mother	Year	County
1	Robt Bell		Tobusky[sic]	Selina Bell	Dead	Choctaw
2	Saml Landis		Non Citizen	No1		
3	Saml Landis		" "	No1		
4	Saml Landis		" "	No1		
5	" "		" "	N°1		
6	" "		" "	N°1		
7						
8		No2 on 1896 roll W^m H Landis				
9		N°5 Born Aug 4, 1902: enrolled Oct. 2, 1902				
10		N°6 Born Aug 4, 1902: enrolled Oct. 2, 1902				
11		N°s 5-6 are twins				
12						
13						
14					for #1 to 4	
15				Date of Application for Enrollment.	Sept 6th 1899	
16						
17						

Choctaw By Blood Enrollment Cards 1898-1914

RESIDENCE: Tobusky[sic]	COUNTY. **Choctaw Nation**	**Choctaw Roll** (Not Including Freedmen)	CARD NO.
POST OFFICE: Thurman			FIELD NO. 4593

Dawes' Roll No.	NAME		Relationship to Person First Named	AGE	SEX	BLOOD	TRIBAL ENROLLMENT		
							Year	County	No.
12715	1 Miller Serena J	23	Named	20	f	1/4	1896	Tobucksy	913
12716	2 " Alta M	6	D	2	f	1/8			
12717	3 " Joseph J	4	S	1	m	1/8			
	4								
	5								
	6								
	7								
	8								
	9								
	10								
	11								
	12								
	13								
	14								
	15	ENROLLMENT OF NOS. 1 2 - 3 HEREON APPROVED BY THE SECRETARY OF INTERIOR MAR 6 1903							
	16								
	17								

TRIBAL ENROLLMENT OF PARENTS

	Name of Father	Year	County	Name of Mother	Year	County
1	R D Bell		Non Citizen	Selina Bell	Dead	Choctaw
2	Joseph Miller		" "	No 1		
3	Joseph Miller		" "	No 1		
4						
5						
6						
7						
8			No1 on roll 1896 Serena J Bell			
9						
10			For children of No.1 see NB (Mar 3 '05) card #358			
11						
12						
13						
14						
15					Date of Application for Enrollment.	
16					Sept 6th 99	
17	McAlester I.T. 12/24/02					

RESIDENCE:	Tobucksy	COUNTY.					CARD NO.	
POST OFFICE:	Indianola	**Choctaw Nation**				Choctaw Roll _(Not Including Freedmen)_	FIELD NO.	**4594**

Dawes' Roll No.	NAME	Relationship to Person Named	AGE	SEX	BLOOD	TRIBAL ENROLLMENT		
						Year	County	No.
I.W. 1136	1 Hamilton, Alexander B	First Named	44	M	I.W.	1896	Tobucksy	14617
DEAD	2 " Louisa	W	43	F	1/2	1896	"	5367
12718	3 Alley, Elsie 22	D	19	F	1/4	1896	"	5369
12719	4 Hamilton Alexander B Jr 14	S	11	M	1/4	1896	"	5370
12720	5 " Frances 11	D	8	F	1/4	1896	"	5371
12721	6 " Walter L 9	S	6	M	1/4	1896	"	5372
I.W. 762	7 Alley, Brick P (24)	Husband of No 3	24	M	I.W.			

8 ENROLLMENT
9 OF NOS. ~~~ 7 ~~~ HEREON
APPROVED BY THE SECRETARY
10 OF INTERIOR May 7-1904

ENROLLMENT
OF NOS. ~~~ 1 ~~~ HEREON
APPROVED BY THE SECRETARY
OF INTERIOR Nov 16 1904

11 No 7 transferred from Choctaw Card #D 641. See
12 decision of Feby 29, 1904
13 No 2 hereon dismissed under order of
14 the Commission to the Five Civilized
Tribes of March 31, 1905.
15 ENROLLMENT
16 OF NOS. 3 4 5-6 HEREON
APPROVED BY THE SECRETARY
17 OF INTERIOR Mar 6, 1903

TRIBAL ENROLLMENT OF PARENTS

	Name of Father	Year	County	Name of Mother	Year	County
1	Alex B Hamilton		Non Citizen	Lutitia Hamilton		Non Citizen
2	Geo Perkins	Dead	Blue	Jane Perkins	Dead	Blue
3	No 1			No 2		
4	No 1			No 2		
5	No 1			No 2		
6	No 1			No 2		
7	Benj F. Alley		Non Citz	Julia Ann Alley		Non Citz

8 No 1 is now guardian of Minnie Brown on Choctaw Card #4595
9 Letters of guardianship filed February 18, 1903
10 No.1 on roll 1896 Aleck B Hamilton
No.4 " " " Alexander "
11 No 6 " " " Walter "
12 No 1 admitted by Dawes Commission in 1896 as an intermarried
citizen Choctaw Case #1356: No appeal
13 No.3 is now the wife of Brick P Alley on Choctaw Card #D.641 July 19, 1901
14 No 2 died April 10, 1900: Proof of death filed July 30, 1901\
15 No 1 is now the husband of Lillie Jones on Choctaw card #3108
16 Evidence of marriage filed with Choctaw #3108 on Aug 28, 1902
17 Watch No.1: is said to have married out July 19, 1901

Date of Application for Enrollment 9-6-99
↗ 1 to 6
{ For child of Nos 3&7 see NB
{ (Apr 26 '06) Card #231
↗ For child of Nos 3&7 see NB (Mar 3'05) #359

Choctaw By Blood Enrollment Cards 1898-1914

RESIDENCE: Tobucksy COUNTY. **Choctaw Nation** (Not Including Freedmen) Choctaw Roll CARD NO.

POST OFFICE: Indianola   FIELD NO. 4595

Dawes' Roll No.	NAME	Relationship to Person First Named	AGE	SEX	BLOOD	TRIBAL ENROLLMENT Year	County	No.
DEAD.	1 Brown Lutitia J DEAD.		22	f	1/4	1896	Tobucksy	5368
12722	2 " Minnie 3	dau	1mo	F	1/8			
	3							
	4							
	5							
	6							
	7							
	8							
	9							
	10							
	11							

12 No. 1 HEREON DISMISSED UNDER ORDER OF THE COMMISSION TO THE FIVE
13 CIVILIZED TRIBES OF MARCH 31, 1905.

14

15 ENROLLMENT
16 OF NOS. 2 HEREON APPROVED BY THE SECRETARY
17 OF INTERIOR MAR 6 1903

TRIBAL ENROLLMENT OF PARENTS

	Name of Father	Year	County	Name of Mother	Year	County
1	Alex B Hamilton		Tobucksy	Louisa Hamilton		Tobucksy
2	W. B. Brown		Non Cit	No1		
3						
4						
5						
6						
7	On roll 1896, Lutitia G Brown					
8						
9	No1 died March 24, 1900 Proof of death filed August 2, 1901					
10	No2 is now ward of A B Hamilton on Choctaw card #4594 Letters of guardianship filed February 18, 1903.					
11						
12						
13					Date of Application for Enrollment.	
14						
15					Sept 9 - 99	
16					No2 enrolled Nov 2/99	
17						

Choctaw By Blood Enrollment Cards 1898-1914

RESIDENCE: Gains[sic]		COUNTY. **Choctaw Nation**				**Choctaw Roll** *(Not Including Freedmen)*	CARD	
POST OFFICE: Featherston							FIELD	

Dawes' Roll No.	NAME		Relationship to Person	AGE	SEX	BLOOD	TRIBAL ENROLLMENT		
							Year	County	No.
12723	1 Carney Jonas	27	First Named	24	M	FB	1896	Sans Bois	2112
	2								
	3								
	4								
	5								
	6								
	7								
	8								
	9								
	10								
	11								
	12								
	13	ENROLLMENT OF NOS. 1 APPROVED BY THE SECRETARY OF INTERIOR MAR 6 1903 HEREON							
	14								
	15								
	16								
	17								

TRIBAL ENROLLMENT OF PARENTS

	Name of Father	Year	County	Name of Mother	Year	County
1	Tandy Carney	Dead		Eliza Carney	Dead	Choctaw
2						
3						
4						
5						
6						
7	For child of No.1 see NB (March 3 1905) #1231					
8						
9						
10						
11						
12						
13						
14					Date of Application for Enrollment.	
15						
16					Sept 6th 1899	
17	Quinton I.T. 1/23/03					

96

RESIDENCE: Tobucksy	COUNTY.	**Choctaw Nation**	Choctaw Roll	CARD NO.	
POST OFFICE: So McAlester			(Not Including Freedmen)	FIELD NO. **4597**	

Dawes' Roll No.	NAME		Relationship to Person	AGE	SEX	BLOOD	TRIBAL ENROLLMENT		
							Year	County	No.
IW457	1 Bell, Hannah	56	First Named	52	F	I.W.			
14441	2 Pitchlynn, William B	20	Son	17	M	1/4	1896	Tobucksy	10246
14442	3 " Priscilla	18	D	15	F	1/4	1896	"	10247
14443	4 " Ida	17	D	14	F	1/4	1896	"	10248
14444	5 " Leona	13	D	10	F	1/4	1896	"	10249
	6								
	7								
	8	ENROLLMENT OF NOS. 2,3,4 and 5 HEREON APPROVED BY THE SECRETARY OF INTERIOR Apr 11, 1903							
	9								
	10								
	11	ENROLLMENT OF NOS. 1 HEREON APPROVED BY THE SECRETARY OF INTERIOR Sep 12, 1903							
	12								
	13								
	14								
	15								
	16								
	17								

TRIBAL ENROLLMENT OF PARENTS

	Name of Father	Year	County	Name of Mother	Year	County
1	Charles Criger		Non Citizen	Christle Criger		Non Citizen
2	W^m B Pitchlynn	Dead	Tobucksy	No1		
3	W^m B Pitchlynn	"	"	No1		
4	W^m B Pitchlynn	"	"	No1		
5	W^m B Pitchlynn	"	"	No1		
6						
7						
8			2,3,4 and 5			
9			Nos 1 ^ admitted by Dawes Commission			
10			Case 878. No appeal			
11						
12			No2 on roll 1896 W^m B Pitchlynn			
13			No3 " " Precillo "			
14		For child of No3 see NB (Apr 26-06) Card #322			Date of Application for Enrollment.	
15		" " " 2 " " " " " #795				
		" " " 4 " " " " " #796				
16		" " " 2 " " (Mar 3 '05) " #365			Sept 9 - 1899	
17		" " " 4 " " " " " #364				

Choctaw By Blood Enrollment Cards 1898-1914

RESIDENCE: Tobucksy
POST OFFICE: So. McAlester
COUNTY: Choctaw Nation
Choctaw Roll (including Freedmen)
CARD NO.
FIELD NO. 4598

Dawes' Roll No.	NAME	Relationship to Person	AGE	SEX	BLOOD	TRIBAL ENROLLMENT Year	County	No.
12724	1 Bond Edmund M 25	First Named	22	M	1/8	1896	Tobucksy	900
12725	2 Turner Ida F 22	Sister	19	f	1/8	1896	"	895
12726	3 Bond Rex 20	Bro	17	M	1/8	1896	"	896
12727	4 " William W 17	bro	14	M	1/8	1896	"	897
12728	5 " Benjamin F 15	bro	12	M	1/8	1896	"	898
12729	6 " Rebecca A 13	Sister	10	f	1/8	1896	"	899
12730	7 Turner, Yulee 1	Son of No2	1mo	M	1/16			
14827	8 Bond, Richard C 1	Son	2wks	M	1/16			
I.W 681	9 Bond, June H 25	Wife	25	F	IW			
	10 No9 transferred from Choctaw card D657 Jan 19,1904							
	11 See decision of Jan. 2, 1904							
	12 No.1 is now the husband of June H Bond on Choctaw Card #D657 Aug 27, 1901							
	13							
	14							
	15							
	16							
	17							

For child of Nos1&9 see NB (Mar'05) #B66 #B67 No.3

ENROLLMENT OF NOS. 1 2 3 4 5 6-7 HEREON APPROVED BY THE SECRETARY OF INTERIOR MAR 6 1903

ENROLLMENT OF NOS. 8 HEREON APPROVED BY THE SECRETARY OF INTERIOR MAY 20 1903

TRIBAL ENROLLMENT OF PARENTS

	Name of Father	Year	County	Name of Mother	Year	County
1	Geo M Bond			Narcissa Bond	Dead	Tobucksy
2	Geo M Bond			Narcissa Bond	"	"
3	" " "			Do Do		"
4	" " "			Do Do		
5	" " "			Do Do		
6	" " "			Do Do		
7	Andrew J Turner		non citizen	No 2		
8	No1			June H Bond	Inter md wh	
9	O. E. Hornidy	Dead	Noncitizen	Emma Hornidy		noncitizen

10 No2 is now the wife of Andrew J Turner a noncitizen Evidence of marriage filed 3/10/01

11 No1 on 1896 roll as Edmund Mc Bond   Correct name of No.2 Ida "F". See letter of

12 No4 " 1896 " " Wallace Bond Jr   Andrew J. Turner filed Aug. 30, 1901.

No5 " 1896 " " Frank

13 No6 " 1896 " " Rebecca "

ENROLLMENT OF NOS. 9 HEREON APPROVED BY THE SECRETARY OF INTERIOR MAR 26 1904

14 No7 Enrolled Aug 10, 1901

15 Geo M Bond, father of above children on Choctaw car #5332 June 6, 1900

16 No8 Born June 3rd 1902. Enrolled June 19th 1902   Sept 6- 99

Date of Application for Enrollment

17 No5 - Terral I.T.   For child of No2 see NB (Apr 26-06) Card #732

98

Choctaw By Blood Enrollment Cards 1898-1914

RESIDENCE: Tobucksy COUNTY. **Choctaw Nation** **Choctaw Roll** CARD No.
POST OFFICE: Thurman *(Not Including Freedmen)* FIELD No. 4599

Dawes' Roll No.		NAME		Relationship to Person	AGE	SEX	BLOOD	TRIBAL ENROLLMENT		
								Year	County	No.
I.W. 1428	1	Staton John T	27	First Named	25	M	IW	1896	Tobucksy	15035
12731	2	" Susan J	25	Wife	22	f	1/4	1896	"	11292
12732	3	" William F	6	S	3	m	1/8	1896	"	11293
	4									
	5	ENROLLMENT								
	6	OF NOS. ~~~ 1 ~~~ HEREON								
	7	APPROVED BY THE SECRETARY OF INTERIOR JUN 12 1905								
	8									
	9									
	10									
	11									
	12									
	13									
	14									
	15	ENROLLMENT								
	16	OF NOS. 2 - 3 HEREON APPROVED BY THE SECRETARY								
	17	OF INTERIOR MAR 6 1903								

TRIBAL ENROLLMENT OF PARENTS

	Name of Father	Year	County	Name of Mother	Year	County
1	Non Cit			Non Cit		
2	Wᵐ Beams	Dead	Tobucksy	Phoebe C Staton	M[sic]	Tobucksy
3	No1			No2		
4						
5						
6	No1 restored to roll by Departmental authority of January 19, 1909 (File 5-5)					
7	No2 on 1896 roll Wᵐ F Staton					
8	Enrollment of No.1 cancelled by order of Department March 4 1907					
9	As to parents[sic] marriage see enrollment of Phoebe C Staton					
10						
11	No1 denied by Dawes Commission in 1896:					
12	Choctaw case #1072, no appeal					
13	Evidence of marriage between Nᵒˢ 1 and 2 filed Dec 24, 1902					
14						
15					Date of Application for Enrollment.	
16					Sept 6 - 99	
17	P.O. Purdy IT 3/3/03					

RESIDENCE:	Tobucksy	COUNTY.					CARD NO.	
POST OFFICE:	Savanna	**Choctaw Nation**			**Choctaw Roll** (Not Including Freedmen)		FIELD NO. 4600	

Dawes' Roll No.	NAME	Relationship to Person First Named	AGE	SEX	BLOOD	TRIBAL ENROLLMENT		
						Year	County	No.
12733 ₁	Chunn William R ²⁹	Named	26	M	1/32	1896	Tobucksy	2349
I.W. 458 ₂	" Lucy ²⁸	wife	24	f	IW	1896	"	14399
12734 ₃	" William C ²	s	2	m	1/64			
₄								
₅								
₆								
₇								
₈								
₉								
₁₀								
₁₁	ENROLLMENT OF NOS. 2 HEREON APPROVED BY THE SECRETARY OF INTERIOR SEP 12 1903							
₁₂								
₁₃								
₁₄								
₁₅	ENROLLMENT OF NOS. 1 - 3 HEREON APPROVED BY THE SECRETARY OF INTERIOR MAR 6 1903							
₁₆								
₁₇								

	TRIBAL ENROLLMENT OF PARENTS					
	Name of Father	Year	County	Name of Mother	Year	County
₁	Wᵐ Chunn	Dead	Tobucksy	Nancy A Hill		Tobucksy
₂	Jas Cantly		Non-citizen	Mossy Cantly		Noncitizen
₃	No1			No2		
₄						
₅						
₆						
₇	No1 on 1896 roll as Wᵐ R Chunn					
₈	Evidence of birth of No.3 received and filed Feby 14, 1902					
₉						
₁₀	For child of Nos 1 and [sic] see NB (March 3 1905) Card #368					
₁₁						
₁₂						
₁₃						
₁₄						
₁₅				Date of Application for Enrollment.		
₁₆				Sept 6ᵗʰ 1899		
₁₇						

Choctaw By Blood Enrollment Cards 1898-1914

RESIDENCE: Cedar	COUNTY.	**Choctaw Nation**	**Choctaw Roll**	CARD NO.
POST OFFICE: Antlers			*(Not Including Freedmen)*	FIELD NO. 4601

Dawes' Roll No.	NAME	Relationship to Person First Named	AGE	SEX	BLOOD	TRIBAL ENROLLMENT		
						Year	County	No.
1	Cheadle Margaret		56	f	IW			
2								
3								
4								
5								
6								
7								
8								
9								
10								
11								
12								
13								
14								
15								
16								
17								

CANCELLED

Transferred to Chickasaw Card # 1647
Dec 11, 1902

TRIBAL ENROLLMENT OF PARENTS

	Name of Father	Year	County	Name of Mother	Year	County
1	Andy Jones		Non Citizen	Mary Jones		Non Citizen
2						
3						
4						
5						
6						
7						
8			As to marriage see affidavit			
9			of John Ward & Mrs Sarah			
10			York, also testimony of her-			
11			self.			
12			On 1897 Chickasaw Roll, Page 92,			
13			Tishomingo Co, and said to be			
14			a Chickasaw. Dec 9/99			
15				Date of Application for Enrollment.		
16				Sept 6th 99		
17						

Choctaw By Blood Enrollment Cards 1898-1914

RESIDENCE:	Sans Bois	COUNTY.						CARD NO.	
POST OFFICE:	Enterprise	**Choctaw Nation**				**Choctaw Roll** (Not Including Freedmen)		FIELD NO. 4602	

Dawes' Roll No.	NAME			Relationship to Person First Named	AGE	SEX	BLOOD	TRIBAL ENROLLMENT		
								Year	County	No.
12735	1 Durant Wallace		32	First Named	29	M	1/2	1896	Scullyville[sic]	3211
I.W. 459	2 Durant Laura		29	Wife	26	f	IW		"	
12736	3 " Gaines		10	Son	7	m	1/4	1896	"	3212
12737	4 " Etta		8	D	5	f	1/4	1896	"	3213
12738	5 " Green		6	D	3	M	1/4	1896	"	3214
	6									
	7									
	8									
	9									
	10									
	11	ENROLLMENT OF NOS. 2 HEREON								
	12	APPROVED BY THE SECRETARY OF INTERIOR SEP 12 1903								
	13									
	14	ENROLLMENT								
	15	OF NOS. 1 - 3 - 4 - 5 HEREON								
	16	APPROVED BY THE SECRETARY OF INTERIOR MAR 6 1903								
	17									

TRIBAL ENROLLMENT OF PARENTS

	Name of Father	Year	County	Name of Mother	Year	County
1	Chas Durant	Dead	Scullyville[sic]	Cely Durant	Dead	Scullyville[sic]
2	Wesley Martindale		Noncitizen	Fanny Martindale		Non Citizen
3	No 1			No 2		
4	No 1			No 2		
5	No 1			No 2		
6						
7						
8						
9	For child of Nos 1 &2 see NB (Apr 26-06) Card #749					
10						
11						
12						
13						
14						
15				Date of Application for Enrollment.		
16				Sept 6 - 99		
17						

102

Choctaw By Blood Enrollment Cards 1898-1914

RESIDENCE: Tobucksy COUNTY. **Choctaw Nation** **Choctaw Roll** *(Not Including Freedmen)* CARD NO.
POST OFFICE: So McAlester FIELD NO. 4603

Dawes' Roll No.	NAME	Relationship to Person	AGE	SEX	BLOOD	TRIBAL ENROLLMENT		
						Year	County	No.
I.W. 763	1 Cole Preslie B ㊷	First Named	38	m	IW	1896	Tobucksy	14390
14828	2 " Laura 31	Wife	28	f	1/8	1896	"	2323
14445	3 " Bonnie M 9	D	6	f	1/16	1896	"	2324
14446	4 " Rogers L 7	Son	4	m	1/16	1896	"	2325
14829	5 " Preslie L 6	"	2	m	1/16	1896	"	2391
	6							
	7							
	8	ENROLLMENT OF NOS. 3 and 4 HEREON APPROVED BY THE SECRETARY OF INTERIOR APR 11 1903						
	9							
	10							
	11							
	12	ENROLLMENT OF NOS. 2 and 5 HEREON APPROVED BY THE SECRETARY OF INTERIOR MAY 20 1903						
	13							
	14						ENROLLMENT	
	15						OF NOS. ~~~ 1 ~~~ HEREON	
	16						APPROVED BY THE SECRETARY OF INTERIOR MAY -7 1904	
	17							

TRIBAL ENROLLMENT OF PARENTS

	Name of Father	Year	County	Name of Mother	Year	County
1	Monroe W Cole		Non Citizen	Nancy J Cole		Non Citizen
2	Jno W Rogers	Dead	" "	Mary E Rogers		Tobucksy
3	No1			No2		
4	No1			No2		
5	No1			No2		
6						
7						
8			No1 See Decision of March 2 '04			
9	Nos 1,3&4 Admitted by Dawes Commission #714					
10	No1 as Presslie[sic] B Cole No appeal					
11						
12						
13			No4 on 1896 roll Rodgers L Cole			
14			No5 " " " P Lawrence Cole			
			For child of No1 see NB (Apr 26-06) #1163			
15						
16				Date of Application for Enrollment.	Sept 6th 1899	
17	Pauls Valley I.T. 10/22/02					

103

Choctaw By Blood Enrollment Cards 1898-1914

RESIDENCE: Gains[sic]   COUNTY. **Choctaw Nation**   **Choctaw Roll** CARD No.
POST OFFICE: Wilberton[sic]   *(Not Including Freedmen)* FIELD No. 4604

Dawes' Roll No.	NAME	Relationship to Person	AGE	SEX	BLOOD	TRIBAL ENROLLMENT		
						Year	County	No.
I.W.460	1 Edmonds Richard O 70	First Named	67	M	IW	1896	Gains[sic]	14493
12739	2 " Martha J 69	wife	66	f	1/4	1896	"	3695
3								
4								
5								
6								
7								
8								
9								
10	ENROLLMENT							
11	OF NOS. 1 HEREON APPROVED BY THE SECRETARY							
12	OF INTERIOR SEP 12 1903							
13	ENROLLMENT							
14	OF NOS. 2 HEREON APPROVED BY THE SECRETARY							
15	OF INTERIOR MAR 6 1903							
16								
17								

TRIBAL ENROLLMENT OF PARENTS

Name of Father	Year	County	Name of Mother	Year	County
1 Wᵐ F Edmonds		Non Citizen	Mary E Edmonds		Non Citizen
2 Jno Riddle	dead	Gaines	Eve Riddle	dead	Gaines
3					
4					
5					
6					
7					
8					
9					
10	On roll 1896 R.O. Edmonds				
11	As to marriage see his testimony				
12	& that of Jerry Folsom				
13	Dec 6/99 No1 See Dawes Commission				
14	record 1896, Case No 1171.			Date of Application for Enrollment.	
15	No.1 admitted by Dawes Commission in 1896 as an intermarried citizen:				
16	Choctaw case #1171: docket entry in this case reads "Application denied."				
17	but entry on original application is as follows "Admit Richard O. Sept 9 - 1899				
	Edmonds as an intermarried citizen."				

P.O. Sans Bois IT 12/15/02   Kinta IT 11/1/04

104

Choctaw By Blood Enrollment Cards 1898-1914

RESIDENCE: POST OFFICE: Fitzhugh			Choctaw Nation				TRIBAL ENROLLMENT			FIELD No. 4605

(Not Including Freedmen)

Dawes' Roll No.	NAME		Relationship to Person First Named	AGE	SEX	BLOOD	TRIBAL ENROLLMENT Year	County	No.
14261	1 Hendrix Edy	29		26	m	1/8	1896	Atoka	6061
I.W. 461	2 " Nancy	30	wife	26	f	IW			
14262	3 " Clemmie	7	D	4	f	1/16	1896	"	6062
	4								
	5								
	6	ENROLLMENT							
	7	OF NOS. 1 and 3 HEREON APPROVED BY THE SECRETARY							
	8	OF INTERIOR APR 11 1903							
	9								
	10	ENROLLMENT							
	11	OF NOS. 2 HEREON APPROVED BY THE SECRETARY							
	12	OF INTERIOR SEP 12 1903							
	13								
	14								
	15								
	16								
	17								

TRIBAL ENROLLMENT OF PARENTS

	Name of Father	Year	County	Name of Mother	Year	County
1	Jasper Hendrix	IW	Atoka	Belle Hendrix		Atoka
2	Caliph Connell		Non Cit	Senna Connell		Non Citq
3	No1			No2		
4						
5						
6	No2 admitted by Dawes Com, Case #			no appeal		
7	1130 as Nancy Hendricks					
8						
9	No1 admitted by Dawes Com case #1130 as Eddie Hendricks					
10	No3 " " " " " " " Clemmie Hendricks					
11						
12						
13	No1 on 1896 roll Edd Hendrix					
14	No3 " " " Clem Hendrix					
15	No1 admitted by U.S. Indian Agent Feb 8, 1895					
16				Date of Application for Enrollment.	Sept 6th 1899	
17	Center I.T. 11/13/02					

Choctaw By Blood Enrollment Cards 1898-1914

CE: San[sic] Bois, I.T. **Choctaw Nation** *(Not Including Freedmen)* FIELD NO. 460

	NAME		Relationship to Person First Named	AGE	SEX	BLOOD	TRIBAL ENROLLMENT		
							Year	County	No.
1	Bond, Sina	36		33	F	1/2	1896	San[sic] Bois	577
2	" Florence	13	Dau	10	"	1/4	"	" "	578
3	" May	10	"	7	"	1/4	"	" "	579
4	" Bennett F	7	Son	4	M	1/4	"	" "	580
5	" Wallace	4	"	11ᵐ	"	1/4			
6	" Sidney	14	Ward	11	"	1/2	1896	San[sic] Bois	582
7	" Green M	10	"	7	"	1/2	"	" "	583
8	Dyer, Nicholas	20	Ward	17	"	full	"	" "	3153
9	Trahern, Douglas	20	Son	17	"	1/2	"	" "	11816
10	" Martha	17	Dau	14	F	1/2	"	" "	11817
11	Bond, Ridgely	50	Hus	47	M	I.W.	"	" "	14275

12748, 12749, I.W. 462

ENROLLMENT
OF NOS. 1 2 3 4 5 6 7 8 9 10 HEREON
APPROVED BY THE SECRETARY
OF INTERIOR MAR 6 1903

ENROLLMENT
OF NOS. 11 HEREON
APPROVED BY THE SECRETARY
OF INTERIOR SEP 12 1903

TRIBAL ENROLLMENT OF PARENTS

	Name of Father	Year	County	Name of Mother	Year	
1	Dave Colbert	Dd	Chic Ind		Dd	Skully
2	Ridgely Bond		Non Cit	No. 1		
3	" "			" 1		
4	" "			" 1		
5	" "			" 1		
6	Wallace "	Dd	San[sic] Bois	Lily McGilberry	Dd	
7	" "	"	" "	" "	"	
8	Jim Dyer	Dd	" "	Lucy	"	San[sic
9	Lysander Trahern		Skullyville	No. 1		
10	" "		"	" 1		
11	Geo Bond	Dd	Non Cit	Rebecca A Bond	Dd	Non cit
12	For child of No10 see NB (March 3,1905) #1208					
13	For child of Nos 1&11 see NB (Mar 3,1905) #667					
14	No.9 also on 1896 roll, #11925, page 308			No 4 on roll as Bennette Bond		
15	Evidence of marriage between N°1 and 11 filed Feby 14, 1903					
16	Evidence of divorce between N°1 and former husband filed Feby 14, 1903				Date of Application for Enrollment.	No.11 9/12/9 9/6/9
17						1 to 10

106

Choctaw By Blood Enrollment Cards 1898-1914

RESIDENCE: POST OFFICE: McAlester, I.T.	COUNTY, **Choctaw Nation**	**Choctaw Roll** *(Not Including Freedmen)*	CARD NO. FIELD NO. **4607**

Dawes' Roll No.	NAME	Relationship to Person First Named	AGE	SEX	BLOOD	TRIBAL ENROLLMENT		
						Year	County	No.
12750	1 Choate, Christopher C⁴⁵		42	M	1/4	1896	Tobucksy	2374
I.W. 1559	2 " , Amanda ⁵¹	Wife	48	F	I.W.	"	"	14402
12751	3 " , Lewis E ¹⁰	Son	7	M	1/8	1893	"	220
12752	4 " , Jacob G ⁶	"	4	"	1/8			
12753	5 Armstrong, Joseph ¹⁵	Ward	12	"	1/4	1896	Tobucksy	146
	6							
	7 No.2 restored to roll by Departmental authority of January 19, 1909 (File 5-51)							
	8 Enrollment of No2 cancelled by order of Department March 4, 1907							
	9 ENROLLMENT OF NOS. 2 HEREON					ENROLLMENT		
	10 APPROVED BY THE SECRETARY OF INTERIOR Aug 2 1906					OF NOS. 1 3 4-5 HEREON		
	11					APPROVED BY THE SECRETARY OF INTERIOR Mar. 6, 1903		
	12 Dec 6/99 See Dawes Commission							
	13 record for 1896, Case No. 757							
	14							
	15 No2 was remarried to Christopher C Choate							
	16 Nov. 18ᵗʰ 1900							
	17 Evidence of birth of No.4 filed Feb 17, 1902							

TRIBAL ENROLLMENT OF PARENTS

	Name of Father	Year	County	Name of Mother	Year	County
1	Saml S Choate	Dd	Tobucksy	Lydia Choate	Dd	Tobucksy
2	Non Cit			Louisa Lankford		Non Cit
3	No1			No2		
4	" 1			" 2		
5	W. P. Armstrong	Dd	Non Cit	Mary Armstrong	Dd	Tobucksy
6						
7						
8						
9	No2 was rejected by Dawes Com-					
10	mission in 1896: Choctaw Case #757. No appeal.					
11						
12				As to parents[sic] marriage see testimony of		
13	No2 GRANTED			Tandy C Walker Not on roll as Chris C Choat		
14		Apr 16 1906		" 2 " " " Amanda "		
15				" 3 P.22-#220-93-PR Tobucksy Co		
16				as Lewis Choate		Date of Application for Enrollment.
17	P.O. Indianola I.T. 7/9/04			Date of application for enrollment 9/6/99		

Choctaw By Blood Enrollment Cards 1898-1914

RESIDENCE:
POST OFFICE: So McAlester, I.T. **Choctaw Nation** **Choctaw Roll** *(Not Including Freedmen)* CARD NO. FIELD NO. 4608

COUNTY.

Dawes' Roll No.	NAME	Relationship to Person First Named	AGE	SEX	BLOOD	TRIBAL ENROLLMENT		
						Year	County	No.
* 1	Lucsaw, Alice,		54	F	1/4			
* 2	" John M	Son	14	M	1/8			
3								
4								
5								
6								
7								
8								
9								
10								
11								
12								
13								
14	See Loula West Petition							
15	C 95							
16								
17								

TRIBAL ENROLLMENT OF PARENTS

Name of Father	Year	County	Name of Mother	Year	County
1 Wm Scanlon			Alice Scanlon		
2					

* Nos 1 and 2 denied by the Comm in 96 Choc Cit Case #1237
* Nos 1 and 2 Decision of U.S. Court C.D. of Sept 6 1896 vacated and set aside by Decree of Choctaw Chickasaw Cit Court Decr 17 '02. The Choctaw-Chickasaw Citizenship Court on Jan 21st 06 denied Nos 1 and 2 Case #24

Admitted by U.S. Court at So McA Sept 6-97, Case 128
As to residence see her testimony.

Date of Application for Enrollment. 9/6/99

108

Choctaw By Blood Enrollment Cards 1898-1914

RESIDENCE:
POST OFFICE: Krebs, I.T.

COUNTY. **Choctaw Nation**

Choctaw Roll (Not Including Freedmen)

CARD NO.
FIELD No. 460

Dawes' Roll No.		NAME		Relationship to Person	AGE	SEX	BLOOD	TRIBAL ENROLLMENT		
								Year	County	No.
I.W. 463	1	Strong, John B	25	First Named	22	M	I.W.			
12754	2	" Bridget	24	Wife	21	F	1/8	1896	Tobucksy	4686
12755	3	" William H	1	Son	2mo	M	1/16			
	4									
	5									
	6									
	7									
	8									
	9									
	10	ENROLLMENT								
	11	OF NOS. 1 HEREON								
	12	APPROVED BY THE SECRETARY OF INTERIOR SEP 12 1903								
	13	ENROLLMENT								
	14	OF NOS. 2 - 3 HEREON								
	15	APPROVED BY THE SECRETARY OF INTERIOR MAR 6 1903								
	16									
	17									

TRIBAL ENROLLMENT OF PARENTS

	Name of Father	Year	County	Name of Mother		County
1	W^m D Strong		Non Cit	Harriet		Non Cit
2	M H Gleason	-	Tobucksy	Mary E Gleason		Tobucksy
3	Nº1			Nº2		
4						
5						
6						
7						
8						
9	For child of Nos 1&2 see NB (Apr 26-06) Card #690					
10						
11						
12	Nº3 Born Jany 31, 1902; enrolled March 22, 1902					
13					No 2 on roll as Biddy Gleason	
14						
15					Date of Application for Enrollment.	
16						
17						9/6/99

Choctaw By Blood Enrollment Cards 1898-1914

RESIDENCE:			COUNTY.							CARD NO.	
POST OFFICE: Savanna, I.T.			**Choctaw Nation**				**Choctaw Roll** *(Not Including Freedmen)*			FIELD NO. 4610	

Dawes' Roll No.	NAME		Relationship to Person	AGE	SEX	BLOOD	TRIBAL ENROLLMENT		
							Year	County	No.
I.W. 1028	1 Choate, Annie M	28	First Named	25	F	I.W.	1896	Tobucksy	14303
12756	2 " Walter	16	Son	13	M	1/4	"	"	2348
3									
4									
5									
6	Affidavits of N°1, Simon E Lewis, and Solomon H Mackey, relative to								
7	marriage of N°1 to Campbell Choate, filed July 1, 1903								
8									
9									
10	ENROLLMENT								
11	OF NOS. ~~~ 1 ~~~ HEREON APPROVED BY THE SECRETARY								
12	OF INTERIOR OCT 21 1904								
13									
14	ENROLLMENT								
15	OF NOS. 2 HEREON APPROVED BY THE SECRETARY								
16	OF INTERIOR								
17									

TRIBAL ENROLLMENT OF PARENTS

	Name of Father	Year	County	Name of Mother	Year	County
1	Lee Faulkner		Non Cit	Alice Faulkner		Non Cit
2	Campbell Choate	Dd	Tobucksy	No. 1		
3						
4						
5						
6						
7						
8						
9						
10			For child of No1 see NB (Apr 26 '06) Card No. 223			
11			No.1 on roll as Annie M Bailey			
12			Certificate of marriage of Campbell Choate, Choctaw			
13			and Annie Mary Faulkner, on Nov. 7-1884 exhibited, but not in condition to be filed.			
14						
15					Date of Application for Enrollment.	
16						
17	P.O. Holliman Jan 19 1904				9/6/99	

110

Choctaw By Blood Enrollment Cards 1898-1914

RESIDENCE: COUNTY. **Choctaw Nation**   **Choctaw Roll**   CARD NO.
POST OFFICE: So Canadian, I.T.   *(Not Including Freedmen)*   FIELD NO. 4611

Dawes' Roll No.	NAME	Relationship to Person	AGE	SEX	BLOOD	TRIBAL ENROLLMENT		
						Year	County	No.
12757	1 Harlan, Sarah A 73	First Named	70	F	1/8	1896	Tobucksy	5344
	2							
	3							
	4							
	5							
	6							
	7							
	8							
	9							
	10							
	11							
	12							
	13							
	14							
	15							
	16							
	17							

ENROLLMENT
OF NOS.   1   HEREON
APPROVED BY THE SECRETARY
OF INTERIOR   MAR 6 1903

TRIBAL ENROLLMENT OF PARENTS

	Name of Father	Year	County	Name of Mother	Year	County
1	Sampson Moncrief	Dd	Skullyville	Saphira Moncrief	Dd	
2						
3						
4						
5						
6						
7						
8						
9						
10						
11						
12				On roll as Sarah A Harlin		
13						
14						
15						Date of Application for Enrollment.
16						
17						9/6/99

Choctaw By Blood Enrollment Cards 1898-1914

RESIDENCE: Tobucksy   COUNTY. **Choctaw Nation**   **Choctaw Roll**   CARD NO.
POST OFFICE: Savanna, I.T.   *(Not Including Freedmen)*   FIELD NO. 4612

Dawes' Roll No.	NAME	Relationship to Person First Named	AGE	SEX	BLOOD	TRIBAL ENROLLMENT Year	County	No.
I.W. 464 ₁	Chunn, Ollie ²⁴	First Named	20	F	I.W.	1896	Tobucksy	14400
12758 ₂	" Mattie ⁵	Dau	2	F	1/16			
12759 ₃	" Oscar Jr ³	"	2mo	"	1/16			
₄								
₅								
₆								
₇								
₈								
₉								
₁₀	ENROLLMENT							
₁₁	OF NOS. 1 HEREON APPROVED BY THE SECRETARY							
₁₂	OF INTERIOR SEP 12 1903							
₁₃	ENROLLMENT							
₁₄	OF NOS. 2 - 3 HEREON APPROVED BY THE SECRETARY							
₁₅	OF INTERIOR MAR 6 1903							
₁₆								
₁₇								

TRIBAL ENROLLMENT OF PARENTS

	Name of Father	Year	County	Name of Mother	Year	County
₁	Andrew Brewster		Non Cit	Arky Brewster		Tobucksy
₂	Oscar Chunn	Dd	Tobucksy	No.1		
₃	" "	"	"	No.1		
₄						
₅						
₆						
₇						
₈	Father of Nos 2 and 3 on 1896 roll Tobucksy Co No 2350					
₉						
₁₀						
₁₁						
₁₂						
₁₃						
₁₄						
₁₅					No3 enrolled Nov 24/99	
₁₆					Date of Application for Enrollment.	
₁₇						9/6/99

112

Choctaw By Blood Enrollment Cards 1898-1914

RESIDENCE: Tobucksy   COUNTY. **Choctaw Nation**   **Choctaw Roll** *(Not Including Freedmen)*   CARD NO.

POST OFFICE: Scipio   FIELD NO. 4613

Dawes' Roll No.	NAME	Relationship to Person First Named	AGE	SEX	BLOOD	TRIBAL ENROLLMENT		
						Year	County	No.
I.W. 1029	1 Low Hugh D 43	First Named	40	m	IW	1896	Tobucksy	14757
12760	2 Nicar Ola P 16	d	13	f	1/4	1896	"	7870
12761	3 Low Emanuel H 14	s	11	m	1/4	1896	"	7871
12762	4 " Nelia J 12	d	9	f	1/4	1896	"	7872
12763	5 " Frances L M 8	d	5	f	1/4	1896	"	7873
12764	6 " Hugh S 6	s	3	m	1/4	1896	"	7874
12765	7 " Arina E 4	d	8mo	f	1/4			
12766	8 Nicar, Grace M 1	Grand Dau	1mo	F	1/8			
	9							
	10	~~ENROLLMENT~~ OF NOS. ~~~ 1 ~~~ HEREON APPROVED BY THE SECRETARY OF INTERIOR OCT 21 1904						
	11							
	12							
	13	No.2 is now the wife of Christy Nicar a noncitizen.						
	14	Evidence of marriage filed Mch 31, 1902						
	15	For child of No.2 see NB (March 3,1905) #797						
	16	ENROLLMENT OF NOS. 2 3 4 5 6 7-8 HEREON APPROVED BY THE SECRETARY OF INTERIOR MAR 6 1903						

TRIBAL ENROLLMENT OF PARENTS

	Name of Father	Year	County	Name of Mother	Year	County
1	Johnathan Low		Non Citizen	Su An Low		Non Citizen
2	No 1			Melvina Low	dead	Tobucksy
3	No 1			Do Do	"	
4	No 1			Do Do		
5	No 1			Do Do		
6	No 1			Do Do		
7	C. H. Nicar		non-citizen	№2		
8						
9	No2 on 1896 roll Pearl O Low					
10	No3 " " " Manuel "					
11	No4 " " " Janmie "					
	No5 " " " Frances "					
12	No6 " " " Hugh Jr "					
13	Evidence of birth of No.6 received and filed March 4, 1902					#1 to 7
14	" " " No.7 " " March 4, 1902					
15	~~N°8 Born April 7, 1902: enrolled May 7, 1902~~					
16						1 to 7 incl
17	No2 PO Citra IT 4/7/05					Sept 6/99

Date of Application for Enrollment

113

RESIDENCE:		COUNTY.				**Choctaw Roll**		CARD NO.	
POST OFFICE: Enterprise, I.T.		**Choctaw Nation**				(Not Including Freedmen)		FIELD NO. **4614**	

Dawes' Roll No.	NAME	Relationship to Person	AGE	SEX	BLOOD	TRIBAL ENROLLMENT		
						Year	County	No.
12767	1 Riddle, Sam 21	First Named	18	M	1/2	1896	San[sic] Bois	10674
12768	2 " Cephus 18	Bro	15	"	1/2	"	"	10675
DEAD	3 " Selina DEAD 16	Sis	13	F	1/2	"	"	10676
12769	4 " Cillin 13	"	10	"	1/2	"	"	10677
12770	5 " Georgian 8	"	5	"	1/2	"	"	10678
	6							
	7							
	8							
	9							
	10 No.3 hereon dismissed under order of							
	11 the Commission to the Five Civilized Tribes of March 31, 1905.							
	12							
	13 ENROLLMENT							
	14 OF NOS. 1 2 4 5 HEREON APPROVED BY THE SECRETARY							
	15 OF INTERIOR Mar 6, 1903							
	16							
	17							

TRIBAL ENROLLMENT OF PARENTS

	Name of Father	Year	County	Name of Mother	Year	County
1	Jack Riddle		San[sic] Bois	Hokmer	Dd	San[sic] Bois
2	" "		" "	"	"	" "
3	" "		" "	"	"	" "
4	" "		" "	"	"	" "
5	" "		" "	"	"	" "
6						
7						
8	For child of No2 see NB (Mar 3'05) #460					
9						
10				No5 on roll as George Riddle		
11	No.3 Died 1900. Proof of death filed Dec. 30, 1902					
12	Father of these children is Jackson Riddle on Choctaw Freedman Card No.1146					
13						
14						
15					Date of Application for Enrollment.	
16						
17	Quinton I.T. 12/22/02				9/6/00	

Choctaw By Blood Enrollment Cards 1898-1914

RESIDENCE:	Jacks Fork	COUNTY.							

RESIDENCE: **Jacks Fork** COUNTY. **Choctaw Nation** **Choctaw Roll** CARD No.
POST OFFICE: **Stringtown,** I.T. *(Not Including Freedmen)* FIELD No. **4615**

Dawes' Roll No.	NAME	Relationship to Person First Named	AGE	SEX	BLOOD	TRIBAL ENROLLMENT		
						Year	County	No.
✓ ✓	1 Stallings, Wm H.		51	M	1/4			
	2							
	3							
	4							
	5							
	6							
	7							
	8							
	9							
	10							
	11							
	12							
	13							
	14							
	15							
	17							

DENIED CITIZENSHIP BY THE CHOCTAW AND CHICKASAW CITIZENSHIP COURT

Case #77 April 28-1904

TRIBAL ENROLLMENT OF PARENTS

Name of Father	Year	County	Name of Mother	Year	County
1 Jacob Stallings	Dd		Hettie McLaughlin	Dd	
2					
3					
4					
5					
6					
7 No1 denied in 96 Case #820					
8 No.1 is the husband of Hawley Stallings on Choctaw card					
9			Admitted by U.S. Court So M^cA. Aug 25-97-		
			As to residence see his testimony.		
10 Judgment of U.S. Ct admitting No.1 vacated and set aside by Decree of C.C.C. Dec' 17 '02					
11 No.1 admitted by United States Court, Central Dis					
12 Ind Ter, August 25, 1897; Court case #					
13 Not now in C.C.C. Case #77					
14					
15					
16					Date of Application for Enrollment.
17					9/6/99

RESIDENCE: Chickasaw Nation COUNTY.
POST OFFICE: Woodville

Choctaw Nation

Choctaw Roll
(Not Including Freedmen)

CARD NO.
FIELD NO. 4616

Dawes' Roll No.	NAME		Relationship to Person	AGE	SEX	BLOOD	TRIBAL ENROLLMENT		
							Year	County	No.
14447	1 Hendrix William	24	First Named	21	M	1/8	1896	Atoka	6054
14448	" Jennie F	3	Dau	1	F	1/16			
14449	" Lily Bell	1	Dau	1mo	F	1/16			
I.W 1137	" Evelina	22	Wife	22	F	1/16			
5	ENROLLMENT								
6	OF NOS. 1 2 and 3 HEREON								
7	APPROVED BY THE SECRETARY OF INTERIOR APR 11 1903								
8									
9	For child of Nos 1&4 see NB (Apr 26-06) Card #475								
10	" " " " " " " " Mar 3-05) " #566								
11									
12	ENROLLMENT								
13	OF NOS. 4 HEREON APPROVED BY THE SECRETARY								
14	OF INTERIOR NOV 16 1904								
15									
16									
17									

TRIBAL ENROLLMENT OF PARENTS

	Name of Father	Year	County	Name of Mother	Year	County
1	Jasper Hendrix		Non Citizen	Belle Hendrix		Non Citizen
2	No.1			Evalela[sic] Hendrix		" "
3	No.1			" "		" "
4	Bob Voss		Non Citizen	Nann Voss		Non Citizen
5						
6	Admitted by Dawes Commission					
7	Case #1130 as Willie Hendrix. No appeal					
8						
9	On 1896 roll as Willie Hendrix					
10	No.1 is the husband of Evelina Hendrix					
11	on Choctaw card D.447					
12						
13	No2 was born March 9th, 1900 and on April 4, 1900 enrolled on Nov 7th, 1901					
14	Choctaw card #D.447 and transferred to Choctaw #4616				Date of Application for Enrollment. #1	
15	No3 born Oct 19,1901: Enrolled Nov 7th 1901.				7/9/1899	
16	No1 admitted by U.S. Indian Agent Feb 8, 1893					
17	No4 transferred from Choctaw card #D-447 Oct 31, 1904: See decision of Oct 15,1904					
	PO Bebee IT 3/27/05					

Choctaw By Blood Enrollment Cards 1898-1914

RESIDENCE: Tobucksy   COUNTY. **Choctaw Nation**   **Choctaw Roll** *(Not Including Freedmen)*   CARD NO.
POST OFFICE: McAlester   FIELD NO. 4617

Dawes' Roll No.	NAME	Relationship to Person	AGE	SEX	BLOOD	TRIBAL ENROLLMENT		
						Year	County	No.
12771	1 Ansley William H ³⁰	First Named	27	M	1/8	1896	Tobucksy	147
	2							
	3							
	4							
	5							
	6							
	7							
	8							
	9							
	10							
	11							
	12							
	13							
	14							
	15	ENROLLMENT OF NOS. 1 HEREON						
	16	APPROVED BY THE SECRETARY						
	17	OF INTERIOR						

TRIBAL ENROLLMENT OF PARENTS

	Name of Father	Year	County	Name of Mother	Year	County
1	Wm Ansley		Tobucksy	Antonette Ansley		Non-Citizen
2						
3						
4						
5						
6						
7						
8						
9						
10	On 1896 roll W Husey Ansley					
11	As to parents[sic] marriage see enrollment					
12	William Ansley					
13						
14					Date of Application for Enrollment.	
15					7/9 - 1899	
16						
17						

Choctaw By Blood Enrollment Cards 1898-1914

RESIDENCE: Tobucksy COUNTY.
POST OFFICE: McAlester

RESIDENCE: Tobucksy   COUNTY. **Choctaw Nation**   **Choctaw Roll** (Not Including Freedmen)   CARD No.   FIELD No. 4618
POST OFFICE: McAlester

Dawes' Roll No.	NAME	Relationship to Person Named	AGE	SEX	BLOOD	TRIBAL ENROLLMENT Year	County	No.
12772	₁ ~~Wade George W~~ DIED PRIOR TO SEPTEMBER 25, 1902 First Named	~~65~~	~~m~~	~~1/4~~	~~1896~~	~~Tobucksy~~	~~12989~~
12773	₂ Pusley, McAlester 21	G son	18	m	1/2	1896	"	10220
	3							
	4							
	5							
	6							
	7							
	8							
	9							
	10							
	11							
	12							
	13							
	14							
	15	ENROLLMENT OF NOS. 1-2 HEREON APPROVED BY THE SECRETARY OF INTERIOR						
	16							
	17							

TRIBAL ENROLLMENT OF PARENTS

Name of Father	Year	County	Name of Mother	Year	County
1			~~Hannah Wade~~	~~Dead~~	~~Choctaw~~
₂ Geo Pusley	dead	Tobucksy			
3					
4					
5					
6					
7			No1 on roll 1896. Geo. W Wade		
8			No. 1 died Nov 29, 1899: Enrollment cancelled by Department May [illegible]		
9					
10					
11					
12					
13					
14					
15					
16					
17					

Choctaw By Blood Enrollment Cards 1898-1914

RESIDENCE: Tobucksy COUNTY. **Choctaw Nation** Choctaw Roll CARD NO.
POST OFFICE: Celestine (Not Including Freedmen) FIELD NO. 4619

Dawes' Roll No.	NAME		Relationship to Person First Named	AGE	SEX	BLOOD	TRIBAL ENROLLMENT		
							Year	County	No.
12774	1 Ward Silas	49		46	m	3/4	1896	Tobucksy	13022
12775	2 " Mary	29	wife	26	f	3/4	1896	"	13023
	3								
	4								
	5								
	6								
	7								
	8								
	9								
	10								
	11								
	12								
	13								
	14								
	15	ENROLLMENT OF NOS. 1-2 HEREON							
	16	APPROVED BY THE SECRETARY							
	17	OF INTERIOR MAR 6 1903							

TRIBAL ENROLLMENT OF PARENTS

Name of Father	Year	County	Name of Mother	Year	County
1 Silas Ward	Dead	Tobucksy	Lucinda Ward	Dead	Towson
2 Frank Holloway	D	"	Emeline Holloway		Jack forks[sic]
3					
4					
5					
6					
7					
8					
9					
10					
11					
12					
13					
14					
15				Date of Application for Enrollment.		
16				Sept 7- 1899		
17						

RESIDENCE:	Tobucksy	COUNTY.	**Choctaw Nation**				**Choctaw Roll** *(Not Including Freedmen)*		CARD No.	
POST OFFICE:	Savanna I.T.								FIELD No. 4620	

Dawes' Roll No.		NAME		Relationship to Person First Named	AGE	SEX	BLOOD	TRIBAL ENROLLMENT		
								Year	County	No.
12776	1	Towry Juanita	23	First Named	20	f	1/8	1896	Tobucksy	3310
I.W. 764	2	" James W	30	Husband	26	m	IW			
12777	3	" Cecil McK	1	Son	2wks	m	1/16			
	4									
	5									
	6									
	7									
	8									
	9	ENROLLMENT								
	10	OF NOS. ~~~~2~~~~ HEREON APPROVED BY THE SECRETARY								
	11	OF INTERIOR MAY -7 1904								
	12									
	13									
	14	ENROLLMENT								
	15	OF NOS. 1 - 3 APPROVED BY THE SECRETARY								
	16	OF INTERIOR MAR 6 1903								
	17									

TRIBAL ENROLLMENT OF PARENTS

	Name of Father	Year	County	Name of Mother	Year	County
1	Jas S Davis	IW	Tobucksy	Annie Davis		Tobucksy
2	G C Towry		Non Cit	Margaret L Towry		Non Cit
3	No.2			No.1		
4						
5						
6						
7						
8						
9	No1 on 1896 roll as Juneta[sic] Davis					
10	No2 See Decision of March 2 '04					
11	No2 as to residence see his testimony					
12	No.3 Born Feby 8, 1902: enrolled Feby 24, 1902					
13	Affidavit of Nº1 relative to her marriage to Nº2 filed June 2, 1903					
14	Certified copy of divorce proceedings between Nº2 and his former wife filed June 2, 1903					
15					Date of Application for Enrollment.	
16	PO Buffalo IT 3/3/05			Sept 7th 1899		
17	PO Gans[sic] IT 3/19/04					

Choctaw By Blood Enrollment Cards 1898-1914

RESIDENCE: Tobucksy	COUNTY.							
POST OFFICE: McAlester								

RESIDENCE: Tobucksy   COUNTY. **Choctaw Nation**   **Choctaw Roll** (Not Including Freedmen)   CARD NO.
POST OFFICE: McAlester   FIELD NO. 4621

Dawes' Roll No.	NAME	Relationship to Person	AGE	SEX	BLOOD	TRIBAL ENROLLMENT		
						Year	County	No.
12778	1 Stanton Arthur 21	First Named	18	m	1/16	1896	Tobucksy	11271
12779	2 Bullard Susan F 19	Sister	16	f	1/16	1896	"	11272
12780	3 Stanton Katie C 17	Sister	14	f	1/16	1896	"	11273
12781	4 Bullard, Clarence R 1	Son of No.2	2mo	m	1/32			
	5							
	6							
	7							
	8							
	9							
	10							
	11							
	12							
	13							
	14	ENROLLMENT						
	15	OF NOS. 1 2 3 - 4 HEREON APPROVED BY THE SECRETARY						
	16	OF INTERIOR MAR 6 1903						
	17							

TRIBAL ENROLLMENT OF PARENTS

	Name of Father	Year	County	Name of Mother	Year	County
1	Wm Stanton	Dead	Tobucksy	Martha A Edwards		IW
2	" "	"	"	Do Do		
3	" "	"	"	Do Do		
4	Frank Bullard		Non Citizen	No2		
5						
6						
7						
8						
9	No1 On 1896 roll Arthur Stenton					
10	No2 " " " Susan " now wife of Frank Bullard: Evidence of marriage requested June 26 '02					
11	No3 " " " Katie " " " " filed July 14th '02					
12	No4 Born April 26th 1902: Enrolled June 24th 1902					
13	For children of No2 see NB (March 3, 1905) #1139					
14						
15					#1 to 3 inc	
16				Date of Application for Enrollment.	9-7-1899	
17						

Choctaw By Blood Enrollment Cards 1898-1914

See Choctaw Card No. 4729

RESIDENCE: Tobucksy   COUNTY. **Choctaw Nation**   **Choctaw Roll**   CARD NO.

POST OFFICE: McAlester   (Not Including Freedmen)   FIELD NO. **4622**

Dawes' Roll No.	NAME	Relationship to Person First Named	AGE	SEX	BLOOD	TRIBAL ENROLLMENT		
						Year	County	No.
15978	1 Coleman, Richard B ⁵⁶	First Named	53	M	1/4	1896	Tobucksy	2305
I.W. 1586	2 " Eva ⁵⁶	Wife	53	F	I.W.	1896	"	14391
15979	3 Walker, Ida C ²⁶	D	23	F	1/8	1896	"	2306
15980	4 Coleman, Bennetta ²³	D	20	F	1/8	1896	"	2307
15981	5 Cooper, Bettie A ²¹	D	18	F	1/8	1896	"	2308
15982	6 Coleman, Henry A ¹⁹	S	16	M	1/8	1896	"	2309
15983	7 " Willie N ¹⁶	D	13	F	1896	ENROLLMENT		2310
15984	8 Cooper, Richard W ¹	GrandSon	1wk	M	1/16	OF NOS. ~~~ 2 ~~~ HEREON		
15985	9 Walker, Coleman Carlota ¹	Gr Dau	1mo	F	1/16	APPROVED BY THE SECRETARY OF INTERIOR Nov. 26, 1906		

Enrollment of No. 2 Cancelled by order of Department Mch 4, 1907. Enrollment of Nos 1 and 8 to 9 inclusive cancelled by order of Department of February 23, 1907

Enrollment of Nos 1,3,4,5,6,7,8 only granted by decision of Commission of Aug 8, 1904 (Chairman Bixby dissenting.)

Copy of decision forwarded attorney for applicants and attorneys for Choctaw & Chickasaw Nations, Aug 8, 1904   Children of No5 on NB Cards (Apr 26-06) #400 & 284

Aug 25,1904 Record forwarded Department

Oct 13,1904 Case referred to Attorney General   Child of No7 on NB (Apr 26-06) #401

Oct 24,1904: Attorney General desires brief   Child of No3 on NB (Apr 26 '06) #402

17 No8 born Nov 13, 1901: Enrolled Nov. 22d, 1901

TRIBAL ENROLLMENT OF PARENTS

Name of Father	Year	County	Name of Mother	Year	County
1 F. S. Coleman	Ded		Ann E Coleman		Non Citizen
2 Geo W. Withers		Non Citizen	Susan G Withers		Non Citizen
3 No1			No2		
4 No1			No2	Nos 1 to 9 inclusive restored to	
5 No1		ENROLLMENT OF NOS. 1,3,4,5,6,7,8 and 9 HEREON	No2	roll by Departmental authority	
6 No1		APPROVED BY THE SECRETARY	No2	of February 20, 1909 (File 5-51)	
7 No1		OF INTERIOR Jan 16, 1906	No2	No.2 GRANTED	
8 Ole C Cooper		Non Citizen	No5	Aug 24, 1906	
9 F. C. Walker		Non Citizen	No3		
10	No5 on 1896 roll Betta Coleman		No3 is now the wife of F. C. Walker - on-citizen		
11	No6 " " " Henry "		Evidence of marriage filed Oct 31, 1902		
12	No7 " " " Willie "		No9 Born Sept 22,1902 enrolled Oct 31, 1902		
13	No5 is now the wife of Ole C Cooper, a non-citizen, Nov 22d,1901				
14	All admitted by Act of Choctaw Council Approved Nov 8-1899				
15	March 15,1906 Department directs enrollment of Nos 1,3,4,5,6,7,8 and 9 as citizens by blood				
16	No2 denied by Dawes Commission in 1896 Choctaw Case #971: No appeal				
17	Nov 14 1904: Brief of applicants & attorneys for Choctaw and Chickasaw forwarded Dept.			Sept 7th 1899	Date of Application for Enrollment

Mar 27,1905: Decision of Commission of Aug 8,1904 enrolling Nos 1,3,4,5,6,7,8 and 9 affirmed by Secty of Interior

Choctaw By Blood Enrollment Cards 1898-1914

Dawes' Roll No.	NAME	Relationship to Person	AGE	SEX	BLOOD	TRIBAL ENROLLMENT		
						Year	County	No.
DEAD	1 Moore Charles F	First Named	33	M	1/2	1896	Tobucksy	8550
IW846	2 " Nannie 36	wife	33	f	IW	1896	"	14813
12782	3 " Henry 13	son	10	M	1/4	1896	"	8551
12783	4 " Virgil 11	son	8	M	1/4	1896	"	8552
12784	5 " Mattie 6	D	3	f	1/4	1896	"	8564
12785	6 " Susan 4	D	1½	f	1/4			
12786	7 " Ella 2	Dau	3mo	F	1/4			
	8							
	9							
	10 Decision Prepared Dec 8-03							
	11 ENROLLMENT							
	12 OF NOS. 2 HEREON APPROVED BY THE SECRETARY							
	13 OF INTERIOR May 21, 1904							
	14 ENROLLMENT							
	15 OF NOS. 3 4 5 6 7 HEREON APPROVED BY THE SECRETARY							
	16 OF INTERIOR Mar 6 1903							
	17							

TRIBAL ENROLLMENT OF PARENTS

	Name of Father	Year	County	Name of Mother	Year	County
1	Lyman Moore	Dead	Scullyville[sic]	Jenny Moore	Dead	Scullyville[sic]
2	Jas Bethel		Non Citizen	Jane Bethel		Non Citizen
3	No1			No2		
4	No1			No2		
5	No1			No2		
6	No1			No2		
7	No1			No2		
8						
9						
10						
11	No1 on roll 1896. Chas F Moore					
12	Certificate of marriage exhibited of				#1 to 6	
13	Frank Moore & Miss Nannie Bethel June 13 1886 in due form & satisfactory but not				Date of Application for Enrollment.	
14	in condition to file					
15	No1 died December 26th 1899. Proof filed Oct 26 1900				Sept 7 1899	
16	No7 Enrolled Oct 26th 1900 No. 1 Hereon Dismissed under order					
17	of the Commission to the Five Civilized Tribes of March 31, 1905					

Choctaw By Blood Enrollment Cards 1898-1914

RESIDENCE: Sans Bois   COUNTY. **Choctaw Nation**   **Choctaw Roll**   CARD NO.
POST OFFICE: Bower   *(Not Including Freedmen)*   FIELD NO. **4624**

Dawes' Roll No.	NAME	Relationship to Person First Named	AGE	SEX	BLOOD	TRIBAL ENROLLMENT		
						Year	County	No.
IW765	1 Beck, Joseph G ㊷	First Named	38	M	IW	1896	Sans Bois	14280
12787	2 " Frances ³²	Wife	29	f	1/2	1896	" "	670
12788	3 " John ¹⁵	Son	12	M	1/4	1896	" "	671
12789	4 " Oliver ¹³	"	10	M	1/4	1896	" "	672
12790	5 " Samuel ¹¹	"	8	M	1/4	1896	" "	673
12791	6 " Tandy ⁹	"	6	M	1/4	1896	" "	674
12792	7 " Gilbert ⁷	"	4	M	1/4	1896	" "	675
12793	8 " Wallace ⁶	"	2	M	1/4	~~1896~~	" "	
	9							
	10	ENROLLMENT						
	11	OF NOS. ~ 1 ~ HEREON APPROVED BY THE SECRETARY						
	12	OF INTERIOR May 7 - 1904						
	13							
	14	ENROLLMENT						
	15	OF NOS. 2,3,4,5,6,7-8 HEREON APPROVED BY THE SECRETARY						
	16	OF INTERIOR Mar 6 1903						
	17							

TRIBAL ENROLLMENT OF PARENTS

	Name of Father	Year	County	Name of Mother	Year	County
1	Thos Beck		Non Citizen	Eliza Beck		Non Citizen
2	Stephen Woods	ded	Wade	Eliza Woods	Choctaw	Wade
3	No1			No2		
4	No1			No2		
5	No1			No2		
6	No1			No2		
7	No1			No2		
8	No1			No2		
9						
10	No1 on roll 1896 Joe G. Beck					
11	No5 on roll 1896 Sam Beck					
12	No1 See Decision of March 2 '04					
13	As to marriage see testimony of No1 & that of G. W. Dukes					Date of Application for Enrollment.
14						
15	For children of Nos 1 and 2 see NB (March 3 '05) #369					Date of application for enrollment 9-7-99
16						
17						

Choctaw By Blood Enrollment Cards 1898-1914

RESIDENCE:	Atoka	COUNTY.					
POST OFFICE:	Kiowa						

Choctaw Nation

Choctaw Roll (Not Including Freedmen)

CARD NO.

FIELD NO. 4625

Dawes' Roll No.	NAME		Relationship to Person	AGE	SEX	BLOOD	TRIBAL ENROLLMENT		
							Year	County	No.
12794	1 Reynolds Ada	29	First Named	26	f	1/8	1896	Atoka	10993
12795	2 " Ruford I	8	Son	5	m	1/16	1896	"	10994
I.W. 682	3 " Hiram C	44	Hus	44	m	I.W.			
	4								
	5								
	6								
	7								
	8								
	9								
	10	ENROLLMENT							
	11	OF NOS. 3 HEREON APPROVED BY THE SECRETARY							
	12	OF INTERIOR MAR 26 1904							
	13								
	14	ENROLLMENT							
	15	OF NOS. 1 - 2 HEREON APPROVED BY THE SECRETARY OF INTERIOR MAR 6 1903							
	16								
	17								

TRIBAL ENROLLMENT OF PARENTS

	Name of Father	Year	County	Name of Mother	Year	County
1	Cooper		Non Citizen	Emma Cooper	Choctaw	Atoka
2	Hiram C Reynolds		Atoka	No1		Atoka
3	B.C. Reynolds		noncitizen	Sarah Reynolds		noncitizen
4						
5						
6						
7						
8	No2 on roll 1896 Ruford Reynolds					
9						
10	No.1 is the wife of Hiram C Reynolds on Choctaw card #D.456					
11	No3 transferred from Choctaw card D 456 January 25, 1904					
12	See decision of January 7, 1904					
13						
14						
15					Date of Application for Enrollment	9 - 6 -99
16						
17						

Choctaw By Blood Enrollment Cards 1898-1914

RESIDENCE: Tobucksy   COUNTY. Choctaw **Nation**   **Choctaw Roll** CARD No.
POST OFFICE: Alderson   (Not Including Freedmen) FIELD No. 4626

Dawes' Roll No.	NAME	Relationship to Person Named	AGE	SEX	BLOOD	TRIBAL ENROLLMENT Year	County	No.
12796	1 Prepgrass Agnes 43	First Named	40	f	1/2	1893	Tobucksy	479
I.W. 683	2 " John H 43	Hus	43	m	I.W.			
	3							
	4							
	5							
	6							
	7							
	8							
	9							
	10	ENROLLMENT						
	11	OF NOS. 2 HEREON APPROVED BY THE SECRETARY						
	12	OF INTERIOR MAR 26 1904						
	13	ENROLLMENT						
	14	OF NOS. 1 HEREON APPROVED BY THE SECRETARY						
	15	OF INTERIOR MAR 6 1903						
	16							
	17							

TRIBAL ENROLLMENT OF PARENTS

	Name of Father	Year	County	Name of Mother	Year	County
1	Dave Colbert	dead	Scullyville[sic]	Amey Colbert	dead	Choctaw
2	Rudolph Prepgrass	Dead	Noncitizen	Marie Prepgrass	Dead	Noncitizen
3						
4						
5						
6	On page 54 #479- 93 Payroll of					
7	Tobucksy Co as Agnes Krogsdale.					
8						
9	No.1 is now the wife of John H Prepgrass on Choctaw card #D.668					
10	No.2 transferred from Choctaw card D668 January 25, 1904 See decision of January 7, 1904					
11						
12						
13				Date of Application for Enrollment.		
14						
15				9- 7 - 99		
16						
17	No1 Dow IT 11/1/04					

Choctaw By Blood Enrollment Cards 1898-1914

RESIDENCE: Tobucksy   COUNTY. **Choctaw Nation**   **Choctaw Roll** CARD No.
POST OFFICE: Krebs   *(Not Including Freedmen)* FIELD No. **4627**

Dawes' Roll No.	NAME	Relationship to Person	AGE	SEX	BLOOD	TRIBAL ENROLLMENT		
						Year	County	No.
15926	1 Foreman William 11	First Named	8	M	1/8	1893	Sans Bois, p 28	285
	2							
	3							
	4							
	5							
	6							
	7							
	8							
	9							
	10							
	11							
	12							
	13							
	14							
	15							
	16							
	17							

ENROLLMENT
OF NOS. One HEREON
APPROVED BY THE SECRETARY
OF INTERIOR AUG 23 1905

TRIBAL ENROLLMENT OF PARENTS

Name of Father	Year	County	Name of Mother	Year	County
1 Saml Foreman	Cherokee	Tobucksy	Sillian Victoria	Choctaw	Dead
2					
3					
4	On payroll 1893 San[sic] Bois Co p 28 No 285 as Wm Foreman				
5					
6					
7	This child also on Cherokee roll with its father Saml Foreman				
8	On Cherokee D-2571 "listed from information."				
9					
10					
11					
12 Canadian- Nos 655 (son) Father - Samuel Foreman (Cherokee Roll - 1896)					
13				Date of Application for Enrollment.	
14				9- 7- 99	
15					
16					
17 P.O. Texanna I.T. 4/13/05					

Choctaw By Blood Enrollment Cards 1898-1914

RESIDENCE: Atoka   COUNTY. **Choctaw Nation**   **Choctaw Roll**   CARD NO.
POST OFFICE: Stonewall   *(Not Including Freedmen)*   FIELD NO. 4628

Dawes' Roll No.	NAME	Relationship to Person First Named	AGE	SEX	BLOOD	TRIBAL ENROLLMENT		
						Year	County	No.
DP	1 Riddle George A	Named	20	M	IW			
	2							
	3							
	4							
	5	DISMISSED						
	6							
	7	JAN 23 1905						
	8							
	9							
	10	No						
	11							
	12							
	13							
	14							
	15							
	16							
	17							

TRIBAL ENROLLMENT OF PARENTS

Name of Father	Year	County	Name of Mother	Year	County
1 Joseph Riddle		Non Citizen	Matilda C Riddle		Non Citizen
2					
3					
4					
5					
6					
7 Wife denied by Commission in Choctaw 1896 case No 8					
8 Wife Rosa Belle Bottom admitted by					
9 U S Court at Ardmore Dec 22-1896 on Choctaw card #5022. Denied by C.C.C.C. in 75T See her enrollment & place her on card with Husband.					
10					
11					
12					
13					
14					
15					
16					
17					

128

Choctaw By Blood Enrollment Cards 1898-1914

RESIDENCE: Sans Bois   COUNTY. **Choctaw Nation**   **Choctaw Roll**   CARD NO.
POST OFFICE: Enterprise   *(Not Including Freedmen)*   FIELD NO. 4629

Dawes' Roll No.	NAME	Relationship to Person First Named	AGE	SEX	BLOOD	TRIBAL ENROLLMENT		
						Year	County	No.
1	Southard Ida M	Named	16	f	1/4			
2	" Engle	Son	4mo	m	1/8			
3								
4								
5								
6								
7								
8								
9								
10								
11								
12								
13								
14								
15								
16								

DISMISSED
SEP 23 1904
Record forwarded Secty of Interior
Oct. 9th 1904

CANCELLED

[illegible] transferred to Choctaw card #5917

APR 17 1905

TRIBAL ENROLLMENT OF PARENTS

	Name of Father	Year	County	Name of Mother	Year	County
1	Henry Cummings		San[sic] Bois	Donia Cummings	Dead	San[sic] Bois
2	[?] T. Southard		non citizen	Nº1		
3						
4		On Payroll 1893 San[sic] Bois Co				
5		page 94 No 937 as Ida May Cummings				
6						
7		No1 admitted as a citizen by blood by U.S. Court				
8		District, I.T. at South McAlester, I.T. Aug 25th 1897: Court				
9		Case #176				
10		No.1 admitted as Ida M Cummins				
11		No 1 is the daughter of Henry A Cummings on Choctaw card #2622				
12		Nº2 Born May 31, 1901. Enrolled Oct. 15, 1902				
13		No1 admitted in 96 Case #963				
14		No1 No appeal to C.C.C.C.				
15					Date of Application for Enrollment.	
16					9-6-99	
17	Besbee Anzina[sic] 8/20/02					

Choctaw By Blood Enrollment Cards 1898-1914

RESIDENCE: Tobucksy COUNTY. **Choctaw Nation** **Choctaw** Roll CARD NO.
POST OFFICE: McAlester *(Not Including Freedmen)* FIELD NO. 4630

Dawes' Roll No.	NAME	Relationship to Person Named	AGE	SEX	BLOOD	TRIBAL ENROLLMENT		
						Year	County	No.
12797	1 Arndt Mary E 32	First Named	29	f	1/8	1896	Tobucksy	114
12798	2 " Samuel F 16	d	13	f	1/16	1896	"	115
12799	3 " Myrtle M 12	d	9	f	1/16	1896	"	116
12800	4 " Fannie J 10	d	7	f	1/16	1896	"	117
12801	5 " William F 8	son	5	m	1/16	1896	"	118
12802	6 " Fred C 6	son	3	m	1/16	1896	"	119
12803	7 " Aran L 4	d	1½	f	1/16			
	8							
	9							
	10							
	11							
	12	ENROLLMENT						
	13	OF NOS. 1,2,3,4,5,6,7 HEREON APPROVED BY THE SECRETARY						
	14	OF INTERIOR MAR 6 1903						
	15							
	16							
	17							

TRIBAL ENROLLMENT OF PARENTS

	Name of Father	Year	County	Name of Mother	Year	County
1	B F Jones	dead	Tobucksy	Jennie C Jones	Ded	Tobucksy
2	Wm Arndt		Non Citizen	No 1		
3	Do Do		Do Do	No1		
4	Do Do		Do Do	No1		
5	Do Do		Do Do	No1		
6	Do Do		Do Do	No1		
7	Do Do		Do Do	No1		
8						
9				Jennie C. Jones a Cherokee		
10	No2 on 1896 roll Sam F Arndt					
11	No5 " " Wm F "					
12						
13	As to parents[sic] marriage see testimony of Tandy Walker					
14					Date of Application for Enrollment.	
15	For child of No1 see NB (Apr 26-06) Card #704				9 - 7 - 99	
16	" " " " " " (Mar 3 '05) " #370					
17						

130

Choctaw By Blood Enrollment Cards 1898-1914

RESIDENCE: San[sic] Bois COUNTY. **Choctaw Nation** **Choctaw Roll** *(Not Including Freedmen)* CARD NO.

POST OFFICE: San Bois, I.T. FIELD NO. 4631

Dawes' Roll No.	NAME		Relationship to Person	AGE	SEX	BLOOD	TRIBAL ENROLLMENT		
							Year	County	No.
I.W. 465	1 Neill, Samuel E	29	First Named	26	M	I.W.			
12804	2 " Dolly	22	Wife	19	F	1/16	1893	Towson	18
12805	3 Bond, Beulah	4	St. Dau	8ᵐ	F	1/32			
12806	4 Neill Ola	2	Dau	3w	F	1/32			
12807	5 " Ottice Emmett	1	Son	1mo	M	1/32			
	6								
	7								
	8								
	9								
	10								
	11	ENROLLMENT OF NOS. 1 HEREON APPROVED BY THE SECRETARY OF INTERIOR SEP 12 1903							
	12								
	13								
	14	ENROLLMENT OF NOS. 2 3 4 - 5 HEREON APPROVED BY THE SECRETARY OF INTERIOR MAR 6 1903							
	15								
	16								
	17								

TRIBAL ENROLLMENT OF PARENTS

	Name of Father	Year	County	Name of Mother	Year	County
1	Geo. W. Neill	Dd	Non Cit	Mary Neill	Dd	Non Cit
2	Seaton	"	San[sic] Bois	Seaton	"	Tobucksy
3	Wallace Bond	"	" "	No.2		
4	No.1			No.2		
5	No.1			No.2		
6						
7						
8			No.2 on P. 54 #16-93-P.R. Towson Co as Dolly Seaton			
9	No.2 also on 1896 census roll, Choctaw Nation,					
10	as Frankie Mae Bond; page 16; #581					
11	No.4 Enrolled Dec. 8th 1900					
12	No.5 born Nov. 30, 1901; Enrolled Dec. 27, 1901					
13	Evidence of birth of No.3 received and filed March 17, 1902					
	For child of Nos 1&2 see NB (Apr 26-06) Card #395					
14						
15						
16					#1 to 3 inc	
17				Date of Application for Enrollment.		9/7/00

131

RESIDENCE:			COUNTY.							CARD NO.	
POST OFFICE:	Mc Alester, I.T.		**Choctaw Nation**				**Choctaw Roll** *(Not Including Freedmen)*			FIELD NO. **4632**	

Dawes' Roll No.	NAME		Relationship to Person	AGE	SEX	BLOOD	TRIBAL ENROLLMENT		
							Year	County	No.
IW1347	1 Reed, James H	65	First Named	63	M	I.W.			
12808	2 " Maggie	39	Wife	36	F	full	1896	Tobucksy	10756
	3								
	4								
	5								
	6								
	7								
	8								
	9								
	10	ENROLLMENT							
	11	OF NOS. 1 HEREON APPROVED BY THE SECRETARY							
	12	OF INTERIOR Mar 14 1905							
	13	ENROLLMENT							
	14	OF NOS. 2 HEREON							
	15	APPROVED BY THE SECRETARY OF INTERIOR Mar 6 1903							
	16								
	17								

TRIBAL ENROLLMENT OF PARENTS

	Name of Father	Year	County	Name of Mother	Year	County
1	Jesse W Reed	Dd	Non Cit	Sarah Reed	Dd	Non Cit
2	Saml. Folsom	"	Blue	Tennessee Folsom	"	Blue
3						
4						
5						
6						
7						
8						
9						
10						
11						
12				No1 Admitted by Dawes Comm #692		
13				Appeal dismissed.		
14						
15						
16					Date of Application for Enrollment.	
17					9/7/99	

Choctaw By Blood Enrollment Cards 1898-1914

Dawes' Roll No.	NAME	Relationship to Person	AGE	SEX	BLOOD	TRIBAL ENROLLMENT		
						Year	County	No.
I.W. 466 ₁	Hailey, Daniel M ⁶²	First Named	59	M	I.W.	1896	Tobucksy	14610
12809 ₂	" Helen M ⁵²	Wife	49	F	1/16	"	"	5338
12810 ₃	" Edward S ³²	Son	29	M	1/32	"	"	5339
12811 ₄	" Walter P ²⁶	"	23	"	1/32	"	"	5341
12812 ₅	" Hattie ²³	Dau	20	F	1/32	"	"	5342
I.W. 766 ₆	" Grace C ㉖	Wife of N°4	26	F	I.W.			
I.W. 1138 ₇	" Minnie L ²⁰	Wife of No.3	20	F	I.W.			
₈								
₉								
₁₀								

₁₁
    ENROLLMENT
    OF NOS. I   HEREON
₁₂ APPROVED BY THE SECRETARY
    OF INTERIOR   SEP 12 1903
₁₃

₁₄ ENROLLMENT
OF NOS. 2-3-4-5   HEREON
APPROVED BY THE SECRETARY
OF INTERIOR   MAR 6 1903
₁₇

ENROLLMENT
OF NOS. ~~~~6~~~~ HEREON
APPROVED BY THE SECRETARY
OF INTERIOR   MAY -7 1904

ENROLLMENT
OF NOS. ~~~~7~~~~ HEREON
APPROVED BY THE SECRETARY
OF INTERIOR   NOV 16 1904

TRIBAL ENROLLMENT OF PARENTS

	Name of Father	Year	County	Name of Mother	Year	County
₁		Dd	Non Cit			Non Cit
₂	R.S. McCarty	"	" "	Mary A McCarty		Skullyville
₃	No.1			No.2		
₄	" 1			" 2		
₅	" 1			" 2		
₆	O.D. Moulton		non-citizen			non-citizen
₇	Jas S Mundy		" "	Rose Mundy		" "
₈						
₉						

₁₀   No3 is the husband of Minnie L Hailey on Choctaw Card #D644 Aug 8,1901
₁₁   For child of Nos 1&6 see NB (Mar 3'05) card #371   No1 on roll as Dan M Hailey
                                        " 4 " " " Walter "
₁₂   N°6 transferred from Choctaw card #D514 See decision of Feby 29, 1904
₁₃   No.7 transferred from Choctaw card #D-644, Oct 31, 1904: See decision of Oct 15, 1904
₁₄
₁₅
₁₆   Date of Application for Enrollment.
₁₇   No4 Haileyville IT   9/7/99
            6/20/05

133

Choctaw By Blood Enrollment Cards 1898-1914

RESIDENCE: COUNTY.   **Choctaw Nation**   **Choctaw Roll**   CARD NO.
POST OFFICE: So McAlester, I.T.   *(Not Including Freedmen)*   FIELD NO. **4634**

Dawes' Roll No.	NAME	Relationship to Person	AGE	SEX	BLOOD	TRIBAL ENROLLMENT		
						Year	County	No.
12813	1 Hailey, William E ³¹	First Named	28	M	1/32	1896	Tobucksy	5340
12814	2 Thomas, Edward G ¹⁴	Ward	11	M	1/8	"	"	12038
12815	3 " Jennie I ¹⁷	"	14	F	1/8	"	"	12037
IW767	4 Hailey, Stella Doyle ㉑	Wife of No 1	20	F	IW			
	5							
	6							
	7							
	8							
	9							
	10							
	11							
	12							
	13							
	14							
	15							
	16							
	17							

> ENROLLMENT
> OF NOS. ~~~ 4 ~~~ HEREON
> APPROVED BY THE SECRETARY
> OF INTERIOR May 7 1904

> ENROLLMENT
> OF NOS. 1, 2, 3 HEREON
> APPROVED BY THE SECRETARY
> OF INTERIOR Mar. 6 1903

TRIBAL ENROLLMENT OF PARENTS

	Name of Father	Year	County	Name of Mother	Year	County
1	D. M. Hailey		Tobucksy	H. M. Hailey		Tobucksy
2	Ed. L. Thomas		Non Cit	Minnie I Thomas	Dd	"
3	" " "		" "	" " "	"	"
4	Edmund H Doyle		Non Citizen	Sue J Doyle		Non-citizen
5						
6						
7	No1 is now the husband of Stella Doyle Hailey on Choctaw card #D.737					
8						June 27, 1902
9	No.4 transferred from Choctaw card #D737; see decision of Feby. 27, 1904					
10						
11	No.1 on roll as Wᵐ E Hailey					
12	For child of Nos 1 and 4 see NB (Mar 3 '05) #372					
13						
14						
15						#1 to 3
16					Date of Application for Enrollment.	9/7/99
17						

134

Choctaw By Blood Enrollment Cards 1898-1914

| RESIDENCE: | | COUNTY. | **Choctaw Nation** | | | | **Choctaw Roll** | | CARD NO. | |
| POST OFFICE: | So McAlester, I.T. | | | | | | *(Not Including Freedmen)* | | FIELD NO. | 4635 |

Dawes' Roll No.	NAME	Relationship to Person First Named	AGE	SEX	BLOOD	TRIBAL ENROLLMENT		
						Year	County	No.
*	1 Mitchell, Samuel	First Named	29	M	1/16			
	2 " Haden Loyd	Son	1	"	1/32			
	3							
	4							
	5							
No2	6 DISMISSED MAY 27 1904							
	7							
	8							
	9							
	10							
	11							
	12							
	13							
	14							
	15							
	16							
	17							

TRIBAL ENROLLMENT OF PARENTS

	Name of Father	Year	County	Name of Mother	Year	County
1	W. C. Mitchell		Tobucksy	M.A. Mitchell		Tobucksy
2	No.1			Belle Mitchell		"
3	DENIED CITIZENSHIP BY THE CHOCTAW AND					
4	CHICKASAW CITIZENSHIP COURT					
5						Mar 28 '04
6	No1 denied in 96 Case #1284					
7			No1 Admitted by U.S. Court at So McA. Sept 9,97			
8			Case No. 104 = As to residence and birth of child see his testimony also as to remarriage of wife			
9			on Card D-450 -			
10	Judgment of U.S. Ct admitting No1 vacated and set aside by Decree of C.C.C.C. Decr 17 '02					
11	No1 now in C.C.C.C. case #37					
12	No1 Denied by C.C.C.C. March 28th '04					
13						
14						
15						
16						Date of Application for Enrollment.
17						9/7/99

135

Choctaw By Blood Enrollment Cards 1898-1914

POST OFFICE: McAlester, I.T. COUNTY. **Choctaw Nation** **Choctaw Roll** *(Not Including Freedmen)* CARD NO. FIELD NO. 4636

Dawes' Roll No.	NAME	Relationship to Person First Named	AGE	SEX	BLOOD	TRIBAL ENROLLMENT		
						Year	County	No.
12816	1 Fairlie, Elizabeth 24		21	F	1/4	1896	Tobucksy	4051
12817	2 " Minta M 4	Dau	6^m	F	1/8			
12818	3 " Mamie 2	Dau	5mo	F	1/8			
	4							
	5							
	6							
	7							
	8							
	9							
	10							
	11							
	12							
	13	ENROLLMENT OF NOS. 1 - 2 - 3 HEREON						
	14	APPROVED BY THE SECRETARY						
	15	OF INTERIOR MAR 6 1903						
	16							
	17							

TRIBAL ENROLLMENT OF PARENTS

	Name of Father	Year	County	Name of Mother	Year	County
1	J. Whelchel		Non Cit	Mary Whelchel	Dd	Tobucksy
2	G. W. Fairlie		" "	No.1		
3	" " "		" "	No.1		
4						
5						
6						
7						
8						
9						
10	For child of No.1 see NB (Mar 3 '05) Card #373					
11				No.1 on roll as Elizabeth Fairly.		
12	~~Evidence of birth of No.2 received and filed April 2, 1902.~~					
13	N^o3 Born Oct. 30, 1901; enrolled April 2, 1902					
14						
15					#1 to 2	
16					Date of Application for Enrollment.	
17					9/7/99	

Choctaw By Blood Enrollment Cards 1898-1914

RESIDENCE:		COUNTY.			CARD No.
POST OFFICE: Scipio, I.T.		**Choctaw Nation**	**Choctaw Roll** *(Not Including Freedmen)*		FIELD No. 4637

Dawes' Roll No.	NAME		Relationship to Person	AGE	SEX	BLOOD	TRIBAL ENROLLMENT		
							Year	County	No.
12819	1 Silmon, Lee	35	First Named	32	M	Full	1896	Tobucksy	11274
12820	2 " Millie	27	Wife	24	F	"	"	"	11305
12821	3 " Ike	5	Son	2	M	"			
12822	4 " Jefferson	2	Son	11mo	M	"			
	5								
	6								
	7								
	8								
	9								
	10								
	11								
	12								
	13	ENROLLMENT OF NOS. 1 2 3 - 4 HEREON APPROVED BY THE SECRETARY OF INTERIOR MAR 6 1903							
	14								
	15								
	16								
	17								

TRIBAL ENROLLMENT OF PARENTS

	Name of Father	Year	County	Name of Mother	Year	County
1	Silmon	Dd	Miss	Maria Lewis	Dd	Miss
2	Wallace Sam	"	Tobucksy	Fannie Sam		Tobucksy
3	No.1			No.2		
4	No.1			No.2		
5						
6	For children of Nos 1 and 2 see NB (Mar 3 '05) #374					
7						
8						
9				No.1 Admitted by Council Act #39, approved Nov. 4-92		
10				" 2 On roll a Millie Sam		
11				No.2 Admitted by Council Act #15, approved Apl. 8-91 as Millie Sam		
12				No.4 Enrolled April 18, 1901.		
13						
14						
15						#1 to 3
16						Date of Application for Enrollment.
17	Carbon I.T. 12/24/02					9/7/99

Choctaw By Blood Enrollment Cards 1898-1914

Dawes' Roll No.	NAME			Relationship to Person	AGE	SEX	BLOOD	TRIBAL ENROLLMENT		
								Year	County	No.
12823	1 Davis, William H		29	First Named	26	M	1/8	1896	Tobucksy	3315
12824	2 " Eugene		5	Son	2	"	1/16			
	3									
	4									
	5									
	6									
	7									
	8									
	9									
	10									
	11									
	12									
	13									
	14									
	15									
	16									
	17									

ENROLLMENT
OF NOS. 1 - 2 HEREON
APPROVED BY THE SECRETARY
OF INTERIOR MAR 6 1903

TRIBAL ENROLLMENT OF PARENTS

	Name of Father	Year	County	Name of Mother	Year	County
1	J. S. Davis		Tobucksy	Annie Davis		Tobucksy
2	No.1			Emma Davis		Non cit.
3						
4						
5						
6						
7						
8						
9						
10			No.1 on as William Davis			
11			Evidence of marriage to be supplied.			
12		Sept 1/99	" " " filed			
13						
14						
15					Date of Application for Enrollment.	
16						
17					9/7/99	

138

Choctaw By Blood Enrollment Cards 1898-1914

RESIDENCE:		COUNTY.								
POST OFFICE: McAlester, I.T.		**Choctaw Nation**				Choctaw Roll *(Not Including Freedmen)*		CARD NO. FIELD NO. 4639		

Dawes' Roll No.	NAME		Relationship to Person	AGE	SEX	BLOOD	TRIBAL ENROLLMENT		
							Year	County	No.
I.W. 467	1 Barnett, Joseph A	56	First Named	54	M	I.W.	1896	Tobucksy	14301
12825	2 " Amelia	51	Wife	48	F	1/4	"	"	894
	3								
	4								
	5								
	6								
	7								
	8								
	9								
	10								
	11	ENROLLMENT							
	12	OF NOS. 1 HEREON APPROVED BY THE SECRETARY							
	13	OF INTERIOR SEP 12 1903							
	14	ENROLLMENT							
	15	OF NOS. 2 HEREON APPROVED BY THE SECRETARY							
	16	OF INTERIOR MAR 6 1903							
	17								

TRIBAL ENROLLMENT OF PARENTS

	Name of Father	Year	County	Name of Mother	Year	County
1	Josiah Barnett	Dd	Non Cit.	Fannie Barnett	Dd	Non Cit
2	Wm Holloway	"	Skullyville	Rebecca Holsten	"	Sugar Loaf
3						
4						
5						
6	No.1 admitted by Dawes Commission in 1896 as an					
7	intermarried citizen: case #904: no appeal					
8						
9						
10						
11			No.1 on roll as Josiah A Barnett			
12			~~As to name and name in license see his testimony~~ No.2 on roll as Amelia Bennett.			
13						
14						
15						
16					Date of Application for Enrollment.	
17						9/7/99

Choctaw By Blood Enrollment Cards 1898-1914

RESIDENCE:
POST OFFICE: McAlester, I.T.   COUNTY. **Choctaw Nation**   Choctaw Roll (Not including Freedmen)   FIELD NO. 4640

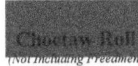

Dawes' Roll No.		NAME		Relationship to Person First Named	AGE	SEX	BLOOD	TRIBAL ENROLLMENT		
								Year	County	No.
I.W.468	1	Wood, Thomas L	50	First Named	47	M	I.W.	1896	Tobucksy	15158
12826	2	" Priscilla C	56	Wife	53	F	1/8	1896	Tobucksy	12994
12827	3	Kellogg, Carlton B	23	St. Son	20	M	1/16	"	"	7509
	4									
	5									
	6									
	7									
	8									
	9									
	10									

ENROLLMENT
OF NOS.   1   HEREON
APPROVED BY THE SECRETARY
OF INTERIOR   SEP 12 1903

ENROLLMENT
OF NOS.   2 - 3   HEREON
APPROVED BY THE SECRETARY
OF INTERIOR   MAR 6 1903

TRIBAL ENROLLMENT OF PARENTS

	Name of Father	Year	County	Name of Mother	Year	County
1	Jno. T. Wood		Non Cit	Fatina Wood		Non cit
2	L.G. Harris	Dd	Eagle	Elizab. Pitchlynn	Dd	Eagle
3	Amasa Kellogg	"	Tobucksy	No.2		
4						
5						
6						
7						
8	For child of No3 see NB (Apr 26-06) Card #639					
9						
10		No.1 Admitted by Dawes Comm #499 as T. L. Wood No appeal				
11		" 2 on roll as Pricilla C Woods				
12		" 3 on roll as Carlton Kellogg				
13		" 1 on 1896 roll as Thomas L Wood.				
14						
15					Date of Application for Enrollment.	
16						
17	No2 PO Elna I.T. 11/1/04					9/7/99

Stringtown 12/23/02

140

Choctaw By Blood Enrollment Cards 1898-1914

| RESIDENCE: POST OFFICE: McAlester, I.T. | COUNTY. **Choctaw Nation** | | | | **Choctaw Roll** (Not Including Freedmen) | CARD NO. FIELD NO. 4641 |

Dawes' Roll No.	NAME	Relationship to Person	AGE	SEX	BLOOD	TRIBAL ENROLLMENT Year	County	No.
12828	1 Sexton, Jonas 35	First Named	32	M	3/4	1896	Tobucksy	11297
DEAD.	2 " Thompson	Son	3wks	M	3/8			
I.W. 768	3 " Jessie L 20	Wife	20	F	I.W.			
	4							
	5							
	6							
	7							
	8	No._2_ HEREON DISMISSED UNDER						
	9	ORDER OF THE COMMISSION TO THE FIVE CIVILIZED TRIBES OF MARCH 31, 1905.						
	10	ENROLLMENT						
	11	OF NOS. ~~~ 3 ~~~ HEREON						
	12	APPROVED BY THE SECRETARY OF INTERIOR MAY -7 1904						
	13							
	14	ENROLLMENT						
	15	OF NOS. 1 HEREON APPROVED BY THE SECRETARY						
	16	OF INTERIOR MAR 6 1903						
	17							

TRIBAL ENROLLMENT OF PARENTS

Name of Father	Year	County	Name of Mother	Year	County
1 Chas Sexton	Dd	Tobucksy	Holemna	Dd	Tobucksy
2 No 1			Jessee L Sexton		Non Citz
3 George Ratliff		non-citizen	Martha Ratliff	dead	non-citizen
4					
5					
6 No.1 is the husband of Jessie L Sexton on Choctaw card #D.700					
7					
8					
9					
10 No.1 is married to Jessee L Mikinley[sic] a non citz Evidence of marriage					
11 filed Jan 24, 1902					
12 No.2 born Jan 4, 1902: Enrolled Jan 24, 1902					
13 N°2 Died July 30, 1902, proof of death filed Oct 20, 1902. Additional affidavit filed Dec. 23, 1902					
14 No.3 transferred from Choctaw card #D.700: See decision of Feby. 27, 1904					
For child of Nos 1&3 see NB (Apr 26-06) Card #439					
15 " " " " " " " (Mar 3-05) " #375					
16					Date of Application for Enrollment.
17					9/7/99

141

Choctaw By Blood Enrollment Cards 1898-1914

Dawes' Roll No.	NAME	Relationship to Person First Named	AGE	SEX	BLOOD	TRIBAL ENROLLMENT Year	County	No.
DEAD.	1 Sloan, Napoleon B	Named	41	M	I.W.	1896	Tobucksy	15037
12829	2 " Lizzie 60	Wife	57	F	1/2	1896	"	3699
12830	3 " Edward P 19	Son	16	M	1/4	1896	"	3700
12831	4 Gotcher Susan E 26	St. Dau	23	F	3/4	1896	Tobucksy	10259
12832	5 Gotcher, Clarence E 2	Son of N°4	2	M	3/8			
12833	6 " Horace E 1	Son of N°4	1	M	3/8			
12834	7 " Elizabeth E 1	Dau of N°4	6wks	F	3/8			
	8							
	9							
	10							
	11							
	12							
	13							
	14							
	15							
	16							
	17							

ENROLLMENT
OF NOS. 2,3,4,5,6,7 HEREON
APPROVED BY THE SECRETARY
OF INTERIOR　MAR 6 1903

NO. 1 HEREON DISMISSED UNDER
ORDER OF THE COMMISSION TO THE FIVE
CIVILIZED TRIBES OF MARCH 31, 1905.

Card 442
364
5550

For child of No.4 see NB (Mar 3'05) card #376
For child of No4 see NB (Apr 26-06) Card #751

TRIBAL ENROLLMENT OF PARENTS

	Name of Father	Year	County	Name of Mother	Year	County
1	Warden Sloan	Dd	Non Cit	Elizab. Sloan	Dd	Non Cit
2	Nich. Hampton	"	Tobucksy	Hokti	"	Tobucksy
3	No.1			No.2		
4	Wm Pusley			" 2		
5	W.E. Gotcher		non-citizen	N°4		
6	" "		" "	N°4		
7	" "		" "	N°4		
8						
9						
10	No2 on 1896 roll as Lizzie Eslone			No1 on roll as N. B. Sloan		
11	No3 " 1896 " " Edmund "			No2 On p. 90-#770-93 F.R. Tobucksy Co		
12	No1 was admitted as an intermarried citizen by Dawes Commission Choctaw Case #833. No appeal			" 3 " " 80-#693- " " " " " as Ed. Sian[sic]		
13	N°4 is now the wife of Walter H Gotcher a noncitizen married in November 1899: See					
14	testimony of W.E. Gotcher taken Oct 7, 1902. Evidence of marriage to be supplied, filed Jan 6, 1903					
15	N°5 Born Nov 29,1900. Enrolled Oct 8, 1902					
16	N°6 Born Nov 5, 1901, enrolled Oct 8, 1902					
17	No7 Born Aug 21,1902. Enrolled Oct 8,1902					
	No.1 died Sept 18, 1902. Proof of death filed Dec. 23, 1902				Date of Application for Enrollment.	9/7/99

Choctaw By Blood Enrollment Cards 1898-1914

| RESIDENCE: POST OFFICE: So McAlester, I.T. | COUNTY. **Choctaw Nation** | | **Choctaw Roll** *(Not Including Freedmen)* | CARD NO. FIELD NO. 4643 |

Dawes' Roll No.	NAME		Relationship to Person	AGE	SEX	BLOOD	TRIBAL ENROLLMENT		
							Year	County	No.
I.W. 469	1 Redpath, William	30	First Named	27	M	I.W.	1896	Tobucksy	14967
12835	" Sula L	29	Wife	26	F	1/8	"	"	10757
12836	" Lula	7	Dau	4	F	1/16	"	"	10758
12837	" Willie	5	Son	1	M	1/16			
12838	" Roy Cecil	2	Son	8m	M	1/16			
12839	" Ruth	1	Dau	7wks	F	1/16			
7									
8									
9									
10									
11	ENROLLMENT OF NOS. 1 HEREON APPROVED BY THE SECRETARY								
12	OF INTERIOR SEP 12 1903								
13									
14	ENROLLMENT								
15	OF NOS. 2 3 4 5 - 6 HEREON APPROVED BY THE SECRETARY								
16	OF INTERIOR MAR 6 1903								
17									

TRIBAL ENROLLMENT OF PARENTS

	Name of Father	Year	County	Name of Mother	Year	County
1	Jno Redpath		Non Cit	Maggie Redpath		Non Cit
2	Mike Gleason		Tobucksy	Mary E Gleason	Dd	Tobucksy
3	No.1			No.2		
4	" 1			" 2		
5	No1			No2		
6	Nº1			Nº2		
7						
8						
9						
10	Admitted by Dawes Com #693-on 96 Roll as Wᵐ Redpath No appeal					
11	No2 on roll as Lula L Redpath					
12	" 3 " " " Lula Redpath					
13	No5 Enrolled January 10th 1901 Evidence of birth of Nº4 received and filed March 20, 1902					
14	Nº6 Born July 25, 1902; enrolled Sept 6, 1902					
15						
16					Date of Application for Enrollment.	
17					9/7/99	

143

Choctaw By Blood Enrollment Cards 1898-1914

RESIDENCE:		COUNTY.	**Choctaw Nation**		**Choctaw Roll**		CARD No.
POST OFFICE: So McAlester, IT					*(Not Including Freedmen)*		FIELD No. **4644**

Dawes' Roll No.	NAME	Relationship to Person First Named	AGE	SEX	BLOOD	TRIBAL ENROLLMENT Year	County	No.
12840 1	Wright, Allen ³⁴		31	M	1/2	1896	Gaines	12935
12841 2	" James B ²⁵	Bro	22	"	1/2	1896	Atoka	14015
I.W. 196 3	" Helen Skiles	Wife	29	F	IW			
4								
5	CITIZENSHIP CERTIFICATE ISSUED FOR NO. 2 APR 22 1903							
6								
NSHIP CERTIFICATE FOR NO 3 JUL 13 1903	CITIZENSHIP CERTIFICATE ISSUED FOR NO 1 APR 25 1903							
9								
10								
11	ENROLLMENT OF NOS. 3 HEREON APPROVED BY THE SECRETARY OF INTERIOR JUN 13 1903							
12								
13								
14								
15	ENROLLMENT OF NOS. 1 & 2 HEREON APPROVED BY THE SECRETARY OF INTERIOR MAR 6 1903							
16								
17								

TRIBAL ENROLLMENT OF PARENTS

	Name of Father	Year	County	Name of Mother	Year	County
1	Allen Wright	Dd	Atoka	Harriet N Wright	Dd	Atoka
2	" "	"	"	" " "	"	"
3	Thos D Skiles	Dead	non-citz	Kate W Skiles		non citz
4						
5						
6						
7						
8						
9	No.1 is now the husband of Helen Skiles Wright on Choctaw card #D.702					
10	As to parents[sic] marriage see enrollment of Mrs. Anna Ludlow. No2 on roll as J. B. Wright					
11	No3 transferred from Choc card #D703 See decision of April 22, 1903					
12						
13						
14						
15						
16						
17					9/7/99	

144

Choctaw By Blood Enrollment Cards 1898-1914

RESIDENCE:		COUNTY.								
POST OFFICE: McAlester, I.T.		**Choctaw Nation**				**Choctaw Roll** (Not Including Freedmen)	CARD NO. FIELD NO. 4645			

Dawes' Roll No.	NAME		Relationship to Person	AGE	SEX	BLOOD	TRIBAL ENROLLMENT		
							Year	County	No.
12842	1 York, Sampson	37	First Named	34	M	Full	1896	Tobucksy	14216
12843	2 " Sebian	32	Wife	29	F	"	"	"	14217
12844	3 " Levi	13	Son	10	M	"	"	"	14218
12845	4 " Rosa	11	Dau	8	F	"	"	"	14219
12846	5 " Minnie	5	"	2	"	"			
	6								
	7								
	8								
	9								
	10								
	11								
	12								
	13								
	14								
	15	ENROLLMENT							
	16	OF NOS. 1 2 3 4 - 5 HEREON APPROVED BY THE SECRETARY OF INTERIOR							
	17								

TRIBAL ENROLLMENT OF PARENTS

	Name of Father	Year	County	Name of Mother		County
1	Tom York	Dd	Tobucksy	Mina York		
2	Sol. Wilson	"	"	Sally Wilson		
3	No.1			No.2		
4	" 1			" 2		
5	" 1			" 2		
6						
7						
8						
9			Nos 1-2-3 and 4- admitted by Act Council #39			
10			approved Nov. 4-92			
11			No.2 on roll as Sabien York			
12			~~Evidence of birth of No.5 received and filed July 30, 1901~~			
13						
14						
15					Date of Application for Enrollment.	
16						
17	PO Krebs Okla					9/7/99

RESIDENCE:			COUNTY.							
POST OFFICE: McAlester, I.T.				**Choctaw Nation**		**Choctaw Roll** *(Not Including Freedmen)*		CARD No. FIELD No. 4646		

Dawes' Roll No.	NAME		Relationship to Person First Named	AGE	SEX	BLOOD	TRIBAL ENROLLMENT		
							Year	County	No.
12847	1 York, Mina	83		80	F	Full	1896	Tobucksy	14214
12848	2 " Lillie	13	Gr. Dau	10	"	"	"	"	14215
	3								
	4								
	5								
	6								
	7								
	8								
	9								
	10								
	11								
	12								
	13								
	14								
	15	1 - 2							
	16								
	17								

TRIBAL ENROLLMENT OF PARENTS

	Name of Father	Year	County	Name of Mother	Year	County
1		Dd			Dd	
2	Chas York	"	Gaines	Nicey York	"	Miss
3						
4						
5						
6						
7						
8						
9						
10						
11				No.1 on roll as Minnie York, and admitted by		
12				Act Council #39, approved Nov. 4-92		
13						
14						
15						
16						
17				Date of Application for Enrollment		9/7/99

146

Choctaw By Blood Enrollment Cards 1898-1914

| RESIDENCE: | Tobucksy | COUNTY. | | | | | | |
| POST OFFICE: | Stuart, I.T. | | | | | | | |

Choctaw Nation   Choctaw Roll *(Not Including Freedmen)*

CARD NO. FIELD NO. 4647

Dawes' Roll No.	NAME	Relationship to Person First Named	AGE	SEX	BLOOD	TRIBAL ENROLLMENT		
---	---	---	---	---	---	Year	County	No.
DEAD.	1 Nail, Benjamin J	~~DEAD~~	24	M	Full	1896	Tobucksy	9603
I.W. 1348	2 Messick, Mary F 23	Wife	20	F	I.W.			
12849	3 Nail, Joel W 4	Son	9ᵐ	M	1/2			
	4							
	5							
	6							
	7							
	8	No. 1 HEREON DISMISSED UNDER ORDER OF THE COMMISSION TO THE FIVE CIVILIZED TRIBES OF MARCH 31, 1905.						
	9							
	10							
	11	ENROLLMENT						
	12	OF NOS. 2 HEREON						
	13	APPROVED BY THE SECRETARY OF INTERIOR MAR 14 1905						
	14							
	15	ENROLLMENT						
	16	OF NOS. 3 HEREON APPROVED BY THE SECRETARY						
	17	OF INTERIOR MAR 6 1905						

TRIBAL ENROLLMENT OF PARENTS

	Name of Father	Year	County	Name of Mother	Year	County
1	Joel Nail	Dd	Tobucksy	Melvina Quincy		Tobucksy
2	W.F. Langley		Non Cit	L. C. Langley		Non Cit
3	No.1			No.2		
4						
5						
6						
7						
8						
9						
10						
11					No.1 on roll as Benjamin Nail.	
12					As to marriage see testimony	
13			No.1 died Jan 23d, 1900: see	of No.1 and of A. Telle.		
14			letter attached	3/9, 1900		
15			Birth affidavit of No.3 received and filed March 10th, 1900.			
16			See Choctaw #D-471		Date of Application for Enrollment.	
17	P.O. Kosoma[sic] I.T. 3/11/05					9/7/99

P.O. Atoka I.T. 11/8/04

147

Choctaw By Blood Enrollment Cards 1898-1914

RESIDENCE:	Chick Nation	COUNTY.					CARD NO.	
POST OFFICE:	Washita, I.T.	**Choctaw Nation**				Choctaw Roll (Not Including Freedmen)	FIELD NO. 4648	

Dawes' Roll No.	NAME	Relationship to Person	AGE	SEX	BLOOD	TRIBAL ENROLLMENT		
						Year	County	No.
I.W. 684 ₁	Sadler, John F ⁴²	First Named	38	M	I.W.			
12850 ₂	" Mettie[sic] ²³	Wife	20	F	1/32	1896	Chick Dist.	14158
12851 ₃	" Alex Matthew ³	Son	7mo	M	1/64			
12852 ₄	" Gracie Ellen ¹	Dau	16mo	F	1/64			
₅								
₆	DECISION PREPARED							
₇								
₈								
₉								
₁₀	ENROLLMENT							
₁₁	OF NOS. 1 HEREON APPROVED BY THE SECRETARY							
₁₂	OF INTERIOR MAR 26 1904							
₁₃								
₁₄	ENROLLMENT OF NOS. 2 3 - 4 HEREON							
₁₅	APPROVED BY THE SECRETARY OF INTERIOR							
₁₆								
₁₇								

	TRIBAL ENROLLMENT OF PARENTS					
	Name of Father	Year	County	Name of Mother	Year	County
₁	J. A. Sadler		Non Cit	Sally Sadler	Dd	Non Cit
₂	Matt Wolf		Chick Dist	Ellen Wolf		Chick. Dist
₃	No.1			No.2		
₄	Nº1			Nº2		
₅						
₆						
₇						
₈						
₉						
₁₀	No1 - As to marriage see his testimony					
₁₁	No2 on 1896 roll as Nettie Wolf					
₁₂	No.3 Enrolled July 16th 1900					
₁₃	Nº4 Born March 30 1901 enrolled July 29, 1902 Evidence of marriage between Nºˢ1 and 2 in accordance					
₁₄	with tribal laws Chickasaw Nation filed Oct. 31, 1902					
₁₅						
₁₆				Date of Application for Enrollment.		
₁₇	Dec 27. 02 P.O. Davis IT			9/7/99		

148

Choctaw By Blood Enrollment Cards 1898-1914

RESIDENCE: Scullyville[sic] COUNTY. **Choctaw Nation** **Choctaw Roll** RD NO.
POST OFFICE: Panama _(Not Including Freedmen)_ LD NO. 4649

Dawes' Roll No.	NAME	Relationship to Person First Named	AGE	SEX	BLOOD	TRIBAL ENROLLMENT		
						Year	County	No.
12853	1 Jones Benjamin F ²⁵	Named	22	M	1/8	1896	Tobucksy	6641
12854	2 " William F ⁶	Son	3	M	1/16	1896	"	6642
	3							
	4							
	5							
	6							
	7							
	8							
	9							
	10							
	11							
	12							
	13							
	14							
	15							
	16							
	17							

ENROLLMENT
OF NOS. 1 - 2 HEREON
APPROVED BY THE SECRETARY
OF INTERIOR MAR 6 1903

TRIBAL ENROLLMENT OF PARENTS

	Name of Father	Year	County	Name of ...	Year	County
1	B J Jones	dead	Tobucksy	Jennie C Jones	dead	Cherokee
2	No1			Rebecca J Jones	W	Noncitizen
3						
4						
5						
6						
7	No1 on 1896 roll Benj F Jones					
8	No2 " " " Willy F "					
9						
10	As to parents[sic] marriage see testimony of Wm Arndt.					
11						
12	As to No1 ~~see~~ parents[sic] marriage see ~~testimony~~ enrollment of May E Arndt.					
13						
14						
15					Date of Application for Enrollment.	
16						
17					Sept. 7, 189c	

Address in card of William Arnold McAlester IT

Choctaw By Blood Enrollment Cards 1898-1914

RESIDENCE:	Tobucksy	COUNTY.	**Choctaw Nation**				**Choctaw Roll**	CARD NO.	
POST OFFICE:	Carbon						*(Not Including Freedmen)*	FIELD NO. 4650	

Dawes' Roll No.	NAME	Relationship to Person Named	AGE	SEX	BLOOD	TRIBAL ENROLLMENT		
						Year	County	No.
✓ ✓	1 Phebus Margaret	* First Named	35	f	I.W.			
15588	2 Jefferson Phoebe 14	D	11	f	1/4	1896	Tobucksy	6669
15589	3 " Emiline 16	D	13	f	1/4	1896	"	6668
✓ DP	4 Phebus Laura E	D	8mo	f	1/4			
	5							
Nº	6							
	7							
⌐	8							
	9							
No.4	10							
	11							
	12							
	13							
	14							
	15							
	16							
	17							

DENIED CITIZENSHIP BY THE CHOCTAW AND
CHICKASAW CITIZENSHIP COURT

DISMISSED MAY 27 1904

ENROLLMENT
OF NOS. 2 and 3 HEREON
APPROVED BY THE SECRETARY
OF INTERIOR SEP 22 1904

For child of No.3 see NB
(Apr 26 '06) Card #1176

TRIBAL ENROLLMENT OF PARENTS

Name of Father	Year	County	Name of Mother	Year	County
1 Wiley Garvin	dead	Non Citizen	Liddy Garvin		Gaines
2 M G Jefferson	dead	Tobucksy	No1		
3 " " "	"	"	No1		
4 W M Phebus	"	"	No1		
5					
6 No1 admitted in 96 Case #988					
7 No1 Admitted by US Court at So McAlester Aug 25/97					
8 Case #187, as Margaret Welch. As to residence and birth of child see her testimony.					
9 As to parents[sic] marriage see testimony of No1 & Wiley Garvin					
10 Judgment of U.S. Ct admitting No1 vacated and set aside by Decree of Choctaw Chickasaw Citizenship Court Dec 17'02					
11 No1 is now wife of W M Phebus a noncitizen 12/24/02					
12 Sallie Welch, daughter of No1 see Choctaw 3424					
13 Nos 2 and 3 admitted by Dawes Com in 1896 Case No 988					
14 M.G. Jefferson not father of No.4					
15 Nº1 also on Choctaw card #D982 as an applicant for enrollment as a citizen by intermarriage					
16 No.4 transferred to Choctaw card #5176 12/5/04			See N 122	Date of Application for Enrollment.
17					9/6 - 99

150

Choctaw By Blood Enrollment Cards 1898-1914

RESIDENCE: Tobucksy COUNTY. **Choctaw Nation** Choctaw Roll (Not Including Freedmen)
POST OFFICE: Hartshorn[sic]   CARD No. FIELD No. 4651

Dawes' Roll No.	NAME	Relationship to Person First Named	AGE	SEX	BLOOD	TRIBAL ENROLLMENT		
						Year	County	No.
12855	₁ Freeman Maria J ³¹	First Named	28	f	3/4	1896	Sugar Loaf	11966
12856	₂ " Ada M ³	D	22mo	f	3/8			
12857	₃ Turner Jackson ⁷	S	4	m	3/8	1896	Sugar Loaf	11967
12858	₄ Freeman Alexander J ¹	Son	1mo	M	3/8			
I.W. 1139	₅ " Jasper N ³⁰	Husband	30	M	I.W.			
	6							
	7							
	8	No1 on 1896 roll Maria J Turner						
	9							
	10							
	11							
	12							
	13	ENROLLMENT						
	14	OF NOS. 1 - 2 - 3 - 4 HEREON						
	15	APPROVED BY THE SECRETARY OF INTERIOR MAR 6 1903			ENROLLMENT				
	16				OF NOS. ~~~ 5 ~~~ HEREON APPROVED BY THE SECRETARY				
	17				OF INTERIOR NOV 16 1904				

TRIBAL ENROLLMENT OF PARENTS

	Name of Father	Year	County	Name of Mother	Year	County
₁	Sml H McCasson		Sugar Loaf	Eliza McCasson		Sugar Loaf
₂	Jasper N Freeman	IW	Tobucksy	No1		
₃	Geo Turner		Non-Citizen	No1		
₄	Jasper Freeman		" "	N°1		
₅	Danl Freeman		" "	E.L. Freeman		Non-citizen
6						
7						
8						
9						
10						
11	No. 3 was admitted in 1896 as a citizen by blood					
12	by Dawes Commission: Choctaw Case #292: No appeal					
13	N°4 Born March 22, 1902: enrolled April 24, 1902					
	No.1 is the wife of Jasper N Freeman on Choctaw card #D.460. July 5, 1902					
14	No 5 transferred from Choctaw card #D-460 Oct 31, 1904: See decision of Oct. 15, 1904					
15	For child of Nos 1&5 see NB (Apr 26-06) Card #579				Date of Application for Enrollment.	#1 to 3
16	" " " " " " (Mar 3-05) " #377					
17	P.O. Horne IT 3/10/05					9-7-99

No5 P.O. Atoka IT 3/9/04

Choctaw By Blood Enrollment Cards 1898-1914

Dawes' Roll No.	NAME	Relationship to Person First Named	AGE	SEX	BLOOD	TRIBAL ENROLLMENT		
						Year	County	No.
* 1	Dobbs Amanda M		27	f				
2	" Mary Elizabeth	Dau	1mo	"				
3								
4								
5								
6	MAY 27 1904 DISMISSED							
7								
8								
9								
10								
11								
12								
13								
14								
15								
16								
17								

TRIBAL ENROLLMENT OF PARENTS

	Name of Father	Year	County	Name of Mother	Year	County
1	W C Mitchell		Tobucksy	Mary Mitchell		Tobucky[sic]
2	J K Dobbs		Non Citz	No1		
3	DENIED CITIZENSHIP BY THE CHOCTAW AND					
4	No1 CHICKASAW CITIZENSHIP COURT Mar 28'04					
5						
6						
7	No1 denied in 96 Case #1284					
8	Admitted by the US Court So McAlester					
9	Case #104. As to residence see testimony					
10	Judgement of U.S. Ct admitting No1 vacated and set aside by Decree in C.C.C.C. Dec 17 '02					
11	No1 adm. in C.C.C.C. Case #157					
12	No1 Denied by C.C.C.C March 28th '04					
13						
14						
15						
16						
17						

Date of Application for Enrollment.
Sept 7 - 99
No2 enrolled Oct 27/99

RESIDENCE: Tobucksy COUNTY.
POST OFFICE: McAlester

Choctaw Nation

Choctaw Roll (Not Including Freedmen)

CARD No.
FIELD No. 4652

152

Choctaw By Blood Enrollment Cards 1898-1914

RESIDENCE: COUNTY. **Choctaw Nation**   **Choctaw Roll**   CARD No.

POST OFFICE: Wilburton, I.T.   (Not Including Freedmen)   FIELD No. 4653

Dawes' Roll No.	NAME	Relationship to Person First Named	AGE	SEX	BLOOD	TRIBAL ENROLLMENT		
						Year	County	No.
✓ ✓	1 Vinson, Miranda ✳		50	F	1/8			
	2							
	3							
	4							
	5							
	6							
	7							
	8							
	9							
	10							
	11							
	12							
	13							
	14							
	15							
	16							
	17							

Case #60 April 26 04

DENIED CITIZENSHIP BY THE CHOCTAW AND CHICKASAW CITIZENSHIP COURT

TRIBAL ENROLLMENT OF PARENTS

	Name of Father	Year	County	Name of Mother	Year	County
1	J. W. Garvin	Dd	Non Cit	Lydia Garvin		Tobucksy
2						
3						
4						
5						
6						
7	No1 denied in 96 Case #988					
8			Admitted by U.S. Court			
9			As to residence see			
	Judgment of U.S. Cr. admitting No1 reversed and set aside by Decree of C.C.C.C. Dec' 17'02					
10	No1 now in C.C.C.C. Case #60					
11						
12						
13						
14						
15						
16					Date of Application for Enrollment.	
17					9/7/99	

Choctaw By Blood Enrollment Cards 1898-1914

RESIDENCE:
POST OFFICE: Cherryvale, I.T.

COUNTY. **Choctaw Nation**

Choctaw Roll (Not Including Freedmen)

CARD NO.
FIELD NO. 4654

Dawes' Roll No.	NAME	Relationship to Person First Named	AGE	SEX	BLOOD	TRIBAL ENROLLMENT		
						Year	County	No.
1	Garvin, Lydia	Named	81	F	1/4			
2								
3								
4								
5								
6								
7								
8								
9								
10								
11								
12								
13								
14								
15								
16								
17								

TRIBAL ENROLLMENT OF PARENTS

	Name of Father	Year	County	Name of Mother	Year	County
1	Abraham Moss	Dd		Phoebe Moss	Dd	
2						
3						
4						
5						
6						
7	No 1 denied in 96 Case #988					
8		Admitted by U.S. Court at So McAlester Aug 25-97 Case #187				
9		Residence satisfactory in testimony taken				
10	No 1 now in C.C.C.C. Case #60					
11						
12						
13						
14						
15						
16				Date of Application for Enrollment.		
17				9/7/99		

154

Choctaw By Blood Enrollment Cards 1898-1914

RESIDENCE:

POST OFFICE: Wilburton, I.T.   COUNTY, **Choctaw Nation**   **Choctaw Roll** (Not Including Freedmen)   CARD NO. FIELD NO. 4655

Dawes' Roll No.	NAME	Relationship to Person First Named	AGE	SEX	BLOOD	TRIBAL ENROLLMENT		
						Year	County	No.
✓✓ 1	Garvin, Wiley A	Named	44	M	1/8			
2								
3								
4								
5								
6								
7								
8								
9								
10								
11								
12								
13								
14								
15								
16								
17								

DENIED CITIZENSHIP BY THE CHOCTAW AND CHICKASAW CITIZENSHIP COURT Case #60 April 1904

TRIBAL ENROLLMENT OF PARENTS

	Name of Father	Year	County	Name of Mother	Year	County
1	J. W. Garvin	Dd		Lydia Garvin		Tobucksy
2						
3						
4						
5						
6						
7	No1 Denied in 96 Case #988					
8			Admitted by U.S. Court at So MᶜA Aug25-97 Case #187			
9			as Wiley Allen Garvin.			
10			As to residence see his testimony.			
			Judgment of U.S. Ct admitting No1 vacated and set aside by Decree of C.C.C. Dec' 17 '02			
11			No1 now in C.C.C. Case #60			
12						
13						
14						
15						
16					Date of Application for Enrollment.	
17					9/7/99	

Choctaw By Blood Enrollment Cards 1898-1914

RESIDENCE:			COUNTY.				
POST OFFICE: Stuart, I.T.			**Choctaw Nation**		Choctaw *(Not Including F*		

Dawes' Roll No.	NAME		Relationship to Person	AGE	SEX	BLOOD	TRIBAL ENROLLMENT		
							Year	County	No.
12859	1 Wright, Eslam	38	First Named	35	M	Full	1896	Atoka	13983
	2								
	3								
	4								
	5								
	13								
	14	OF NOS. APPROVE	MENT HEREON RETARY						
	15	OF INTERIOR	6 1903						
	16								
	17								

TRIBAL ENROLLMENT OF PARENTS

	Name of Father	Year	County	Name of Mother	Year	County
1	Aaron Wright	Dd	Atoka		Dd	Atoka
2						
3						
4						
5						
6						
7						
8						
9	Nº1 is the husband of Frances Wade on Choctaw card #63.					
10						
11				On roll as Eastlim Wright		
12						
13						
14						
15						
16				Date of Application for Enr		
17						

Choctaw By Blood Enrollment Cards 1898-1914

RESIDENCE:	House Correction COUNTY.								
POST OFFICE:	Detroit, Mich.	**Choctaw Nation**				**Choctaw Roll** (Not Including Freedmen)	CARD NO. FIELD NO. 4657		

Dawes' Roll No.	NAME	Relationship to Person	AGE	SEX	BLOOD	TRIBAL ENROLLMENT		
						Year	County	No.
12860	1 Wright, Cephus 28	First Named	25	M	Full	1893	Atoka	1074
	2							
	3							
	4							
	5							
	6							
	7							
	8							
	9							
	10							
	11							
	12							
	13							
	14	ENROLLMENT OF NOS. 1 HEREON						
	15	APPROVED BY THE SECRETARY						
	16	OF INTERIOR MAR 6 1903						
	17							

TRIBAL ENROLLMENT OF PARENTS

	Name of Father	Year	County	Name of Mother	Year	County
1	Aaron Wright	Dd	Atoka		Dd	Atoka
2						
3						
4						
5						
6						
7						
8						
9						
10						
11						
12			On p. 113 #1074-93, P.R. Atoka Co. as Sephus Wright.			
13			In Detroit house of correction for life.			
14						
15						
16					Date of Application for Enrollment.	
17					9/7/99	

Died prior to September 25, 1902 not entitled to land or money
(See Indian Office letter Aug 5-1910, D.C. #1110-1910)

Choctaw By Blood Enrollment Cards 1898-1914

RESIDENCE:		COUNTY. **Choctaw Nation**				**Choctaw Roll** (Not Including Freedmen)	CARD NO.	
POST OFFICE:							FIELD NO. 4658	

Dawes' Roll No.	NAME	Relationship to Person First Named	AGE	SEX	BLOOD	TRIBAL ENROLLMENT		
						Year	County	No.
1	Garvin, Robert H	Named	36	M	1/8			
2								
3								
4								
5								
6								
7								
8								
9								
10								
11								
12								
13								
14								
16								
17								

DENIED CITIZENSHIP BY THE CHOCTAW AND CHICKASAW CITIZENSHIP COURT

TRIBAL ENROLLMENT OF PARENTS

	Name of Father	Year	County	Name of Mother	Year	County
1	J.W. Garvin	Dd		Lydia Garvin		Tobucksy
2						

No1 denied in 96 Case #988

Admitted by U.S. Court at So M°A Aug 25-97 Case #187 as Robert Hawkins Garvin
As to residence see his testimony.

Judgment of U.S. Ct admitting No1 vacated and set aside by Decree of C.C.C.C. Dec 17 '02

No1 now in C.C.C.C. Case #60

Date of Application for Enrollment. 9/7/99

No1 PO Abelburton[sic] I.T. 11/1/04

158

Choctaw By Blood Enrollment Cards 1898-1914

Choctaw Nation

Choctaw Roll
(Not Including Freedmen)

CARD No.
FIELD No. 4659

Dawes' Roll No.	NAME	Relationship to Person First Named	AGE	SEX	BLOOD	TRIBAL ENROLLMENT Year	County	No.
12861	1 Compelube Columbus 40	Named	37	M	F B	1896	Tobucksy	7480
DEAD.	2 " Ellen DEAD	wife	25	f	3/4	1896	"	7481
12862	3 " Nicholas 14	Son	11	M	7/8	1896	"	7482
12863	4 " Henry 12	"	9	M	7/8	1896	"	7483
12864	5 " Joshua 8	"	5	M	7/8	1896	"	7484
12865	6 " Martin 30	brother	27	M	F B	1896	"	7508
	7							
	8							
	9 No. 2 HEREON DISMISSED UNDER							
	10 ORDER OF THE COMMISSION TO THE FIVE							
	11 CIVILIZED TRIBES OF MARCH 31, 1905.							
	12							
	13							
	14 ENROLLMENT OF NOS. 1 3 4 5- 6 HEREON							
	APPROVED BY THE SECRETARY							
	15 OF INTERIOR MAR 6 1903							
	16							
	17							

TRIBAL ENROLLMENT OF PARENTS

Name of Father	Year	County	Name of Mother	Year	County
1 J Compelube	dead	Tobucksy			
2 Nicholas Pusley	Dead	Gaines	Elsie Pusley	Dead	Gaines
3 No1			No2		
4 No1			No2		
5 No1			No2		
6 J Compelube	Dead	Tobucksy	Betsy Compelube	Dcd	Tobucksy
7					
8 No1 on 1896 roll Columbus Kampelubbi					
9 No2 " " " Ellen "			No2 Evidence of Death filed June 24th 1902 Died Sept 7th 1901		
10 No3 " " " Nicholas "			For child of No.1 see NB (Mar 3'05) Card #378		
No4 " " " Henry "					
11 No5 " " " Joshua "					
12 No6 " " " Martin "					
13					
14					
15				Date of Application for Enrollment.	
16				Sept 7- 99	
17					

Choctaw By Blood Enrollment Cards 1898-1914

RESIDENCE:	Tobucksy	COUNTY.							CARD No.	
POST OFFICE:	McAlester		Choctaw Nation				Choctaw Roll *(Not Including Freedmen)*		FIELD No. 4660	

Dawes' Roll No.	NAME		Relationship to Person Named	AGE	SEX	BLOOD	TRIBAL ENROLLMENT		
							Year	County	No.
12866	1 Pusley Sallie	24	First Named	21	f	FB	1893	Tobucksy	472
12867	2 Compelube Nellie	8	S[sic]	5	f	FB	1896	Tobucksy	7497
DEAD	3 Pusley Edward	DEAD	~~S~~	~~1~~	~~M~~	~~FB~~			
*12868	4 Compelube Bettie	1	~~Dau~~ Son	2mo	~~F~~ M	Full			
	5								
	6								
	7								
	8								
	9	No3 Hereon Dismissed under order of							
	10	the Commission to the Five Civilized							
	11	Tribes of March 31, 1905.							
	12								
	13	ENROLLMENT							
	14	OF NOS. 1-2-4 HEREON APPROVED BY THE SECRETARY							
	15	OF INTERIOR Mar 6 1903							
	16								
	17								

	TRIBAL ENROLLMENT OF PARENTS					
	Name of Father	Year	County	Name of Mother	Year	County
1	Nicholas Pusley	Ded	Gaines	Elsie Pusley	dead	Gaines
2				No1		
3				~~No1~~		
4	Columbus Compolabbee[sic]	1896	Tobucksy	No1		
5						
6						
7						
8						
9						
10	No1 on Payroll 1893 Tobucksy Co page 53					
11	No 472 as Sally Pusley					
12						
13	No2 on 1896 roll as Nellie Kampolubbi[sic]			#1 to 3		
14	No4 Born March 6,1902: enrolled May 27, 1902			Date of Application for Enrollment.		
15	No4 Illegitimate			Sept 7- 99		
16	~~No3 Died Oct. 13, 1899, proof of death filed Feby 18, 1903~~					
17	For child of No1 see NB (Mar 3 1905) Card #378					
	* 11-19-23 No4 Sex changed from "F" to "M" by Departmental authority of Nov 8,1923 (7124)					

2868 should be enrolled as male

Choctaw By Blood Enrollment Cards 1898-1914

RESIDENCE: Tobucksy COUNTY. **Choctaw Nation** **Choctaw Roll** *(Not Including Freedmen)* CARD No.
POST OFFICE: McAlester FIELD NO. **4661**

Dawes' Roll No.	NAME	Relationship to Person First Named	AGE	SEX	BLOOD	TRIBAL ENROLLMENT Year	TRIBAL ENROLLMENT County	TRIBAL ENROLLMENT No.
12869	1 Pusley Nancy 28	First Named	25	f	FB	1896	Tobucksy	10223
12870	2 James Fred 8	son	5	M	1/2	1896	"	6665
12871	3 Pusley, Nancy Jr 3	Dau	6wks	F	1/2			
12872	4 Compelube Martha 1	Dau	2mo	F	Full			
	5							
	6							
	7							
	8							
	9							
	10							
	11							
	12							
	13							
	14							
	15							
	16							
	17							

ENROLLMENT OF NOS. 1 2 3 4 HEREON
APPROVED BY THE SECRETARY
OF INTERIOR Mar 6 1903

TRIBAL ENROLLMENT OF PARENTS

	Name of Father	Year	County	Name of Mother	Year	County
1	Nicholas Pusly[sic]	Dcd	Gains[sic]	Elsie Pusly	Dcd	Gains[sic]
2				No1		
3	Pusley		Choctaw	No1		
4	Columbus Compalabee[sic]	1896	Tobucksy	No1		
5						
6						
7						
8						
9			No4 Born March 16, 1902; enrolled May 27, 1902			
10			No4 Illegitimate			
11			For child of No1 see NB (Apr 26-06) Card #617			
12						
13						
14						
15				No3 enrolled Nov. 24/99		
16				Date of Application for Enrollment	Sept 7- 99	
17					1 & 2	

Choctaw By Blood Enrollment Cards 1898-1914

RESIDENCE:	Gaines	COUNTY.							
POST OFFICE:	Simpson		**Choctaw Nation**				**Choctaw Roll** (Not Including Freedmen)	CARD NO. FIELD NO. **4662**	

Dawes' Roll No.	NAME		Relationship to Person	AGE	SEX	BLOOD	TRIBAL ENROLLMENT		
							Year	County	No.
12873	1 Wade Simon	30	First Named	27	M	Full	1896	Gaines	12984
12874	2 " Sally	23	wife	20	f	Full	1896	Sans Bois	11835
12875	3 " Lonena	4	D	1	f	Full			
15943	4 " Henry		son	2	M	Full			
	5								
	6								
	7								
	8	ENROLLMENT							
	9	OF NOS. ~~~ 4 ~~~ HEREON							
		APPROVED BY THE SECRETARY							
	10	OF INTERIOR Nov 24 1905							
	11								
	12	ENROLLMENT							
	13	OF NOS. 1 - 2 - 3 HEREON APPROVED BY THE SECRETARY							
	14	OF INTERIOR Mar 6 1903							
	15								
	16								
	17								

TRIBAL ENROLLMENT OF PARENTS

	Name of Father	Year	County	Name of Mother	Year	County
1	Nicholas Wade		Gaines	Betsy Wade	Dead	Gaines
2	Isaac Thompson	Dcd	Sugar Loaf	Eliza Thompson	"	Sugar Loaf
3	No1			No2		
4	No1			No2		
5						
6						
7						
8						
9	No1 on 1896 roll Simeon Wade					
10	No2 " " " Sally Thompson					
11	No4 was born March 13, 1900: application received and name placed on this card March 25, 1905 under provisions of act of Congress approved March 3, 1905					
12						
13						
14						
15					#1 to 3 inc	
16				Date of Application for Enrollment.	Sept 7 - 99	
17	Krebs I.T. 12/23/02					

P.O. Carbon I.T. 3/26/04

162

Choctaw By Blood Enrollment Cards 1898-1914

RESIDENCE: Tobucksy   COUNTY. **Choctaw Nation**   **Choctaw Roll** CARD NO.
POST OFFICE: Indianola   *(Not Including Freedmen)*   FIELD NO. 4663

Dawes' Roll No.	NAME	Relationship to Person First Named	AGE	SEX	BLOOD	TRIBAL ENROLLMENT		
						Year	County	No.
I.W. 847	1 Williams Thomas H 40	First Named	36	M	IW	1896	Sans Bois	15140
12876	2 " Mary E 24	wife	21	f	1/2	1896	" "	12679
12877	3 " Darthula 5	d	2	f	1/4			
12878	4 " Aurelia 3	d	4 day	f	1/4			
12879	5 " Leo McC 1	son	1 mo	M	1/4			
	6							
	7				No (1) DECISION PREPARED Dec 8 '03			
	8	ENROLLMENT						
	9	OF NOS. 1 HEREON						
	10	APPROVED BY THE SECRETARY OF INTERIOR MAY 21 1904						
	11							
	12							
	13	ENROLLMENT						
	14	OF NOS. 2 3 4 - 5 HEREON APPROVED BY THE SECRETARY						
	15	OF INTERIOR MAR 6 1903						
	16							
	17							

TRIBAL ENROLLMENT OF PARENTS

	Name of Father	Year	County	Name of Mother	Year	County
1	R T Williams		Non Cit	Susan Williams		Non Cit
2	Frank Perry		Sans Bois	Bicey Perry		Sans Bois
3	No1			No2		
4	No1			No2		
5	No.1			No.2		
6						
7						
8	No1 on 1896 roll Tom H Williams					
9	No2 " " " Mary Do.					
10	No.5 born Jany 7, 1902: Enrolled Feby 10, 1902 For child of nos 1&2 see NB (Apr 26, 1906) Card No. 103.					
11						
12						
13						
14				P.O. address of No1 Vireton I.T. Jany 2, 1901.		
15				Date of Application for Enrollment.		
16				Sept 7 - 99		
17	P.O. address No1 Vireton I.T. Jany 2, 1901					

PO Massey OF 2/25/04

163

Choctaw By Blood Enrollment Cards 1898-1914

RESIDENCE:	Gaines Co	COUNTY.							
POST OFFICE:	Wilburton								

COUNTY. Choctaw Nation **Choctaw Roll** *(Not Including Freedmen)* **CARD NO.** **FIELD NO. 4664**

Dawes' Roll No.	NAME	Relationship to Person First Named	AGE	SEX	BLOOD	TRIBAL ENROLLMENT		
						Year	County	No.
IW794*	1 Rockett Louis ⑫	First Named	39	M	IW			
15792	2 " Ida M ²⁷	wife	24	f	AW	1896	Gaines	10741
DEAD	3 " Thompson M	son	6	M	1/2	1896	Gaines	10742
16216	4 " Louis Henry	son	6	M	White	ENROLLMENT		
16217	5 " Ross Lee	son	4	F[sic]	"	OF NOS. ~~~2~~~ HEREON APPROVED BY THE SECRETARY		
16218	6 " Francis Marion	son	2m	M	"	OF INTERIOR Jan 5 1906		

May 22,1905 Record as to [...] as to No2 remanded by Department for further hearing July
testimony taken Nov 15,1905 14,1905. Further [sic]
Report to Department as to No2 *No1 Admitted by the U.S.Court at So Mᶜ Alester Aug 25,
Jan 5,1906 Department affirms 1896 Case #212 & by Dawes Commission No 1183
decision of Commission enrolling No2 *No1 Decision of the U.S.Court C.D. admitting No1 of
No4 born Dec 6,1896 Aug 25,1897 vacated and set aside by Decree of Choctaw
No5 born June 9,1898 Chickasaw Cit Court Decr 17 1902. The Choctaw-Chick-
No4 Proof of Birth filed Dec 22,1902 asaw Court on Jan 20,1904 admitted No1 as a citizen by
No5 proof of birth filed Jany 2,1903 intermarriage of the Choctaw Nation Case #26
Mar 15,1905: See letter of Dept withholding approval of enrollment of No2 Mar 21,1905. Report to
Dept as to No2 and decisions enrolling her forwarded.

TRIBAL ENROLLMENT OF PARENTS

	Name of Father	Year	County	Name of Mother	Year	County
1	J B Rockett		Non Cit	U. A. Rockett		Non Cit
2	Henry Moore		" "	M. f[sic]. Moore		" "
3	No1		Gaines	Lizzie Rockett	Ded	Gaines
4	No1	ENROLLMENT		No2	ENROLLMENT	
5	No1	OF NOS. 1 HEREON APPROVED BY THE SECRETARY		No2	OF NOS. 4, 5 & 6 HEREON APPROVED BY THE SECRETARY	
6	No1	OF INTERIOR May 9 1904		No2	OF INTERIOR Mar 4, 1907	

7 No 2 admitted in 1896 as a citizen by blood; no appeal
8 No.2 Admitted by Dawes Commission Case #1183
9 No.3 died August 11,1900. Proof of death filed Dec 30,1902.
10 *No1 was admitted by U.S.Court Central District Ind Ter So Mᶜ Alester I.T.
11 August 25, 1897, Court Case #121 Louis Rockett et al
12 No6 Born Sept 24,1902 Enrolled Dec 24, 1902
13 For children of Nos 1&2 see NB 1023 (Act Apr 26-06)

			No.3 Hereon Dismissed under order of the Commission to the Five Civilized Tribes of March 31, 1905.	Date of Application for Enrollment. Sept 7-99	

164

Choctaw By Blood Enrollment Cards 1898-1914

RESIDENCE: Sans Bois	COUNTY.	Choctaw Nation	Choctaw Roll	CARD No.
POST OFFICE: Whitefield			(Not Including Freedmen)	FIELD No. 4665

Dawes' Roll No.	NAME	Relationship to Person First Named	AGE	SEX	BLOOD	TRIBAL ENROLLMENT		
						Year	County	No.
DEAD.	1 ~~King Hiram~~ DEAD 49		~~46~~	~~M~~	~~1/4~~	~~1896~~	~~Sans Bois~~	~~7429~~
12880	2 " Charles 23	Son	20	M	1/4	1896	" "	7430
12881	3 " Harris 18	"	15	M	1/4	1896	" "	7431
12882	4 " Martha C 14	D	11	f	1/4	1896	" "	7432
12883	5 " Mary E 12	D	9	f	1/4	1896	" "	7433
12884	6 " Rupell 9	S	6	M	1/4	1896	" "	7434
	7							
	8							
	9							
	10							
	11							
	12 No. 1 HEREON DISMISSED UNDER							
	13 ORDER OF THE COMMISSION TO THE FIVE							
	14 CIVILIZED TRIBES OF MARCH 31, 1905.							
	15 ENROLLMENT							
	16 OF NOS. 2 3 4 5 - 6 HEREON							
	17 APPROVED BY THE SECRETARY OF INTERIOR MAR 6 1903							

TRIBAL ENROLLMENT OF PARENTS

	Name of Father	Year	County	Name of Mother	Year	County
1	~~Jefferson King~~	~~Dcd~~	~~Sans Bois~~	~~Martha Folsom~~		~~San[sic] Bois~~
2	No1		" "	Martha King	Dcd	" "
3	No1		" "	Do Do		" "
4	No1		" "	Eliza King	Dcd	Non Citizen
5	No1		" "	" "		" " "
6	No1		" "	" "		" " "
7						
8			No4 on roll 1896 Mattie King			
9			No6 " " " Rupel "			
10			For child of No2 see NB (Apr 26-06) Card #407			
11			" " " No4 " " " " " #534			
12			As to parents[sic] marriage see certificate herewith filed			
13			No 1 Died Dec 1900: Proof of death filed Dec 23, 1902			
14			For child of No.5 see NB (April 26, 1906) No. 535			
15						
16					Date of Application for Enrollment	
17			Date of application for enrollment	Sept 8-99		

No3 P.O. Chickasha IT 1/19/06

RESIDENCE: Sans Bois   COUNTY. **Choctaw Nation**   **Choctaw Roll** CARD NO.
POST OFFICE: ~~Enterprise~~   (Not Including Freedmen) FIELD NO. 4666

Dawes' Roll No.		NAME		Relationship to Person	AGE	SEX	BLOOD	TRIBAL ENROLLMENT		
								Year	County	No.
12885	1	King William S	25	First Named	22	M	1/2	1896	San[sic] Bois	7422
I.W. 769	2	" Sarah J		wife	25	f	IW	1896	" "	14715
12886	3	" Eva Ethel	1	Dau	6wks	f	1/4			
	4									
	5									
	6									
	7									
	8	ENROLLMENT								
	9	OF NOS. ~~2~~ HEREON APPROVED BY THE SECRETARY								
	10	OF INTERIOR MAY -7 1904								
	11									
	12									
	13	ENROLLMENT								
	14	OF NOS. 1 - 3 HEREON								
	15	APPROVED BY THE SECRETARY OF INTERIOR MAR ...								
	16									
	17									

TRIBAL ENROLLMENT OF PARENTS

	Name of Father	Year	County	Name of Mother	Year	County
1	Hiram King		San[sic] Bois	Martha King	Dcd	San[sic] Bois
2	Joe Pryor		Non Cit	Viney Pryor		Non Cit
3	No.1			No 2		
4						
5						
6			No2 see decision of March 2 '04			
7			No1 on 1896 roll William King			
8			No2 " " " Janey "			
9			No.3 Enrolled September 7, 1901			
10			No2 See Decision of March 2 '1904			
			For child of Nos 1&2 see NB (March 3, 1905) #1114			
11						
12						
13					Date of Application for Enrollment.	
14						
15					Sept 8 - 99	
16						
17	12-23-02 PO Quinton IT					

Choctaw By Blood Enrollment Cards 1898-1914

RESIDENCE:	Tobucksy	COUNTY.								
POST OFFICE:	McAlester									

Choctaw Nation
Choctaw Roll (Not Including Freedmen)
CARD No. FIELD No. 4667

Dawes' Roll No.	NAME	Relationship to Person First Named	AGE	SEX	BLOOD	TRIBAL ENROLLMENT		
						Year	County	No.
12887	1 Fulton Eliza 52	First Named	49	f	1/4	1896	Tobucksy	4056
	2							
	3							
	4							
	5							
	6							
	7							
	8							
	9							
	10							
	11							
	12							
	13							
	14							
	15							
	16							
	17							

ENROLLMENT OF NOS. 1 HEREON APPROVED BY THE SECRETARY OF INTERIOR MAR 6 1903

TRIBAL ENROLLMENT OF PARENTS

	Name of Father	Year	County	Name of Mother	Year	County
1	Allen Stanton	Dcd	Sugar Loaf		Dcd	Sugar Loaf
2						
3						
4						
5						
6						
7						
8						
9						
10						
11						
12						
13						
14						
15					Date of Application for Enrollment.	
16						
17						

Dawes' Roll No.	NAME	Relationship to Person First Named	AGE	SEX	BLOOD	TRIBAL ENROLLMENT		
						Year	County	No.
12888	1 Sam Fannie 46	Named	43	f	Full	1896	Tobucksy	11304
12889	2 Perteet Lizzie 18	d	15	f	"	1896	"	11308
12890	3 Sam Eliza A 16	d	13	f	"	1896	"	11309
12891	4 " Ace 14	S	11	M	"	1896	"	11310
12892	5 Perteet, Clarence 1	Gr Son	8wks	M	1/2			
	6							
	7							
	8							
	9							
	10							
	11							
	12							
	13							
	14							
	15							
	16							
	17							

POST OFFICE: Krebs   Choctaw Nation   (Not Including Freedmen)   FIELD NO. 4668

ENROLLMENT
OF NOS. 1 2 3 4 - 5 HEREON
APPROVED BY THE SECRETARY
OF INTERIOR MAR 6 1903

TRIBAL ENROLLMENT OF PARENTS

	Name of Father	Year	County	Name of Mother	Year	County
1	Willis	Dcd	Non-Cit	Fara Ann		Choctaw
2	Wallace Sam	"	Tobucksy	No 1		Tobucksy
3	Do Do	"	"	No 1		
4	Do Do	"	"	No 1		
5	John Perteet		non-citizen	Nº2		
6						
7	Nos. 1, 2, 3 and 4 Admitted by Act of Council #15 Approved Apil[sic] 8/91					
8	Nº2 is now the wife of John Perteet a noncitizen Evidence of marriage filed May 10,1902					
9	Nº5 Born March 28, 1902: enrolled May 10, 1902					
10	No3 on roll 1896 Ely Ann Sam No4 " " " Ease "					
11	For child of No3 see NB (Apr 26-06) Card #771					
12	" " " 2 " " (Mar 3 '05) " #393					
13				Date of Application for Enrollment. For Nos 1 to 4 incl		
14				Sept 8th 99		
15						
16						
17						

Choctaw By Blood Enrollment Cards 1898-1914

RESIDENCE: San[sic] Bois	COUNTY.				CARD NO.
POST OFFICE: Whitefield	**Choctaw Nation**		**Choctaw Roll** (Not Including Freedmen)		FIELD NO. **4669**

Dawes' Roll No.	NAME	Relationship to Person First Named	AGE	SEX	BLOOD	TRIBAL ENROLLMENT		
						Year	County	No.
DEAD. 1	Hughart, Nancy DEAD.		27	F	1/2			
12893 2	" Clarence C [13]	S	10	M	1/4	1893	San[sic] Bois	954
12894 3	" Levi [11]	"	8	"	1/4	1893	"	955
12895 4	" Birdie E [9]	D	6	F	1/4	1893	"	956
14905 5	" Odie	"	2	"	1/4			
12896 6	" Boyd [3]	Son	4mo	M	1/4			
7								
IP CERTIFICATE NO. 2-3-4-5-6 UG 29 1903								
10								
11	ENROLLMENT OF NOS. 2-3-4 & 6 HEREON APPROVED BY THE SECRETARY OF INTERIOR MAR 6 1903							
12								
13								
14	ENROLLMENT OF NOS. 5 HEREON APPROVED BY THE SECRETARY OF INTERIOR MAY 21 1903							
15								
16								
17								

	TRIBAL ENROLLMENT OF PARENTS					
	Name of Father	Year	County	Name of Mother	Year	County
1	Jasper Crowder	Dcd	San[sic] Bois	Sarah Crowder	Dcd	San Bois
2	R. L. Hughart		Non Cit	No.1		
3	" " "		" "	No.1		
4	" " "		" "	No.1		
5	" " "		" "	No.1		
6	" " "		" "	No.1		
7						
8						
9	No.1 On San[sic] Bois Payroll 1893 p 98 No 953					
10	No.2 " " " " " p.98 " 954 Clarence Hughart					
11	No.3 " " " " " p.98 " 955					
12	No.4 " " " " " p.98 " 956 Gertie Hughart					
13	No.6 Enrolled June 23, 1900					
	No.1 Died February 29, 1900. Evidence of death filed April 15, 1901					
14	Nº5 Born June 15, 1897: proof of birth filed March 1, 1903					
15						
16						Sept 8/99
17						

RESIDENCE:	Sans Bois	COUNTY.						CARD No.	
POST OFFICE:	Enterprise	**Choctaw Nation**				Choctaw Roll (Not Including Freedmen)		FIELD No. 4670	

Dawes' Roll No.	NAME		Relationship to Person	AGE	SEX	BLOOD	TRIBAL ENROLLMENT		
							Year	County	No.
12897	1 Bench Sallie	73	First Named	70	f	Full	1896	Sans Bois	683
12898	2 Dixon Eliza	33	D	30	f	"	1896	" "	684
12899	3 " Wallace	18	G Son	15	M	1/2	1896	" "	3177
12900	4 " Albert	1	Son of Nº3	2wks	M	1/4			
I.W. 1263	5 " Amber	19	Wife of No 3	19	F	I.W.			
	6								
	7								
	8								
	9	ENROLLMENT OF NOS. 5 HEREON APPROVED BY THE SECRETARY OF INTERIOR DEC 30 1904							
	10								
	11								
	12								
	13	ENROLLMENT OF NOS. 1 2 3 4 HEREON APPROVED BY THE SECRETARY OF INTERIOR MAR 6 1903							
	14								
	15								
	16								
	17								

	TRIBAL ENROLLMENT OF PARENTS					
Name of Father		Year	County	Name of Mother	Year	County
1 James Goings		Dcd	Kiamitia	Nancy Goings	Dcd	Choctaw
2 Dixon		"	"	No1		
3 Silas Dixon		"	San[sic] Bois	Betty James		Non Cit
4 Nº3				Amber Dixon		" "
5 Bud Harris			Non-Citz	Ellen Harris		" "
6						
7 No2 on 1896 roll Sissy Bench						
8						
9 As to No3 parents[sic] marriage see No1 testimony						

For child of Nos 3 and 5 see NB (Mar 3,1905) #394

Nº3 is now the husband of Amber Dixon non-citizen Evidence of

marriage filed Sept 23, 1902

Nº4 Born Sept 5, 1902; enrolled Sept 23, 1902

1 to 3 inc

Amber Dixon, wife of Nº3, is enrolled on Choctaw Card #D820 - October 23, 1902

Date of Application for Enrollment. Sept 8/99

No5 originally listed for enrollment Oct. 23,1902 on Choctaw

card #D-820; transferred to this card Dec 15,1904 See decision of Nov 26, 1904

No3 PO Wesley I.T. 1/28/04

Choctaw By Blood Enrollment Cards 1898-1914

RESIDENCE: COUNTY. **Choctaw Nation**   **Choctaw Roll**   CARD No.

POST OFFICE: Russellville, I.T.   (Not Including Freedmen)   FIELD No. 4671

Dawes' Roll No.	NAME	Relationship to Person First	AGE	SEX	BLOOD	TRIBAL ENROLLMENT Year	County	No.
1	Thomas, Daisy L	Named	18	F	I.W.			
2								
3								
4								
5								
6								
7								
8								
9								
10								
11								
12								
13								
14								
15								
16								
17								

Nov 28 '04 3794

DENIED CITIZENSHIP BY THE CHOCTAW AND CHICKASAW CITIZENSHIP COURT

TRIBAL ENROLLMENT OF PARENTS

	Name of Father	Year	County	Name of Mother	Year	County
1	C. C. Payne		Non Cit	J. M. Payne		Non Cit
2						
3						
4						
5						
6						
7						
8						
9						
10	No 1 denied in 96 Case #400					
11	Admitted by U.S. Court at So McA Aug 25-97 Case #240.					
12	as Daisy L. Payne					
13	As to residence see testimony of Christopher C. Payne					
14	Judgement of U.S. C admitting No 1 vacated and set aside by Decree of Choctaw Chickasaw Citizenship Court Dec 17'02					
	No 1 now in C.C.C.C Case #37					
15						
16						
17						

Date of Application for Enrollment. 9/7/99

171

Choctaw By Blood Enrollment Cards 1898-1914

RESIDENCE:
POST OFFICE:

COUNTY. **Choctaw Nation**

Choctaw Roll
(Not Including Freedmen)

CARD NO.

FIELD NO. 4672

Dawes' Roll No.	NAME	Relationship to Person First Named	AGE	SEX	BLOOD	TRIBAL ENROLLMENT		
						Year	County	No.
1	Payne, Louie O	Named	16	M	None			
2	" Jesse H	Bro	13	"	"			
3	" Joanna M	Sis	11	F	"			
4	" Willie E	Bro	9	M	"			
5	" Gussie L	Sis	5	F	"			
6								
7								
8								
9								
10								
11								
12								
13								
14								
15								
16								
17								

TRIBAL ENROLLMENT OF PARENTS

	Name of Father	Year	County	Name of Mother	Year	County
1	C. C. Payne		Non Cit	J. M. Payne		Non Cit
2						
3						
4						
5						
6						
7	Nos 1 to 5 incl. denied in 96 Case #400					
8	Admitted by U.S. Court at So MᶜA Aug 25-97 Case No. 240					
9	No.2 as Jessie H Payne					
	As to residence see testimony of father.					
10	Judgment of U.S. Court No. 240 vacated and set aside by Decree of Choctaw Chickasaw Citizenship Court Dec 1702					
11	No 1 to 5 incl now in C.C.C. Case #37					
12						
13						
14						
15						
16				Date of Application for Enrollment.		
17				9/7/99		

172

Choctaw By Blood Enrollment Cards 1898-1914

Dawes' Roll No.	NAME	Relationship to Person First Named	AGE	SEX	BLOOD	TRIBAL ENROLLMENT Year	County	No.
12901	1 Riggs, Samuel 9	First Named	6	M	1/8	1896	Atoka	10997
12902	2 " Lee 7	Bro	4	"	"	"	"	10998
12903	3 " Wilson 6	Bro	2	"	"			
12904	4 Mathis, Mary J 21	1/2 Sis	18	F	"	1896	Atoka	8839
12905	5 " Eliza 20	"	17	F	"	"	"	8840
12906	6 " Susan F 18	"	15	F	"	"	"	8841
12907	7 " Josephine 14	"	11	"	"	"	"	8842
	8							
	9							
	10							
	11							
	12							
	13							
	14							
	15	ENROLLMENT OF NOS. 1,2,3,4,5,6-7 HEREON APPROVED BY THE SECRETARY OF INTERIOR Mar 6 1903							
	16							
	17							

TRIBAL ENROLLMENT OF PARENTS

	Name of Father	Year	County	Name of Mother	Year	County
1	Tom Riggs		non-cit	Angie Riggs	Dd	Atoka
2	" "		" "	" "	"	"
3	" "		" "	" "	"	"
4	Dan Mathis	Dd	Chic "	" "	"	"
5	" "	"	" "	" "	"	"
6	" "	"	" "	" "	"	"
7	" "	"	" "	" "	"	"
8						
9						
10						
11						
12	Mother of these children on 1896 Choctaw roll No 10996					
13	No.1 on roll as Sammie Riggs					
14	For child of No4 see NB (Apr 26-06) Card #440 " 4 " " Jennie Mathis					
15	" " " " 5 " (Mar 3-05) " #395 " 6 " " Susa "					
16	" 5 " " Liza "					
17	P.O. Story, I.T.			Date of application for enrollment		

Date of Application for Enrollment.

9/7/99

Choctaw By Blood Enrollment Cards 1898-1914

RESIDENCE:
POST OFFICE: Krebs, I. T.

COUNTY. **Choctaw Nation**

Choctaw Roll
(Not Including Freedmen)

CARD NO.
FIELD NO. 4674

Dawes' Roll No.	NAME		Relationship to Person	AGE	SEX	BLOOD	TRIBAL ENROLLMENT		
							Year	County	No.
12908	1 Frye, Lewis	22	First Named	19	M	Full	1896	Blue	4391
	2								
	3								
	4								
	5								
	6								
	7								
	8								
	9								
	10								
	11								
	12								
	13	ENROLLMENT							
	14	OF NOS. 1 HEREON APPROVED BY THE SECRETARY							
	15	OF INTERIOR MAR 6 1903							
	16								
	17								

TRIBAL ENROLLMENT OF PARENTS

	Name of Father	Year	County	Name of Mother	Year	County
1	Pusley Frye	Dd	Blue	Bessie Frye	Dd	Blue
2						
3						
4						
5						
6	No.1 also on 1896 Choctaw roll, page 85, #3564 as Lewis Dyer					
7						
8						
9						
10						
11						
12				On roll as Lewis Fry.		
13						
14						
15						
16					Date of Application for Enrollment.	
17					9/7/99	

RESIDENCE: COUNTY. **Choctaw Nation** **Choctaw Roll** (Not Including Freedmen) CARD NO.
POST OFFICE: So M^c^Alester, I.T. FIELD NO. 4675

Dawes' Roll No.	NAME		Relationship to Person First Named	AGE	SEX	BLOOD	TRIBAL ENROLLMENT Year	County	No.
12909	1 Beams, George W	34		31	M	1/4	1896	Tobucksy	907
I.W. 470	2 " Sallie	25	Wife	22	F	I.W.	"	"	14302
12910	3 " Edna M	5	Dau	2	F	1/8			
12911	4 " Edgar A	1	Son	7m	M	1/8			
	5								
	6								
	7								
	8								
	9 ENROLLMENT								
	10 OF NOS. 2 HEREON								
	APPROVED BY THE SECRETARY								
	11 OF INTERIOR SEP 12 1903								
	12								
	13 ENROLLMENT								
	14 OF NOS. 1-3-4 HEREON								
	APPROVED BY THE SECRETARY								
	15 OF INTERIOR MAR 6 1903								
	16								
	17								

TRIBAL ENROLLMENT OF PARENTS

Name of Father	Year	County	Name of Mother	Year	County
1 Isom Beams	Dd	Tobucksy	Mary Beams	Dd	Tobucksy
2 Ric^h^ Holloway	"	Non Cit	Holloway		Non Cit
3 No.1			No.2		
4 " 1			" 2		
5					
6					
7					
8					
9 Evidence of marriage between G. W. Beams and					
10 Sallie Lewis filed Jany. 3, 1903.					
11			On roll as Geo. W. Beams.		
For children of Nos 1 and 2 see NB (Mar 3 '05) #396					
12					
13					
14					
15					
16					Date of Application for Enrollment.
17					9/7/99

Choctaw By Blood Enrollment Cards 1898-1914

RESIDENCE:
POST OFFICE: Stigler, I.T.

COUNTY. **Choctaw Nation**

Choctaw Roll CARD NO.
(Not Including Freedmen) FIELD NO. 4

Dawes' Roll No.	NAME	Relationship to Person First Named	AGE	SEX	BLOOD	TRIBAL ENROLLMENT		
						Year	County	No.
I.W. 471	1 Turner, James M 45		42	M	I.W.			
12912	2 " James A 10	Son	7	"	1/8	1896	San[sic] Bois	11836
	3							
	4							
	5							
	6							
	7							
	8							
	9							
	10							
	11							
	12	ENROLLMENT OF NOS. 1 HEREON APPROVED BY THE SECRETARY OF INTERIOR SEP 12 1903						
	13							
	14							
	15	ENROLLMENT OF NOS. 2 HEREON APPROVED BY THE SECRETARY OF INTERIOR MAR 6 1903						
	16							
	17							

TRIBAL ENROLLMENT OF PARENTS

	Name of Father	Year	County	Name of Mother	Year	
1	Thos. T. Turner		Non Cit	Martha Turner		
2	No.1			Sallie A Turner	Dd	
3						
4						
5						
6						
7						
8	Evidence of marriage between N°1 and Sallie A Harris received and					
9	filed Feby 10, 1903.					
10				Nos 1&2 Admitted by Dawes Comm #281. No appeal		
11				As to marriage see his testimony		
				No.2 on 96 roll as James Turner.		
12	For child of No1 see NB (Apr 26 '06) #1256.					
13						
14						
15						Date of Application for Enrollment.
16						
17	Quinton I.T. 1/3/03					9/7/99

176

Choctaw By Blood Enrollment Cards 1898-1914

| RESIDENCE: | Creek Nation | | | | | Choctaw Roll | CARD No. | |
| POST OFFICE: | Senora, I.T. | | | | Choctaw Nation | *(Not Including Freedmen)* | FIELD No. 46|77 |

Dawes' Roll No.	NAME		Relationship to Person	AGE	SEX	BLOOD	TRIBAL ENROLLMENT		
							Year	County	No.
12913	1 Beams, Charles	27	First Named	24	M	1/4	1896	Tobucksy	945
D18/5/12	2 " Tissie M		Dau	1	F	1/8			
	3								
	4 **DECISION RENDERED.**								
	Apr 28,1906 Record forwarded Department								
	6 No2 REFUSED APR 28 1906								
	7								
	8								
	9 ACTION APPROVED BY ... NOV 30 [Illegible]								
	10								
	11								
	12								
	13								
	14								
	15 ENROLLMENT								
	OF NOS. 1 HEREON								
	16 APPROVED BY THE SECRETARY								
	17 OF INTERIOR MAR 1903								

TRIBAL ENROLLMENT OF PARENTS

	Name of Father	Year	County	Name of Mother	Year	Coun
1	Isom Beams	Dd	Tobucksy	Mary Beams	Dd	Tobucksy
2	No1			Annie -Bean[sic]		Creek
3						
4						
5						
6						
7				No2 placed hereon in accordance with the provisions of the Act		
8				of Congress approved March 3, 1905		
9						
10				No2 Application also made for her enrollment as a citizen of the		
11				Creek Nation		
12						
13				No1 Died February - 1910: Proof of death filed 3/7/12		
14						
15						
16					Date of Application for Enrollment.	
17	Henrietta I.T. 12/24/02				9/7/99	

Choctaw By Blood Enrollment Cards 1898-1914

RESIDENCE:
POST OFFICE: McAlester, I.T. COUNTY. **Choctaw Nation** **Choctaw Roll** (Not Including Freedmen) CARD NO. FIELD NO. 4678

Dawes' Roll No.	NAME	Relationship to Person	AGE	SEX	BLOOD	TRIBAL ENROLLMENT		
						Year	County	No.
12914	1 Wilson, Sallie	First Named 42	39	F	Full	1896	Tobucksy	13046
DEAD.	2 " Tillie	Dau	8	"	"	"	"	13049
	3							
	4							
	5							
	6							
	7							
	8							
	9							
	10							
	11 No. 2 HEREON DISMISSED UNDER							
	12 ORDER OF THE COMMISSION TO THE FIVE CIVILIZED TRIBES OF MARCH 31, 1905.							
	13							
	14 ENROLLMENT							
	15 OF NOS. 1 HEREON APPROVED BY THE SECRETARY							
	16 OF INTERIOR MAR 6 1903							
	17							

TRIBAL ENROLLMENT OF PARENTS

	Name of Father	Year	County	Name of Mother	Year	County
1		Dd			Dd	
2	Sol. Wilson	"	Tobucksy	No.1		
3						
4						
5						
6						
7						
8	No.2 Died February, 1900: Proof of death filed Dec. 30, 1902.					
9						
10						
11						
12						
13						
14						
15						
16						
17				Date of Application for Enrollment.		9/7/99

Choctaw By Blood Enrollment Cards 1898-1914

RESIDENCE: Tobucksy COUNTY. **Choctaw Nation** | Choctaw Roll _(Not Including Freedmen)_ CARD No.
POST OFFICE: South Canadian | | FIELD No. 4679

Dawes' Roll No.	NAME	Relationship to Person First Named	AGE	SEX	BLOOD	TRIBAL ENROLLMENT		
						Year	County	No.
DEAD 1	Cheadie Elias R	DEAD	40	M	1/4	1896	Tobucksy	2363
2								
3								
4								
5								
6								
7								
8								
9	No. 1 HEREON DISMISSED UNDER ORDER OF THE COMMISSION TO THE FIVE							
10	CIVILIZED TRIBES OF MARCH 31, 1905.							
11								
12								
13								
14								
15								
16								
17								

CANCELLED

Applicant died prior to ratification of Choctaw-Chickasaw agreement Sept. 25, 1902

TRIBAL ENROLLMENT OF PARENTS

	Name of Father	Year	County	Name of Mother	Year	County
1	James S Cheadle	dead	Tobucksy	Susan Cheadle	Dead	Tobucksy
2						
3						
4						
5						
6						
7						
8						
9						
10	No1 is husband of Lucy B Cheadle on Chickasaw					
11	card #772, and father of children thereon.					
12						
13	No 1 Died Aug 23, 1902: proof of death filed Sept 6, 1902.			Date of Application for Enrollment.		
14						
15				Sept 8th 1899		
16						
17						

Choctaw By Blood Enrollment Cards 1898-1914

RESIDENCE: Sans Bois   COUNTY. **Choctaw Nation**   Choctaw Roll CARD NO.
POST OFFICE: Whitefield   *(Not Including Freedmen)* FIELD NO. 4680

Dawes' Roll No.	NAME	Relationship to Person First Named	AGE	SEX	BLOOD	TRIBAL ENROLLMENT Year	County	No.
12915	1 Folsom Starns W ⁶³	First Named	60	M	1/4	1896	Sans Bois	3844
12916	2 " Martha M ⁶⁸	wife	65	f	1/8	1896	" "	3845
	3							
	4							
	5							
	6							
	7							
	8							
	9							
	10							
	11							
	12							
	13							
	14							
	15							
	16							
	17							

ENROLLMENT
OF NOS. 1 & 2 HEREON
APPROVED BY THE SECRETARY
OF INTERIOR MAR 6 1903

TRIBAL ENROLLMENT OF PARENTS						
Name of Father	Year	County	Name of Mother	Year	County	
1 Watt Folsom	Dcd	Sans Bois	Elizabeth Folsom	Dcd	Sans Bois	
2 Harris Crowder	"	"	Nancy Crowder		Choctaw	
3						
4						
5						
6						
7	No1 on 1896 roll S W Folsum					
8	No2 " " " Mattie Folsum					
9						
10						
11						
12						
13						
14				Date of Application for Enrollment.		
15				Sept 8/99		
16						
17						

Choctaw By Blood Enrollment Cards 1898-1914

RESIDENCE:	Tobucksy	COUNTY.	**Choctaw Nation**	**Choctaw Roll** (Not Including Freedmen)	CARD NO.
POST OFFICE:	Thurman				FIELD NO. 4681

Dawes' Roll No.	NAME		Relationship to Person First Named	AGE	SEX	BLOOD	TRIBAL ENROLLMENT		
							Year	County	No.
12917	1 Bell	Thomas W ²⁷	First Named	24	M	1/4	1896	Tobucksy	912
I.W. 1030	2 "	Mary Viola ²⁴	Wife	21	F	IW			
12918	3 "	Robert W ¹	Son	1	M	1/8			
12919	4 "	Nancy S ³	Dau	3	F	1/8			
	5								
	6								
	7	ENROLLMENT							
	8	OF NOS. ~~ 2 ~~ HEREON							
		APPROVED BY THE SECRETARY							
	9	OF INTERIOR OCT 21 1904							
	10								
	11								
	12								
	13	ENROLLMENT							
	14	OF NOS. 1, 3 & 4 HEREON							
		APPROVED BY THE SECRETARY							
	15	OF INTERIOR MAR 6 1903							
	16								
	17								

TRIBAL ENROLLMENT OF PARENTS

	Name of Father	Year	County	Name of Mother	Year	County
1	Robt D Bell		Non cit	Salina Bell	Dcd	Tobucksy
2	WP Nichols		Non cit	Nancy A Nichols		U S Cit
3	Nº1			Nº2		
4	No 1			No 2		
5						
6						
7						
8	Nº3 Born Sept 4, 1901: enrolled Oct. 2, 1902					
9	No4 Born Decʳ 16 1899: Evidence of Birth filed Decʳ 22ⁿᵈ 1902					
10	For children of Nos 1 and 2 see NB (March 3, 1905) #1297					
11						
12						
13						
14						
15						
16				Date of Application for Enrollment.	Sept 8ᵗʰ 99	
17	Amy I.T. 12/22/02					

PO Allen IT 4/17/05

Choctaw By Blood Enrollment Cards 1898-1914

RESIDENCE: Tobucksy   COUNTY. **Choctaw Nation**   **Choctaw Roll** (Not Including Freedmen)   CARD No.
POST OFFICE: Savanna   FIELD No. **4682**

Dawes' Roll No.	NAME	Relationship to Person Named	AGE	SEX	BLOOD	TRIBAL ENROLLMENT		
						Year	County	No.
12920	1 Mackey, Solomon H 49	First Named	46	M	1/2	1896	Tobucksy	9205
12921	2 " Elizabeth H 39	Wife	36	f	1/2	1896	"	9206
12922	3 " David M 22	Son	19	M	1/2	1896	"	9207
12923	4 " Benjamin P 21	"	18	M	1/2	1896	"	9208
12924	5 " Willis S 19	"	16	M	1/2	1896	"	9209
12925	6 " Beulah A 16	S[sic]	13	f	1/2	1896	"	9210
12926	7 " Solomon H Jr 14	S	11	M	1/2	1896	"	9211
12927	8 " Narcissa E 10	S[sic]	7	f	1/2	1896	"	9212
12928	9 " Malina A 7	S[sic]	4	f	1/2	1896	"	9213
12929	10 " Quida L 5	S[sic]	2	f	1/2		"	
I.W. 848	11 " Belle (21)	Wife of No 4	21	F	IW			
	12				#397			

For children of Nos 4 & 11 see NB (Mar 3-05)

ENROLLMENT
OF NOS. 1,2,3,4,5,6,7,8,9,10 HEREON
APPROVED BY THE SECRETARY
OF INTERIOR Mar. 6, 1903

ENROLLMENT
OF NOS. 11 HEREON
APPROVED BY THE SECRETARY
OF INTERIOR May 21, 1904

TRIBAL ENROLLMENT OF PARENTS

	Name of Father	Year	County	Name of Mother	Year	County
1	M Mackey	Dcd	Blue	Melina Fruney		Blue
2	W. W. Hampton		Blue	Judith Hampton	Dcd	Wade
3	No1			No2		
4	No1			No2		
5	No1			No2		
6	No1			No2		
7	No1			No2		
8	No1			No2		
9	No1			No2		
10	No1			No2		
11	James Cantley	Dead	noncitizen	Mollie Cantley		noncitizen

12   No1 on 1896 roll Soloman H McKey

13 No11 transferred from Choctaw card   No2 " " " Elizabeth H "
14 D963 April 15, 1904, see decision of   No3 " " " David M "
15 March 15, 1904   No4 " " " Ben P "
  No5 " " " Willis W "
16 For child of No5 see NB (Apr 26-06) Card #593   No6 " " " Beulah "   Date of Application for Enrollment.
  No7 " " " Solomon H Jr "
  No8 " " " Narcisa "   Spt 8/99
  No9 " " " Aurilla "

182

Choctaw By Blood Enrollment Cards 1898-1914

RESIDENCE:	Tobucksy	COUNTY.	**Choctaw Nation**			**Choctaw Roll** (Not Including Freedmen)		CARD No.	
POST OFFICE:	Alderson							FIELD No. 4683	

Dawes' Roll No.	NAME		Relationship to Person First Named	AGE	SEX	BLOOD	TRIBAL ENROLLMENT		
							Year	County	No.
I.W. 472	1 Brimage John W	48	First Named	45	M	IW	1896	Tobucksy	14305
14450	2 " Minerva	31	w	28	f	3/4	1896	"	922
14451	3 " Josephine	13	d	10	f	3/8	1896	"	923
14452	4 " Nancy	10	d	7	f	3/8	1896	"	924
14453	5 " Emma	8	d	5	f	3/8	1896	"	925
	6								
	7 ENROLLMENT								
	8 OF NOS. 2 3 4 and 5 HEREON APPROVED BY THE SECRETARY								
	9 OF INTERIOR APR 11 1903								
	10 ENROLLMENT								
	11 OF NOS. 1 HEREON APPROVED BY THE SECRETARY								
	12 OF INTERIOR SEP 12 1903								
	13								
	14								
	15								
	16								
	17								

TRIBAL ENROLLMENT OF PARENTS

Name of Father	Year	County	Name of Mother	Year	County
1 Alex Brimage		Non-Cit	Charity Brimage		US Cit
2 Peter Garland	Dcd	San[sic] Bois	Annie Garland	Dcd	San[sic] Bois
3 No1			No2		
4 No1			No2		
5 No1			No2		
6					
7					
8	Admitted by Dawes Commission				
9	Case #~~609~~ 619 No appeal				
10					
11	No1 on 1896 roll Jno. W. Brimage				
12					
13			Date of Application for Enrollment.		
14					
15				Sept 8/99	
16 PO Craig Okla 3/21/08					
17 PO Coleman IT 12/15/04					

Choctaw By Blood Enrollment Cards 1898-1914

Dawes' Roll No.		NAME		Relationship to Person	AGE	SEX	BLOOD	TRIBAL ENROLLMENT		
								Year	County	No.
12930	1	Pusley William W	28	First Named	25	M	1/2	1896	Tobucksy	10218
Dead	2	" Lenora	DEAD	Wife	21	f	1/4	1896	"	10219
12931	3	" Collins G	5	S	2	M	3/8			
	4	" William E	3	S	10 days	M	3/8			
I.W. 849	5	" Lelan		Wife	16	F	IW			
	6									
	7									
	8	No. 2 and 4 HEREON DISMISSED UNDER								
	9	ORDER OF THE COMMISSION TO THE FIVE								
	10	CIVILIZED TRIBES OF MARCH 31, 1905.								
	11	ENROLLMENT OF NOS. 5 HEREON								
	12	APPROVED BY THE SECRETARY OF INTERIOR MAY 21 1904								
	13									
	14									
	15	ENROLLMENT OF NOS. 1 & 3 HEREON								
	16	APPROVED BY THE SECRETARY OF INTERIOR MAR 6 1903								
	17									

TRIBAL ENROLLMENT OF PARENTS

	Name of Father	Year	County	Name of Mother	Year	County
1	Wᵐ Pusley	dead	Tobucksy	Elizabeth Sloan		Tobucksy
2	T J Ryan	"	U S Cit	Lelia E Dawson		Tobucksy
3	No1			No2		
4	No1			No2		
5	Joseph Hendrix		noncitizen	Margie Hendrix		noncitizen
6						
7						
8	No1 transferred from Choctaw card D971 April 15, 1904 See decision of March 15,					
9	No1 on 1896 roll Wᵐ W Pusly					
10	Affidavit as to birth of No4 filed					
11	and acknowledged Nov 24/99. As to					
12	No3 filed and acknowledged Dec 19/99					
13	No.2 Died Oct 6,1899: Proof of death filed Dec 23, 1902					
14	No.4 " Dec 24/1899: " " " " " "					
15	For children of Nos 1 & 5 see NB (Mar 3,1905) #614			#1 to 4.		
16				Date of Application for Enrollment. Sept 8/99		
17				#5 Dec 23, 1902		

Choctaw By Blood Enrollment Cards 1898-1914

RESIDENCE: COUNTY.   **Choctaw Nation**   Choctaw Roll   CARD NO.

POST OFFICE: Savanna, I.T.   (Not Including Freedmen)   FIELD NO. 4685

Dawes' Roll No.	NAME	Relationship to Person First Named	AGE	SEX	BLOOD	TRIBAL ENROLLMENT Year	TRIBAL ENROLLMENT County	TRIBAL ENROLLMENT No.
I.W. 473	1 McCaull, James M 49	First Named	45	M	I.W.	1896	Tobucksy	14865
12932	2 " Ada 31	Wife	28	F	1/16	"	"	9214
12933	3 " John S 12	Son	9	M	1/32	"	"	9215
12934	4 " Mary A 10	Dau	7	F	1/32	"	"	9216
12935	5 " Ida 7	"	4	"	1/32	"	"	9217
12936	6 " Margaret L 5	"	2	"	1/32			
12937	7 " Leonora 2	Dau	1mo	F	1/32			
	8							
	9							
	10							
	11	ENROLLMENT OF NOS. 1 HEREON						
	12	APPROVED BY THE SECRETARY OF INTERIOR SEP 12 1903						
	13							
	14	ENROLLMENT OF NOS. 2,3,4,5,6,7 HEREON						
	15	APPROVED BY THE SECRETARY OF INTERIOR						
	16							
	17							

TRIBAL ENROLLMENT OF PARENTS

	Name of Father	Year	County	Name of Mother	Year	County
1	Jno. F. McCaull		Non Cit	Marg. McCaull		Non Cit
2	Wm Chunn	Dd	Tobucksy	Nancy A Hill		Tobucksy
3	No.1			No.2		
4	" 1			" 2		
5	" 1			" 2		
6	" 1			" 2		
7	No.1			No.2		
8						
9						
10						
11						
12		No.7 Enrolled Feby 8th, 1901		No.1 on roll as Jas. M. McCaull		
13				" 2 " " " Ada McCall		
14				" 3 " " " Jno. "		
15				" 4 " " " Mary "		
				" 5 " " " Ida "		#1 to 6
16						Date of Application for Enrollment.
17						9/8/99

Choctaw By Blood Enrollment Cards 1898-1914

| RESIDENCE: POST OFFICE: McAlester, I.T. | COUNTY. Choctaw Nation | | Choctaw Roll (Not Including Freedmen) | CARD No. FIELD No. 4686 |

Dawes' Roll No.	NAME	Relationship to Person	AGE	SEX	BLOOD	TRIBAL ENROLLMENT		
						Year	County	No.
12938	1 Coley, Gibson DIED PRIOR TO SEPTEMBER 25, 1902	First Named	18	M	Full	1896	Tobucksy	2969
	2							
	3							
	4							
	5							
	6							
	7							
	8							
	9							
	10							
	11							
	12							
	13							
	14							
	15							
	16							
	17							

ENROLLMENT OF NOS. 1 HEREON APPROVED BY THE SECRETARY OF INTERIOR MAR 6 1903

TRIBAL ENROLLMENT OF PARENTS

Name of Father	Year	County	Name of Mother	Year	County
1 Wilson Coley	Dd	Tobucksy	Coley	Dd	Tobucksy
2					
3					
4					
5					
6 No.1 died prior to Sept 25, 1902; Enrollment cancelled by Department May 2, 1906					
7					
8					
9					
10					
11					
12					
13					
14					
15					
16				Date of Application for Enrollment.	
17				9/8/99	

Choctaw By Blood Enrollment Cards 1898-1914

	NAME		Relationship to Person First Named	AGE	SEX	BLOOD	TRIBAL ENROLLMENT		
							Year	County	No.
1	Williams, Frank	32	First Named	29	M	Full	1896	Atoka	14025
2	" Clemmie	27	Wife	23	F	I.W.			
3	" Wilson	7	Son	4	M	1/2	1896	Atoka	14026
4	" Joe	4	"	1	"	1/2			
5									
6									
7									
8									
9									
10									
11	ENROLLMENT								
12	OF NOS. 2 HEREON APPROVED BY THE SECRETARY								
13	OF INTERIOR MAR 14 1905								
14	ENROLLMENT								
15	OF NOS 1,3,4 HEREON APPROVED BY THE SECRETARY								
16	OF INTERIOR								
17									

TRIBAL ENROLLMENT OF PARENTS

	Name of Father	Year	County	Name of M...	Year	County
1	Silas Annkweatobi	Dd	Kiamitia	Mima		Towson
2	Smith		Non Cit	Ann		Non Cit
3	No.1			No.2		
4	" 1			" 2		
5						
6						
7			No2 separated from her husband			
8			about Oct 1/99			
9						
10						
11						
12						
13						
14						
15						
16				te of Application for Enrollment.		
17				9-8-99		

Choctaw By Blood Enrollment Cards 1898-1914

Dawes' Roll No.	NAME		Relationship to Person	AGE	SEX	BLOOD	TRIBAL ENROLLMENT		
							Year	County	No.
12942	1 Folsom, Simpson	25	First Named	22	M	Full	1896	Tobucksy	4017
I.W.770	2 " Annie	37	Wife	37	F	I.W.			
	3								
	4								
	5								
	6								
	7								
	8								
	9								
	10								
	11	ENROLLMENT							
	12	OF NOS. ~~ 2 ~~ HEREON							
	13	APPROVED BY THE SECRETARY OF INTERIOR MAY 7 1904							
	14								
	15								
	16								
	17								

TRIBAL ENROLLMENT OF PARENTS

	Name of Father	Year	County	Name of Mother	Year	County
1	Rufus Folsom	Dd	Tobucksy	Folsom	Dd	Tobucksy
2	Verney Mackey	dead	non-citizen	Mary Mackey	dead	non-citizen
3						
4						
5						
6						
7						
8						
9	№1 is now the husband of Anna Folsom on Choctaw card #D.711, April 15, 1902					
10	No.2 transferred from Choctaw card #D.711: see decision of Feby 27, 1904					
11						
12						
13				on roll as Sim Folsom		
14						
15						
16				Date of Application for Enrollment.		
17				9/8/99		

RESIDENCE: Chickasaw Nation COUNTY. **Choctaw Nation**   **Choctaw Roll**   CARD NO.
POST OFFICE: Wynnewood   *(Not Including Freedmen)* FIELD NO. **4689**

Dawes' Roll No.	NAME	Relationship to Person First Named	AGE	SEX	BLOOD	TRIBAL ENROLLMENT Year	County	No.
✓ * 1	Miller John H	First Named	28	M	1/8		Court	
✓ * 2	" Delilah E	Wife	27	f	IW		"	
✓ * 3	" Frances	d	7	f	1/16		"	
✓ * 4	" James E	S	6	M	1/16			
DEAD. 5	" Della	d	4	f	1/16			
✓ 6	" Newton	S	2	M	1/16			
✓ 7	" Susan Pearl	Dau	16mo	F	1/16			
✓ 8	" Wallice[sic] W	Son	3wks	M	1/16			
9								
10	Nos 6 to 8 DISMISSED MAY 27 1904							
* 11	Nos. 1 to 5 incl denied in C.C.C.C. Case #61 March 9 '04							
12	DENIED CITIZENSHIP BY THE CHOCTAW AND							
13	2,3,4,5 CHICKASAW CITIZENSHIP COURT Mar 9 '04							
14								
15								
16								
17								

TRIBAL ENROLLMENT OF PARENTS

	Name of Father	Year	County	Name of Mother	Year	County
1	Jas J Miller	dead	Non Citizen	Mary Miller	dead	Non Citizen
2	I. N. Bradburn	"	"	Mahala Bradburn	"	"
3	No 1			No 2		
4	No 1			No 2		
5	No 1			No 2		
6	No 1			No 2		
7	Nº 1			Nº 2		
8	No 1			No 2		
9	Nos 1 to 5 incl denied in 96 Case #1282					
10	Judgment of US Ct admitting No 1 to 5 incl vacated and set aside by Decree of C.C.C.C. Decr 17'02 / Nos 1 to 5 incl dism'd in C.C.C.C. Case #61					
11	Admitted by U S Court at So MᶜAlester					
12	Aug 25-1896 #121					
13	As to residence and birth of child see testimony of No 1.					
14	Nº7 Born Nov 1, 1900; enrolled Feby. 27,1902					
15	Evidence of birth of Nº6 received and filed April 9,1902			Date of Application for Enrollment.		
16	No 8 Born June 3ʳᵈ 1902: Enrolled June 27" 1902			Sept 8/99		
17	Post office address is now Hart. I.T.					

Stringtown I.T. 1/5/03

Choctaw By Blood Enrollment Cards 1898-1914

RESIDENCE: Tobucksy   COUNTY.

POST OFFICE: McAlester

Choctaw Nation

Choctaw Roll *(Not Including Freedmen)*

CARD No.

FIELD No. **4690**

Dawes' Roll No.	NAME		Relationship to Person Named	AGE	SEX	BLOOD	TRIBAL ENROLLMENT		
							Year	County	No.
12943	1 Patterson, James	49	First Named	46	M	1/8	1896	Tobucksy	10250
I.W. 1429	2 " Sophronia	42	W	38	f	I.W.			
12944	3 " Robert	22	S	19	M	1/16	1896	Tobucksy	10251
12945	4 " Jesse J	20	S	17	M	1/16	1896	"	10252
12946	5 " Luke	17	S	14	M	1/16	1896	"	10253
12947	6 " Oscar	13	S	10	M	1/16	1896	"	10254
12948	7 " Lewis	10	S	7	M	1/16	1896	"	10255
12949	8 " Edmund	8	S	5	M	1/16	1896	"	10256
12950	9 " Green	6	S	3	M	1/16	1896	"	10257
12951	10 " Simon L	3	S	1 day	M	1/16			
	11								
	12		ENROLLMENT OF NOS. ~~ 2 ~~ HEREON APPROVED BY THE SECRETARY OF INTERIOR Jun 12 1905						
	13								
	14	ENROLLMENT OF NOS. 1,3,4,5,6,7,8,9,10 HEREON APPROVED BY THE SECRETARY OF INTERIOR Mar. 6, 1903							
	17								

TRIBAL ENROLLMENT OF PARENTS

	Name of Father	Year	County	Name of Mother	Year	County
1	Jas Patterson		Non-Citizen	Sarah Patterson	Dead	Choctaw
2	Jesse Downing		" "	Lizzie Downing		Non Cit
3	No.1			No.2		
4	No.1			No.2		
5	No.1			No.2		
6	No.1			No.2		
7	No.1			No.2		
8	No.1			No.2		
9	No.1			No.2		
10	No.1			No.2		
11						
12			For child of No.3 see NB (Mar 3'05) Card #350			
			No 4 on 1896 roll Jesse Patterson			
13						
14	Nos 1-2-3&4 admitted by Act of Choctaw Council #50				Date of Application for Enrollment.	
15	approved Nov 6th 84					
16	certified copy of Act of Choctaw Council admitting No.1 and family filed Dec 15, 1902 with Choctaw Card #2857				Sept 8/99	
17						

P.O. Alderson I.T. 1/7/05

190

Choctaw By Blood Enrollment Cards 1898-1914

RESIDENCE: Sans Bois   COUNTY. **Choctaw Nation**   **Choctaw Roll**   CARD NO.
POST OFFICE: Stigler   *(Not Including Freedmen)*   FIELD NO. **4691**

Dawes' Roll No.	NAME		Relationship to Person First Named	AGE	SEX	BLOOD	TRIBAL ENROLLMENT		
							Year	County	No.
12952	1 Folsom, Daniel	27	First Named	24	M	1/2	1896	Sans Bois	3841
I.W. 474	2 " Vina	25	wife	22	f	I.W.	1896	" "	14513
12953	3 " Mabel	6	d	3	f	1/4	1896	" "	3842
12954	4 " Iva L	4	d	1½	f	1/4			
12955	5 " Elias Smedley	2	Son	2mo	M	1/4			
12956	6 " Zora E	1	Dau	7mo	F	1/4			
	7								
	8								
	9								
	10								
	11	ENROLLMENT OF NOS. 2 HEREON APPROVED BY THE SECRETARY OF INTERIOR Sep 12 1903							
	12								
	13								
	14	ENROLLMENT OF NOS. 1,3,4,5,6 HEREON APPROVED BY THE SECRETARY OF INTERIOR Mar. 6, 1903							
	15								
	16								
	17								

TRIBAL ENROLLMENT OF PARENTS

	Name of Father	Year	County	Name of Mother	Year	County
1	Elias Folsom		San[sic] Bois	Elzina Folsom	Dead	San[sic] Bois
2	Pink Brewer		Non Citizen	Amanda Brewer		U.S. Citizen
3	No.1			No.2		
4	No.1			No.2		
5	No.1			No.2		
6	No.1			No.2		
7						
8						
9						
10				#1 to 4		
11				Date of Application for Enrollment.		
12				Sept. 8/99		
13						
14						
15						
16	No.5 Enrolled June 26, 1900					
17	No.6 Born Sept. 3, 1901: enrolled April 16, 1902					

Choctaw By Blood Enrollment Cards 1898-1914

RESIDENCE: Tobucksy COUNTY. **Choctaw Nation**
POST OFFICE: Krebs

Choctaw Roll CARD NO.
(Not Including Freedmen) FIELD NO. **4692**

Dawes' Roll No.	NAME		Relationship to Person	AGE	SEX	BLOOD	TRIBAL ENROLLMENT		
							Year	County	No.
12957	1 Riddle, Sallie	63	First Named	60	f	full	1896	Tobucksy	13038
	2								
	3								
	4								
	5								
	6								
	7								
	8								
	9								
	10								
	11								
	12								
	13	ENROLLMENT							
	14	OF NOS. 1 HEREON APPROVED BY THE SECRETARY							
	15	OF INTERIOR Mar 6 1903							
	16								
	17								

TRIBAL ENROLLMENT OF PARENTS

	Name of Father	Year	County	Name of Mother	Year	County
1	Willis	dead	Tobucksy	Liza Ann	dead	Choctaw
2						
3						
4						
5		On roll Sallie Willis				
6						
7						
8						
9		Admitted by Act of Choctaw Council				
10		#15, approved Apl 8th 1891, as Liney Willis				
11						
12						
13						
14					Date of Application for Enrollment.	
15						
16					Sept. 8/99	
17						

192

Choctaw By Blood Enrollment Cards 1898-1914

RESIDENCE: Atoka   COUNTY: **Choctaw Nation**   **Choctaw Roll** *(Not Including Freedmen)*   CARD NO.
POST OFFICE: Atoka   FIELD NO. **4693**

Dawes' Roll No.	NAME	Relationship to Person First Named	AGE	SEX	BLOOD	TRIBAL ENROLLMENT Year	County	No.
12958	1 Edwards, Eli 43	First Named	40	M	1/2	1893	Atoka	242
12959	2 " , Isaac 33	bro	30	M	1/2	1893	"	243
	3							
	4							
	5							
	6							
	7							
	8							
	9							
	10							
	11							
	12							
	13							
	14							
	15							
	16							
	17							

ENROLLMENT
OF NOS. 1&2 HEREON
APPROVED BY THE SECRETARY
OF INTERIOR Mar 6, 1903

TRIBAL ENROLLMENT OF PARENTS

	Name of Father	Year	County	Name of Mother	Year	County
1	Tobias Edwards		Jackson	Rhoda Edwards	dead	Scullyville[sic]
2	Tobias Edwards		"	" "		
3						
4						
5						
6	No.1 on Atoka payroll 93 p. 23 #242, as Ely Edwards					
7	No.2 " " " " #93 p.23 #243					
8						
9						
10	For children of No.1 see NB (March 3,1905) Card #351					
11						
12						
13						
14					Date of Application for Enrollment.	
15						
16					Sept 8/99	
17	P.O. Lehigh I.T. 8/30/05					

Choctaw By Blood Enrollment Cards 1898-1914

RESIDENCE:	Tobucksy	COUNTY.		
POST OFFICE:	Krebbs			

Choctaw Nation

Choctaw Roll (Not Including Freedmen)

CARD No.

FIELD No. **4694**

Dawes' Roll No.	NAME	Relationship to Person	AGE	SEX	BLOOD	TRIBAL ENROLLMENT		
						Year	County	No.
12960 1	Frazier, Amziah	First Named	26	M	Full	1896	Tobucksy	4007
12961 2	" Lou	Wife	21	f	Full	1896	"	11306
DEAD 3	" Jimmie	S	1	M	"			
4								
5								
6								
7								
8								
9								
10								
11								
12								
13								
14								
15								
16								
17								

ENROLLMENT
OF NOS. 1 & 2 HEREON
APPROVED BY THE SECRETARY
OF INTERIOR MAR 6 1903

TRIBAL ENROLLMENT OF PARENTS

	Name of Father	Year	County	Name of Mother	Year	County
1	Sweeny Frazier	Dead	Tobucksy	Louisa Frazier	Dead	Tobucksy
2	Wallace Sam	"	"	Fannie Sam		Do
3	No.1			No.2		
4						
5						
6						
7	No.1 On roll 1896 Ameziah Frazier					
8	No.2 " " " Lou Sam					
9						
10						
11						
12						
13	No.3 died in October 1899. Proof of death filed January 14, 1905.					
14						
15						
16					Sept. 8/99	
17						

Choctaw By Blood Enrollment Cards 1898-1914

RESIDENCE:	COUNTY.							
POST OFFICE: So MᶜAlester, I.T.	**Choctaw Nation**		**Choctaw Roll** (Not Including Freedmen)			CARD NO. FIELD NO. 4695		

Dawes' Roll No.	NAME	Relationship to Person	AGE	SEX	BLOOD	TRIBAL ENROLLMENT		
						Year	County	No.
12962	1 Shults, Sophia 33	First Named	30	F	1/16	1896	Tobucksy	11301
	2							
	3							
	4							
	5							
	6							
	7							
	8							
	9							
	10							
	11							
	12							
	13							
	14							
	15							
	16							
	17							

ENROLLMENT
OF NOS. 1 HEREON
APPROVED BY THE SECRETARY
MAR 6 1903

TRIBAL ENROLLMENT OF PARENTS

	Name of Father	Year	County	Name of Mother	Year	County
1	John Shults	Dd	Non Cit	Paulina Shults	Dd	Tobucksy
2						
3						
4						
5						
6						
7						
8						
9						
10						
11						
12			on roll as Sophia Shetize			
13						
14						
15						
16						Date of Application for Enrollment.
17						9/11/99

Choctaw By Blood Enrollment Cards 1898-1914

Dawes' Roll No.	NAME	Relationship to Person First Named	AGE	SEX	BLOOD	TRIBAL ENROLLMENT		
						Year	County	No.
12963	1 Carney, Serena 24	First Named	21	F	Full	1896	San[sic] Bois	2158
	2							
	3							
	4							
	5							
	6							
	7							
	8							
	9							
	10							
	11							
	12							
	13							
	14							
	15							
	16							
	17							

MAR 6 1903

TRIBAL ENROLLMENT OF PARENTS

	Name of Father	Year	County	Name of Mother	Year	County
1	Billy Willis	Dd	Tobucksy	Malali	Dd	
2						
3						
4						
5						
6						
7						
8						
9						
10						
11						
12						
13						
14						
15						
16						
17						

Date of Application for Enrollment. 9/8/99

Choctaw By Blood Enrollment Cards 1898-1914

RESIDENCE:
POST OFFICE: So. McAlester, I.T.   COUNTY. **Choctaw Nation**   **Choctaw Roll** *(Not Including Freedmen)*   CARD No. FIELD No. **4697**

Dawes' Roll No.	NAME		Relationship to Person	AGE	SEX	BLOOD	TRIBAL ENROLLMENT		
							Year	County	No.
I.W. 475	1 Watson, Amasa	46	First Named	43	M	I.W.	1896	Tobucksy	15159
12964	2 " Frances M	28	Wife	25	F	1/4	1896	"	13002
12965	3 " Mary R	8	Dau	5	F	1/8	1896	"	13003
12966	4 " Amasa H	5	Son	1½	M	1/8			
12967	5 " Sudie F	1	Dau	3wks	F	1/8			
	6								
	7								
	8								
	9								
	10								
	11								
	12								
	13								
	14								
	15								
	16								
	17								

ENROLLMENT OF NOS. 1 HEREON APPROVED BY THE SECRETARY OF INTERIOR SEP 12 1903

ENROLLMENT OF NOS. 2 3 4 5 HEREON APPROVED BY THE SECRETARY OF INTERIOR MAR 6 1905

TRIBAL ENROLLMENT OF PARENTS

	Name of Father	Year	County	Name of Mother	Year	County
1	W. A. Watson		Non Cit	S. A. Watson		Non Cit
2	Ben Jones	Dd	Tobucksy	Jennie Jones	Dd	Tobucksy
3	No.1			No.2		
4	" 1			" 2		
5	No.1			No2		
6						
7						
8						
9						
10						
11			No1 admitted by Dawes Comm. #541 no appeal			
12			X As to parents[sic] marriage see enrollment of Mary			
13			on Cherokee roll - see to this. Also see testimony No.1			
14						
15			No4 Affidavit irregular and returned for			
16			correction. Returned corrected and filed Mar. 14,1900			
17	12/23/02 PO McAlester IT		No 5 Enrolled June 24, 1901		Date of Application for Enrollment.	9/8/99

Evidence of marriage between Nos 1 and 2 filed June 24, 1901

Choctaw By Blood Enrollment Cards 1898-1914

RESIDENCE:	Atoka	COUNTY.	**Choctaw Nation**		**Choctaw Roll**	CARD NO.	
POST OFFICE:	Legal				*(Not Including Freedmen)*	FIELD NO. **4698**	

Dawes' Roll No.	NAME		Relationship to Person	AGE	SEX	BLOOD	TRIBAL ENROLLMENT		
							Year	County	No.
I.W.930	1 King, Mary Y	(58)	First Named	55	f	IW	1896	Atoka	14732
	2								
	3								
	4								
	5								
	6	Take no further action [Illegible...]							
	7	[Illegible...]							
	8	Protest overrules by Jan 23 '04							
		Dept March 28, 1904							
	9								
	10								
	11								
	12	ENROLLMENT OF NOS. 1 HEREON							
	13	APPROVED BY THE SECRETARY							
	14	OF INTERIOR AUG 3 1904							
	15								
	16								
	17								

TRIBAL ENROLLMENT OF PARENTS

	Name of Father	Year	County	Name of Mother	Year	County
1	Robt Cummings	dead	Non Cit	Elizabeth Cummings	Dead	US Cit
2						
3						
4						
5	No 1 on 1885 Roll Sans Bois Co No 383 as Mary King 42 years old					
6	James King 1885 Sans Bois Co No 382					
7	No.1 is divorced wife of Anderson King on Choctaw card					
8	No. 4053, and No 11334 on final roll, approved Mar 10, '03					
9						
10						
11						
12						
13						
14						
15					Date of Application for Enrollment.	
16						
17	PO Ashland IT 2/8/04				9- 8 - 99	

198

Choctaw By Blood Enrollment Cards 1898-1914

RESIDENCE: Atoka   COUNTY. **Choctaw Nation**   **Choctaw Roll** *(Not Including Freedmen)*   CARD NO.
POST OFFICE: Atoka   FIELD NO. 4699

Dawes' Roll No.	NAME	Relationship to Person	AGE	SEX	BLOOD	TRIBAL ENROLLMENT		
						Year	County	No.
12968	1 Harkins Alonzo J 43	First Named	40	M	1/4	1896	Atoka	5947
12969	2 " Nancy J 47	Wife	44	f	1/4	1896	"	5948
12970	3 " Edward S 27	S Son	24	M	1/4	1896	"	5949
	4							
	5							
	6							
	7							
	8							
	9							
	10							
	11							
	12							
	13							
	14							
	15							
	16							
	17							

ENROLLMENT
OF NOS. 1,2,3 HEREON
APPROVED BY THE SECRETARY
OF INTERIOR MAR 6 1903

TRIBAL ENROLLMENT OF PARENTS

	Name of Father	Year	County	Name of Mother	Year	County
1	Clay Harkins	dead	Atoka	Melvina Harkins	Dead	Atoka
2	Jno Spring	"	Wade	Sally A Spring	"	Wade
3	Dave Harkins	"	Atoka	No2		
4						
5						
6						
7	No1 on 1896 roll A J Harkins					
8	No3 " " " Ed S Do					
9						
10						
11						
12						
13						
14						
15				Date of Application for Enrollment.		
16				Sept 9 - 1899		
17						

Choctaw By Blood Enrollment Cards 1898-1914

RESIDENCE: COUNTY. **Choctaw Nation**   **Choctaw Roll**   CARD NO.
POST OFFICE: So McAlester, I.T.   *(Not Including Freedmen)*   FIELD NO. 4700

Dawes' Roll No.	NAME	Relationship to Person First Named	AGE	SEX	BLOOD	TRIBAL ENROLLMENT		
						Year	County	No.
I.W. 931	1 Grant, Henry ⑤⑥	Named	51	M	I.W.	1896	Tobucksy	15097
12971	2 " Minnie 36	Wife	33	F	1/16	"	"	12039
12972	3 " Minnie Jr 13	Dau	10	F	1/32	"	"	12040
12973	4 " Mary 12	"	9	F	1/32	"	"	12041
12974	5 " Frank 10	Son	7	M	1/32	"	"	12042
12975	6 " John 5	"	2	M	1/32			
12976	7 " Charley 2	Son	1mo	M	1/32			
	8							
	9	ENROLLMENT						
	10	OF NOS. 1 HEREON						
	11	APPROVED BY THE SECRETARY OF INTERIOR AUG 3 1904						
	12							
	13							
	14	ENROLLMENT						
	15	OF NOS. 2,3,4,5,6,7 HEREON APPROVED BY THE SECRETARY						
	16	OF INTERIOR MAR 6 1903						
	17							

TRIBAL ENROLLMENT OF PARENTS

	Name of Father	Year	County	Name of Mother	Year	County
1	W. Grant	Dd	Non Cit	Eve Grant	Dd	Non Cit
2	John Shults	"	Atoka	Paulina Shults	"	Atoka
3	No.1			No.2		
4	" 1			" 2		
5	" 1			" 2		
6	" 1			" 2		
7	No.1			No.2		
8						
9						
10				No.4 on roll as Mary A. Grant.		
11	No.7 Enrolled March 7th, 1901					
12						
13						
14	For child of No3 see NB (Apr 26-06) Card #423					
15	" " " " 2 " " (Mar 3'05) " #352				#1 to 6	
16					Date of Application for Enrollment.	
17					9/11/99	

200

Choctaw By Blood Enrollment Cards 1898-1914

RESIDENCE: Atoka COUNTY. **Choctaw Nation** Choctaw Roll CARD No.
POST OFFICE: Legal, I.T. (Not Including Freedmen) FIELD No. 4701

Dawes' Roll No.	NAME		Relationship to Person	AGE	SEX	BLOOD	TRIBAL ENROLLMENT		
							Year	County	No.
12977	1 King, Mack	29	First Named	26	M	Full	1896	San[sic] Bois	7438
12978	2 " Lizzie	21	Wife	18	F	"	"	" "	7439
12979	3 " Josephine	6	Dau	3	F	"	"	" "	7440
~~12980~~	4 DIED PRIOR TO SEPTEMBER 25, 1902 ~~Sophia~~		"	1	F	"			
15850	5 " Rady		"	1	F	"			
	6								
	7								
	8								
	9	ENROLLMENT OF NOS. 5 HEREON							
	10	APPROVED BY THE SECRETARY							
	11	OF INTERIOR JUN 12 1905							
	12								
	13								
	14	ENROLLMENT OF NOS. 1,2,3,4							
	15	APPROVED BY THE SECRETARY							
	16	OF INTERIOR MAR 6 1903							
	17								

TRIBAL ENROLLMENT OF PARENTS

	Name of Father	Year	County	Name of Mother	Year	County
1	Levi King	Dd	Skullyville	Mary King	Dd	San[sic] Bois
2	Jerry Folsom		Sugar Loaf	Nancy Folsom	Dd	" "
3	No.1			No.2		
4	" 1			" 2		
5	" 1			" 2		
6						
7						
8						
9	No.4 died Jan 15, 1903. Enrollment cancelled by Department July 8, 1904					
10	No5 was born July 5, 1902: application received and No5 placed on this					
11	card April 6, 1905, under Act of Congress approved March 3, 1905 For child of No.2 see NB (March 3, 1905) #733 No.1 on roll as Mike King					
12						
13						
14						
15					#1 to 4	
16					Date of Application for Enrollment.	
17	P.O. No2 McCurtain I.T. 3/6/05					9/11/99

Choctaw By Blood Enrollment Cards 1898-1914

Choctaw Nation   Choctaw Roll CARD NO.

ICE: Thurman   *(Not Including Freedmen)* FIELD NO. 4702

NAME	Relationship to Person	AGE	SEX	BLOOD	TRIBAL ENROLLMENT		
					Year	County	No.
1 Byington David J 40	First Named	43	M	Full	1896	Tobucksy	889
2 " Winnie E 31	Wife	28	f	"	1896	"	890
3 " Rosa 19	D	16	f	"	1896	"	891
4 " Simon W 11	S	8	m	"	1896	"	892
5							
6							
7							
8							
9							
10							
11							
12							
13							
14							
15							
16							
17							

ENROLLMENT OF NOS. 1,2,3,4 HEREON APPROVED BY THE SECRETARY OF INTERIOR MAR 6 1903

TRIBAL ENROLLMENT OF PARENTS

Name of Father	Year	County	Name of Mother	Year	County
1 Albert Byington	Dead	Blue	Annie Byington	Dead	Blue
2 Simon Hancock	"	San[sic] Bois	Maggie Hancock		San[sic] Bois
3 No 1			Harriet Byington	Dead	Tobucksy
4 No 1			Do Do		
5					
6					
7					
8	No3 on 1896 roll Rosie E Byington				
9	No4 " " " Simon W Do				
10					
11					
12					
13					
14					
15				Date of Application for Enrollment.	
16					
17				Sep 11, 1899	

Choctaw By Blood Enrollment Cards 1898-1914

RESIDENCE: Atoka COUNTY. **Choctaw Nation** Choctaw Roll CARD
POST OFFICE: Kiowa, I.T. *(Not Including Freedmen)* FIELD

Dawes' Roll No.		NAME		Relationship to Person First Named	AGE	SEX	BLOOD	TRIBAL ENROLLMENT		
								Year	County	No.
I.W. 574	1	Krieger, William	45	First Named	42	M	I.W.	1896	Atoka	14733
12985	2	" Margaret A	34	Wife	31	F	1/32	1893	"	641
12986	3	" Chrystal E	17	Dau	14	"	1/64	1893	"	642
12987	4	" William E	15	Son	12	M	"	1893	"	643
12988	5	" Estelle L	13	Dau	10	F	"	1893	"	644
12989	6	" Ethel L	13	"	10	"	"	1893	"	645
12990	7	" Clarence S	10	Son	7	M	"	1893	"	646
12991	8	" Henry	7	"	3	"	"			
12992	9	" Jesse L	5	"	2	"	"	ENROLLMENT OF NOS. ~~~ 1 ~~~ HEREON APPROVED BY THE SECRETARY		
12993	10	" Mary D	3	Dau	9^{d}	F	"	OF INTERIOR FEB -8 1904		
12993	11	" Karl E	1	Son	1mo	M	"			
	12	ENROLLMENT								
	13	OF NOS. 2 3 4 5 6 7 8 9 10 & 11 HEREON								
	14	APPROVED BY THE SECRETARY OF INTERIOR MAR 19 1903								
	15	No 1 admitted by Dawes Com in 1896								
	16	Case No 1206								
		1 & 2 see NB (March 3 1905) #780								
		~~1901: Enrolled Dec 28, 1901~~								

TRIBAL ENROLLMENT OF PARENTS

	Name of Father	Year	County	Name of Mother	Year	County
1	Chas. Krieger		Non Cit	Mary Krieger		Non Cit
2	J.M. Lowry		Chick. Nat	Maggie McGee	Dd	Red River
3	No.1			No.2		
4	" 1			" 2		
5	" 1			" 2		
6	" 1			" 2		
7	" 1			" 2		
8	" 1			" 2		
9	" 1			" 2		
10	" 1			" 2		
11	" 1			" 2		
12	No.1 on roll as William Kragger			For child of No.3 see NB (March 3,1905) #782		
13	" 2 " p. 62 #641-93 P.R. Atoka Co as Margret A Kreiger[sic]					
14	" 3 " p. 62 #642-93 " " " " " Christina E Krieger.					
15	" 4 " p. 62 #643-93 " " " " " " Laura E Krieger.					#1 to 10 Date of Application for Enrollment.
16	" 5 " p. 62 #644-93 " " " " " " Ethel Krieger.					
17	" 6 " p. 62 #645-93 " " " " " " Clarence Krieger.					9/11/99

Choctaw By Blood Enrollment Cards 1898-1914

RESIDENCE:		COUNTY.							
POST OFFICE: McAlester, I.T.		**Choctaw Nation**				**Choctaw Roll** (Not Including Freedmen)		CARD No. FIELD No. **4704**	

Dawes' Roll No.	NAME	Relationship to Person Named	AGE	SEX	BLOOD	TRIBAL ENROLLMENT		
						Year	County	No.
I.W.476	1 Krieger, Frederick C (51)	First Named	48	M	I.W.	1896	Tobucksy	14723
12995	2 " Catherine M 41	Wife	38	F	1/4	"	"	7498
12996	3 " Rosa E 22	Dau	19	"	1/8	"	"	7499
12997	4 " Arthur B 19	Son	16	M	"	"	"	7500
12998	5 " Charles F 15	"	12	"	"	"	"	7501
12999	6 " Irena 13	Dau	10	F	"	"	"	7502
13000	7 " Dee S 9	Son	6	M	"	"	"	7503
13001	8 " Mattie E 7	Dau	4	F	"	"	"	7504
13002	9 " Francis S 5	Son	2	M	"			
	10							

No.3 now the wife of Isiah Hodges non-citizen. Evidence of marriage filed July 14-1902.

11

12

13 No 1 admitted by Dawes Com in 1896, Case No. 1205

14

ENROLLMENT OF NOS. 2,3,4,5,6,7,8 & 9 HEREON APPROVED BY THE SECRETARY OF INTERIOR Mar. 19, 1903

For child of No.6 see NB (Apr 26 '06) #1288

15

16

17

TRIBAL ENROLLMENT OF PARENTS					
Name of Father	Year	County	Name of Mother	Year	County
1 Chas Krieger		Non Cit	C. M. Kreiger[sic]		Non Cit
2 B. H. Lowry	Dd	Tobucksy	Lucy Lowry	Dd	Tobucksy
3 No.1			No.2		
4 " 1			" 2		
5 " 1			" 2		
6 " 1			" 2		
7 " 1			" 2		
8 " 1			" 2		
9 " 1			" 2		
10					
11			No.1 On roll as Fred C Kraiger		
12			" 2 " " " Minerva		
13			" 3 " " " Rosa A		
			" 4 " " " Arthur A		
14			" 5 " " " Charlie		
15			" 6 " " " Irene		
16			" 7 " " " D. S.		
17			" 8 " " " Mattie		

ENROLLMENT OF NOS. 1 HEREON APPROVED BY THE SECRETARY OF INTERIOR Sep. 12 1903

Date of Application for Enrollment.

9/11/99

Choctaw By Blood Enrollment Cards 1898-1914

RESIDENCE: Atoka   COUNTY. **Choctaw Nation**   **Choctaw Roll**   CARD NO.

POST OFFICE: Atoka   *(Not Including Freedmen)*   FIELD NO. 4705

Dawes' Roll No.	NAME	Relationship to Person First Named	AGE	SEX	BLOOD	TRIBAL ENROLLMENT Year	County	No.
I.W. 477	1 McClendon James W³⁴	First Named	33	M	IW	1896	Atoka	14876
18003	2 " Kate ³¹	wife	28	f	1/4	1896	"	9431
	3							
	4							
	5							
	6							
	7							
	8							
	9							
	10							
	11							
	12							
	13							
	14							
	15							
	16							
	17							

ENROLLMENT
OF NOS.   1   HEREON
APPROVED BY THE SECRETARY
OF INTERIOR   SEP 12 1903

ENROLLMENT
OF NOS. ~ 2 ~ HEREON
APPROVED BY THE SECRETARY
OF INTERIOR   MAR 19 1903

TRIBAL ENROLLMENT OF PARENTS

	Name of Father	Year	County	Name of Mother	Year	County
1						
2	Dave Harkins	Dead	Atoka	Nancy Harkins		Atoka
3						
4						
5						
6						
7	No 1 admitted by Dawes Commission					
8	Case #1294 as J. W. McClendon					
9						
10	No 1 on 1896 roll as J W McClendon					
11	No 2 " " " " Mrs Kate "					
12						
13						
14						
15					Date of Application for Enrollment.	
16					Sept 9 - 1899	
17						

Choctaw By Blood Enrollment Cards 1898-1914

| RESIDENCE: | Atoka | COUNTY. | | **Choctaw Nation** | | | **Choctaw Roll** *(Not Including Freedmen)* | | CARD NO. |
| POST OFFICE: | Atoka | | | | | | | | FIELD NO. **4706** |

Dawes' Roll No.	NAME	Relationship to Person First Named	AGE	SEX	BLOOD	TRIBAL ENROLLMENT		
						Year	County	No.
I.W. 1479	1 Oldham, Minnie ²⁸		25	f	I.W.			
15691	2 Jackson, Annie N ⁷	D	4	f	3/8			
	3							
	4							
	5							
	6							
	7							
	8							
	9							
	10							
	11							
	12							
	13							

ENROLLMENT
OF NOS. ~~ 2 ~~ HEREON
APPROVED BY THE SECRETARY
OF INTERIOR Dec. 2 - 1904

ENROLLMENT
OF NOS. One HEREON
APPROVED BY THE SECRETARY
OF INTERIOR Aug 22 1905

TRIBAL ENROLLMENT OF PARENTS

	Name of Father	Year	County	Name of Mother	Year	County
1	Jno. Gilbert		Non Cit	Lina Gilbert		Non Cit
2	Pete Jackson	dead	Atoka	No.1		
3						
4						
5						
6						
7						

As to marriage & birth of child see
testimony of No.1 & Rebecca Jackson.
Father of No.2 Pete Jackson on 1896 roll, Atoka Co. No. 7313
Nº1 is now the wife of J.G. Oldham a non-citizen. Evidence of
marriage filed May 21, 1902.
No.2 Born Oct. 16, 1896, proof of birth filed March 20,
No.1 formerly wife of Pete Jackson, 1896, Atoka No. 7313, now deceased
For children of No.1 see NB (Apr 26 '06) #1152

Date of Application for Enrollment.
Sept. 9ᵗʰ 1899

Date of Application for Enrollment.

P.O. Tuskahoma

206

Choctaw By Blood Enrollment Cards 1898-1914

Dawes' Roll No.	NAME		Relationship to Person First Named	AGE	SEX	BLOOD	TRIBAL ENROLLMENT		
							Year	County	No.
13004	1 Wilson Emma	28	First Named	25	f	1/4	1896	Gaines	12903
13005	2 Moore John H	11	S	8	m	1/8	1896	"	8543
13006	3 " Oscar	8	S	5	"	1/8	1896	"	8544
13007	4 Argo Louis	13	S	10	"	Full	1896	"	94
	5								
	6								
	7								
	8								
	9								
	10								
	11								
	12								
	13								
	14								
	15								
	16								
	17								

ENROLLMENT
OF NOS. 1 2 3 & 4 HEREON
APPROVED BY THE SECRETARY
OF INTERIOR MAR 19 1903

TRIBAL ENROLLMENT OF PARENTS

	Name of Father	Year	County	Name of Mother	Year	County
1	M J Katubbee	dead	Tobucksy	Margaret Johnson		Tobucksy
2	Jno Moore	"	Non-Citizen	No1		"
3	" "	"	" "	No1		"
4	Dave Thomas	"	Atoka	No1		"
5						
6						
7						
8						
9		No2 on 1896 roll Jno Heny[sic] Moore				
10		No3 " " " G O B "				
11		No4 adopted by William G Argo white man in Probate Court				
12		Sebastian Co Ark July 25-1892				
13						
14					Date of Application for Enrollment.	
15						
16					Sept 9 - 1899	
17						

Choctaw By Blood Enrollment Cards 1898-1914

Choctaw Nation

Choctaw Roll *(Not Including Freedmen)*

CARD No.
FIELD No. 4708

Dawes' Roll No.	NAME	Relationship to Person First Named	AGE	SEX	BLOOD	TRIBAL ENROLLMENT Year	TRIBAL ENROLLMENT County	TRIBAL ENROLLMENT No.
13008	1 Willis Lee ²⁸		20	M	Full	1896	Tobucksy	13037
	2							
	3							
	4							
	5							
	6							
	7							
	8							
	9							
	10							
	11							
	12							
	13							
	14							
	15							
	16							
	17							

ENROLLMENT
OF NOS. 1 HEREON
APPROVED BY THE SECRETARY
OF INTERIOR MAR 19 1903

TRIBAL ENROLLMENT OF PARENTS

Name of Father	Year	County	Name of Mother	Year	County
1 Willis	dead		Emma Willis	Dead	
2					
3					
4					
5					
6	No1 admitted by Act of Choctaw Council of April 8, 1891				
7					
8					
9					
10					
11					
12			Date of Application for Enrollment.	Sept 9 - 1899	
13					
14					
15					
16					
17					

Choctaw By Blood Enrollment Cards 1898-1914

Choctaw Nation

Choctaw Roll (Not Including Freedmen)

CARD NO. FIELD NO. **4709**

Dawes' Roll No.	NAME		Relationship to Person	AGE	SEX	BLOOD	TRIBAL ENROLLMENT		
							Year	County	No.
13009	1 Lewis, Simon E	61	First Named	58	M	1/8	1896	Tobucksy	7875
IW 478	2 " Martha J	41	Wife	38	f	I.W.	1896	"	14958
13010	3 " Simon F	21	S	18	M	1/16	1896	"	7876
13011	4 " George C	19	S	16	M	1/16	1896	"	7877
13012	5 Williams Julia A	16	d	13	f	1/16	1896	"	7878
13013	6 Lewis, Ruth	14	d	11	f	1/16	1896	"	7879
13014	7 " John Calvin	1	Gr. Son	5mo	M	1/32			
I.W. 771	8 Lewis, Rosa	21	Wife of No 3	21	f	I.W.			
	9	ENROLLMENT							
	10	OF NOS. ~~~ 8 ~~~ HEREON APPROVED BY THE SECRETARY							
	11	OF INTERIOR May -7 - 1904							
	12	ENROLLMENT							
	13	OF NOS. 2 HEREON APPROVED BY THE SECRETARY							
	14	OF INTERIOR Sep 12 1903							
	15	ENROLLMENT							
	16	OF NOS. 1,3,4,5,6 & 7 HEREON APPROVED BY THE SECRETARY							
	17	OF INTERIOR Mar 19 1903							

TRIBAL ENROLLMENT OF PARENTS

	Name of Father	Year	County	Name of Mother	Year	County
1	Jno. T.W. Lewis	dead	Scullyville[sic]	Levina Lewis	dead	Cedar
2	Geo D Beard	"	U.S. Citizen	Ann Beard	"	U.S. Citizen
3	No.1			No.2		
4	No.1			No.2		
5	No.1			No.2		
6	No.1			No.2		
7	No.3			Rosa Lee Lewis		white woman
8	Hiram Blauset		noncitizen	Martha Blauset		non citizen

9 For child of No 4 see NB (Apr 26-06) Card #405   For child of No5 see NB (March 3,1905) #757
10 " " " " 3 " " " " " #1155
11 No.1 on 1896 roll Simeon E Lewis
12 3 " " " Simeon F "
13 4 " " " G. Clay "
14 5 " " " Julia E "
No2 admitted by Dawes Com Case #1229
#1 to 6 inc
Sept. 1899
Date of Application for Enrollment.

No.3 is the husband of Rosa Lewis on Choctaw card #D.530
15 No.7 Born Feby 28,1902; enrolled July 25, 1902
No.8 transferred from Choctaw Card #D530: See decision of Feby 29, 1904
16 No.5 is now wife of Robert Williams, a noncitz. Evidence of marriage filed Dec. 30, 1902
17 No.5 P.O. McAlester I.T.

RESIDENCE: Chickasaw Nation COUNTY.
POST OFFICE: Lone Grove

Choctaw Nation

Choctaw Roll
(Not Including Freedmen)

CARD NO.
FIELD NO. **4710**

Dawes' Roll No.	NAME	Relationship to Person First Named	AGE	SEX	BLOOD	TRIBAL ENROLLMENT		
						Year	County	No.
✓ 1	Frazier, Louisa T	Named	19	f			Court	
2	" Henry L	Son	4mo	m				
3								
4								
5								
6								
	#1 - 2 DISMISSED							
8	Sep. 20 1904							
9								
10								
11								
12								
13								
14								
15								
16								
17								

TRIBAL ENROLLMENT OF PARENTS

Name of Father	Year	County	Name of Mother	Year	County
1 Jack Vernon	Dead		Mattie Vernon		Chickasaw Nation
2 Isaac S Frazier		non-citizen	No.1		
3					
4 No.1 denied in 96 Case #250					
5 Admitted by the U.S. Court at So McAlester					
6 Aug 26/1899 Case #98, as Laura T. Vernon					
As to residence see her testimony					
7 Judgement[sic] of U.S. Court admitting No1 vacated and set aside by Decree of Choctaw Chickasaw Citizenship Court Dec 17'02					
8 No.1 should be Louisa T Vernon, and was admitted by the					
9 Court, as Louisa T. Vernon; see original judgment in said case					
10					
11 No 2 Enrolled Aug 29th, 1900					
12 No appeal to C.C.C.C.					
13					
14				Date of Application for Enrollment.	
15					
16				Sept. 9th 1899	
17					

210

Choctaw By Blood Enrollment Cards 1898-1914

RESIDENCE: Tobucksy COUNTY. **Choctaw Nation** Choctaw Roll CARD NO.
POST OFFICE: Savanna (Not Including Freedmen) FIELD No. 4711

Dawes' Roll No.	NAME	Relationship to Person First Named	AGE	SEX	BLOOD	TRIBAL ENROLLMENT		
						Year	County	No.
I.W. 772	1 Culbertson, Jesse W 29	First Named	26	M	IW	1896	Tobucksy	14398
13015	2 " Katie 29	W	26	f	1/16	1896	"	2360
13016	3 " Theophelos P 8	S	5	m	1/32	1896	"	2361
13017	4 " Clyde W 6	S	3	"	1/32	1896	"	2362
13018	5 " Cornelius M 1	Son	1mo	M	1/32			
	6							
	7							
	8 ENROLLMENT							
	9 OF NOS. ~~~ 1 ~~~ HEREON							
	APPROVED BY THE SECRETARY							
	10 OF INTERIOR MAY -7 1904							
	11							
	12 DECISION PREPARED#1 Nov 27, 03							
	13							
	14							
	15 ENROLLMENT							
	OF NOS. 2 3 4 & 5 HEREON							
	16 APPROVED BY THE SECRETARY							
	17 OF INTERIOR MAR 9 1903							

TRIBAL ENROLLMENT OF PARENTS

	Name of Father	Year	County	Name of Mother	Year	County
1	EH Culbertson		Non Cit	H H Culbertson		Non Cit
2	Geo Moncrief	dead	Tobucksy	Moncrief	Dead	Tobucksy
3	No1			No2		
4	No1			No2		
5	No.1			No.2		
6						
7	No1 See Decision of March 2 1904					
8	Evidence of marriage to be supplied					
9						
10	No2 As to parents[sic] marriage see testimony enrollment					
11	Cap R Moncrief					
12						
13	No4 on 1896 roll Clyde Culbertson					
14	No5 Born Feby 23, 1902; enrolled March 27,1902					
15	See affidavit of N°1 as to the name of minister who performed the ceremony				Date of Application	
	of marriage between himself and N°2 filed June 2 1903				for Enrollment.	
16	For child of Nos 1 and 2 see NB (Mar 3 '05) Card #353					
17					Sept. 9 1899	

211

Choctaw By Blood Enrollment Cards 1898-1914

RESIDENCE: Gaines COUNTY. **Choctaw Nation** Choctaw Roll CARD NO.
POST OFFICE: Featherston *(Not Including Freedmen)* FIELD NO. 4712

Dawes' Roll No.	NAME	Relationship to Person	AGE	SEX	BLOOD	Year	County	No.
13019	1 Lewis Easter ⁴¹	First Named	38	f	Full	1896	Gaines	7844
13020	2 " Evelena ¹²	d	9	f	1/2	1896	"	7845
13021	3 McKinney Calvin ²²	S	19	m	1/2	1896	"	9174
13022	4 " Henry ²⁰	S	17	m	1/2	1896	"	9175
13023	5 " Isabella ¹⁸	d	15	f	1/2	1896	"	9176
6								
7								
8								
9								
10								
11								
12								
13								
14								
15								
16								
17								

ENROLLMENT
OF NOS. 1 2 3 4 & 5 HEREON
APPROVED BY THE SECRETARY
OF INTERIOR MAR 19 1903

TRIBAL ENROLLMENT OF PARENTS

	Name of Father	Year	County	Name of Mother	Year	County
1	Rube Anderson	dead	Jacks Fork	Hotima Anderson	Dead	Wade
2	Simon W Lewis	Col	Gaines	No 1		
3	Jerry McKinney	"	Scullyville[sic]	No 1		
4	" "	"	"	No 1		
5	" "	"	"	No 1		
6						
7						
8						
9	For child of No. 5 see NB (Apr 26-06) No 799					
10	" " " " " " " (Mar 3-05) " 1390					
11						
12						
13						
14				Date of Application for Enrollment.		
15				Sept. 9ᵗʰ 1899		
16						
17	No3 P.O. Taff IT 9/23/05					

212

Choctaw By Blood Enrollment Cards 1898-1914

RESIDENCE: Tobucksy   COUNTY. **Choctaw Nation**   **Choctaw Roll**   CARD No.
POST OFFICE: So. McAlester   *(Not Including Freedmen)*   FIELD No. **4713**

Dawes' Roll No.	NAME		Relationship to Person	AGE	SEX	BLOOD	TRIBAL ENROLLMENT		
							Year	County	No.
13024	1 Meadows, Laura	25	First Named	22	F	1/2	1893	Skullyville	351
13025	2 " Leslie	3	S	2mo	M	1/4			
13026	3 " Sherman A	1	Son	4mo	M	1/4			
	4								
	5								
ENSHIP CERTIFICATE FOR N° 1-3 JUL 25 1903	6	ENROLLMENT OF NOS. 1 2 & 3 HEREON APPROVED BY THE SECRETARY OF INTERIOR MAR 19 1903							
	7								
IP CERTIFICATE N-O 29 1904	8								
	9								
	10								
	11								
	12								
	13								
	14								
	15								
	16								
	17								

TRIBAL ENROLLMENT OF PARENTS

	Name of Father	Year	County	Name of Mother	Year	County
1	Jas Ladd		Non Cit	Susan Ladd		Scullyville[sic]
2	Anderson[sic] Meadows		Tobucksy	No.1		
3	Andrew Meadows		Choc. Freedman	No.1		
4						
5						
6						
7						
8						
9	N°1 on pay roll 1893 of Scullyville[sic] Co as Laura Ladd, Page 37, No					
10	Husband of No.1 and father of No.2 is Andrew Meadows on Choctaw freedman card #1151					
11	N°3 Born Jany. 22, 1902: enrolled June 10, 1902					
12						
13						
14						
15						
16						Sept. 9, 1899
17						

Choctaw By Blood Enrollment Cards 1898-1914

RESIDENCE: Blue   COUNTY. **Choctaw Nation**   **Choctaw Roll**   CARD No.

POST OFFICE: Goodland   *(Not Including Freedmen)*   FIELD No. **4714**

Dawes' Roll No.	NAME	Relationship to Person	AGE	SEX	BLOOD	TRIBAL ENROLLMENT		
						Year	County	No.
13027	1 Hayes Thomas 21	First Named	18	M	Full	1896	Blue	5927
	2							
	3							
	4							
	5							
	6							
	7							
	8							
	9							
	10							
	11							
	12							
	13							
	14							
	15	ENROLLMENT OF NOS. 1 HEREON						
	16	APPROVED BY THE SECRETARY						
	17	OF INTERIOR Mar. 19 1903						

TRIBAL ENROLLMENT OF PARENTS

	Name of Father	Year	County	Name of Mother	Year	County
1	Phillip Hays[sic]	Dcd	Blue	Hyosh Hayes	Dcd	Kiamitia
2						
3						
4						
5						
6						
7						
8						
9						
10						
11						
12						
13						
14				Date of Application for Enrollment.		
15				Sept. 9 - 1899		
16						
17						

Choctaw By Blood Enrollment Cards 1898-1914

RESIDENCE:	Tobucksy	COUNTY.	Choctaw Nation	Choctaw Roll	CARD NO.
POST OFFICE:	Savanna			(Not Including Freedmen)	FIELD NO. 4715

Dawes' Roll No.		NAME		Relationship to Person First Named	AGE	SEX	BLOOD	TRIBAL ENROLLMENT		
								Year	County	No.
13028	1	Davis Riley	27	Named	24	M	1/8	1896	Tobucksy	3305
I.W.932	2	" Maggie	28	wife	24	f	IW	1896	"	14462
13029	3	" Annie	7	d	4	f	1/16	1896	"	3306
	4									
	5									
	6									
	7									
	8									
	9	ENROLLMENT								
	10	OF NOS. 2 HEREON								
		APPROVED BY THE SECRETARY								
	11	OF INTERIOR AUG 3 1904								
	12									
	13									
	14									
	15	ENROLLMENT								
	16	OF NOS. 1 & 3 HEREON								
		APPROVED BY THE SECRETARY								
	17	OF INTERIOR MAR 19 1903								

TRIBAL ENROLLMENT OF PARENTS

	Name of Father	Year	County	Name of Mother	Year	County
1	Jas Davis		Tobucksy	Annie Davis		Tobucksy
2	Long	Dcd	Non Cit	Carrie Messick	Dcd	U S Cit
3	No1			No2		
4						
5						
6						
7						
8	Evidence of marriage between Nᵒˢ1 and 2 filed Jany 3, 1903					
9	Affidavit of Nᵒ2 as to residence at time of her marriage to Nᵒ1 filed July 3, 1903 Sept 9- 1899					
10						
11						
12						
13						
14						
15					Date of Application for Enrollment.	
16						
17					Sept. 9, 1899	

Choctaw By Blood Enrollment Cards 1898-1914

RESIDENCE:	Sans Bois	COUNTY.							
POST OFFICE:	Whitefield		**Choctaw Nation**				**Choctaw Roll** (Not Including Freedmen)	CARD NO. FIELD NO.	4716

Dawes' Roll No.	NAME	Relationship to Person	AGE	SEX	BLOOD	TRIBAL ENROLLMENT		
						Year	County	No.
13030	₁ Clark Edwin ²⁴	First Named	21	M	1/4	1896	Sans Bois	2111
I.W. 1350	₂ " Ina Katherine ¹⁶	Wife	16	F	I.W.			
	3							
	4							
	5							
	6							
	7							
	8							
	9							
	10							
	11	ENROLLMENT OF NOS. 2 HEREON APPROVED BY THE SECRETARY OF INTERIOR MAR 14 1905						
	12							
	13							
	14	ENROLLMENT OF NOS. 1 HEREON APPROVED BY THE SECRETARY OF INTERIOR MAR 19 1903						
	15							
	16							
	17							

TRIBAL ENROLLMENT OF PARENTS

	Name of Father	Year	County	Name of Mother	Year	County
1	John P Clark		Sans Bois	Phoebe Clark		Sans Bois
2	J. C. Foster		noncitizen	Maria Foster		noncitizen
3						
4						
5						
6						
7	Nº1 is now the husband of Ina Catherine[sic] Clark on Choctaw Card #D801 Sept 23, 1902					
8	Nos 1 and 2 were married Sept. 17, 1902					
9						
10	No.2 originally listed for enrollment on Choctaw card D-801 Sep 23, 1902					
11	transferred to this card Jan. 29, 1905. See decision of Jan. 13, 1905					
12	Record as to enrollment of No.2 forwarded to Department March 14, 1906					
13	Record returned. See opinion of Assistant Attorney General of March 13, 1906 in case of Omer R Nicholson					
14	For child of Nos 1 and 2 see NB (March 3,1905) #1215					
15				Date of Application for Enrollment.		
16				Sept 6ᵗʰ 99		
17	PO Stigler IT 3/10/05					

216

RESIDENCE: Tobucksy COUNTY. **Choctaw Nation** **Choctaw Roll** CARD NO.
POST OFFICE: McAlester (Not Including Freedmen) FIELD NO. **4717**

Dawes' Roll No.	NAME	Relationship to Person First Named	AGE	SEX	BLOOD	TRIBAL ENROLLMENT		
						Year	County	No.
13031	1 McClure, Alfred W 42	First Named	39	M	3/4	1896	Tobucksy	9185
DEAD	2 " Frances 33	wife	30	f	3/4	1896	"	9186
13032	3 " Henry E 7	son	3	M	3/4	1896	"	9187
13033	4 " Eunice 6	D	3	f	3/4	1896	"	9188
13034	5 " Benjamin B 4	S	1	M	3/4			
13035	6 Fry, Frederick 10	Step son	7	M	3/4	1896	"	4010
	7							
	8							
	9							
	10							
	11 No. 2 hereon dismissed under order							
	12 of the Commission to the Five Civilized							
	13 Tribes of March 31, 1905.							
	14							
	15 ENROLLMENT							
	OF NOS. 1 3 4 5 & 6 HEREON							
	16 APPROVED BY THE SECRETARY							
	17 OF INTERIOR Mar 19 1903							

TRIBAL ENROLLMENT OF PARENTS

	Name of Father	Year	County	Name of Mother	Year	County
1	Wm McClure	Dead	Red River	Lucinda McClure	Dead	Blue
2	Chas Jones	"	Blue	Emily Jones	Dead	Blue
3	No.1			No.2		
4	No.1			No.2		
5	No.1			No.2		
6	Elijah Fry	Dead	Blue	No.2		
7						
8						
9						
10						
11	No.6 on 1896 roll Fred Fry					
12	No.2 Died Oct. 20, 1899: Proof of death filed Dec. 30, 1902					
13	For child of No.1 see N.B. (Apr 26, '06) Card No. 233					
14						
15						
16					6/9 - 99	
17					Date of Application for Enrollment.	

Choctaw By Blood Enrollment Cards 1898-1914

RESIDENCE: Tobucksy   COUNTY.   Choctaw Nation   Roll   CARD No.

POST OFFICE: So. McAlester   (Choctaw Freedmen)   FIELD No. 4718

Dawes' Roll No.	NAME		Relationship to Person First Named	AGE	SEX	BLOOD	TRIBAL ENROLLMENT		
							Year	County	No.
I.W. 1400	1 Kelly William F	48		45	M	IW	1896	Tobucksy	14720
13036	2 " Lorena	33	wife	30	f	1/16	1893	"	464
13037	3 " Faye L	10	d	7	f	1/32	1893	"	465
	4								
	5 Not DISMISSED								
	6								
	7 Such Action rescinded and								
	8								
	9 GRANTED								
	10								
	11								
	12								
	13								
	14								
	15								
	16								
	17								

SEP 23 1904

No 1   MAY 23 1905

ENROLLMENT OF NOS. One HEREON APPROVED BY THE SECRETARY OF INTERIOR AUG 22 1905

ENROLLMENT OF NOS. 2 & 3 HEREON APPROVED BY THE SECRETARY OF INTERIOR MAR 19 1903

TRIBAL ENROLLMENT OF PARENTS						
Name of Father	Year	County	Name of Mother		Year	County
1 Jno Kelly		Non-Citizen	Carry Kelly			Non-Citizen
2 Aaron Harlan		Non-Citizen	Sarah A Harlan			Choctaw
3 No1			No2			
4						
5 No.1 restored to roll by Departmental authority of January 19, 1909 (File 5-51)						
6 Enrollment of No.1 cancelled by order of Department March 4, 1904						
7 No2 on Pay Roll 1893 page 52- #464 Tobucksy Co						
8 No3 " " " " " 465 " "						
9						
10 No1 admitted by Dawes Commission as						
11 W.F. Kelly #1198						
12 Appealed to Central Dist #126. No appeal to C.C.C.C.						
No1 on 1896 roll as W.F. Kelly						
13 Evidence of marriage under Choctaw law of N^{os}1 and 2						
14 received and filed Jany 22, 1903.						
15						
16						
17 PO Massey IT						

218

Choctaw By Blood Enrollment Cards 1898-1914

RESIDENCE: Tobucksy	COUNTY:	**Choctaw Nation**	Choctaw Roll	CARD No.
POST OFFICE: McAlester			(Not including Freedmen)	FIELD No. 4719

Dawes' Roll No.	NAME		Relationship to Person	AGE	SEX	BLOOD	TRIBAL ENROLLMENT		
							Year	County	No.
13038	1 Bevill Alice	44	First Named	41	f	1/8	1896	Tobucksy	875
13039	2 " Jay	24	Son	21	m	1/16	1896	"	876
13040	3 Owens Susie	18	d	15	f	1/16	1896	"	877
13041	4 Bevill Abbie	16	d	13	f	1/16	1896	"	878
13042	5 " Roy	15	S	12	m	1/16	1896	"	879
13043	6 " Ray	12	S	9	m	1/16	1896	"	880
I.W. 1492	7 " Laura		Wife of No. 2	25	F	I.W.			
	8								
	9								
	10								
	11								
	12								
	13								
	14								
	15								
	16								
	17								

ENROLLMENT OF NOS. 1 2 3 4 5 & 6 HEREON APPROVED BY THE SECRETARY OF INTERIOR MAR 19 1903

ENROLLMENT OF NOS. Seven HEREON APPROVED BY THE SECRETARY OF INTERIOR AUG 22 1905

TRIBAL ENROLLMENT OF PARENTS

	Name of Father	Year	County	Name of Mother	Year	County
1	Leonidas Pitchlynn	Dead	Red River	Sophia Pitchlynn	Dead	Red River
2	Joseph Bevill	Do	Non Citizen	No1		
3	" "		" "	No1		
4	" "		" "	No1		
5	" "		" "	No1		
6	" "		" "	No1		
7	James Smith	dead	" "	Drucilla Smith		non citz
8						
9						

No.3 is now the wife of Ed Owens a non-citizen
Evidence of marriage filed Dec 24, 1902
No.7 originally listed for enrollment on Choctaw card #D-970 Dec 23, 1902 transf
this card July 17, 1905 See decision of May 23, 1905.
For child of No4 see NB (Apr 26-06) Card #470
" " " " " " " (Mar 3 '05) " #355
" " " " " " " " " " " #561

#1 to 6 inc

Date of Application for Enrollment. 9-6-99

No7 P.O. Camden Ark 5/23/05

Choctaw By Blood Enrollment Cards 1898-1914

| | RESIDENCE: | Gaines | COUNTY. | Choctaw Nation | Choctaw Roll *(Not Including Freedmen)* | FIELD NO. 4720 |
| POST OFFICE: | Wilburton | | | | | |

	NAME		Relationship to Person First Named	AGE	SEX	BLOOD	TRIBAL ENROLLMENT		
							Year	County	No.
13044	1 Billy Elizabeth	37	First Named	34	f	FB	1896	Tobucksy	881
13045	2 " Williamson	14	Son	11	m	FB	1896	"	920
DEAD.	3 " Annie	20	D	17	f	FB	1896	"	919
13046	4 " Martha	10	D	7	f	FB	1896	"	921
13047	5 Moore Robert	7	G son	4	m	FB	1896	"	8565
	6								
	7								
	8								
	9								
	10								
	11	No. 3 HEREON DISMISSED UNDER							
	12	ORDER OF THE COMMISSION TO THE FIVE							
	13	CIVILIZED TRIBES OF MARCH 31, 1905.							
	14								
	15	ENROLLMENT							
	16	OF NOS. 1 2 4 and 5 HEREON APPROVED BY THE SECRETARY							
	17	OF INTERIOR MAR 19 1903							

TRIBAL ENROLLMENT OF PARENTS

	Name of Father	Year	County	Name of Mother	Year	County
1	Wᵐ Joel	dead	Sugar Loaf	Mandy Joel	dead	Sugar Loaf
2	Robinson Billy	"	Sugar Loaf	No1		
3	Do Do	"	" "	No1		
4	Do Do	"	" "	No1		
5	Jesse Moore			No3		
6						
7						
8			No.5 on 1896 Choctaw roll page 213 #8565 as Lee R. Moore			
9						
10						
11						
12			No2 on roll 1896 William Billy			
13			No3 died March - 1900: proof of death filed Dec 19, 1902			
14						
15				Date of Application for Enrollment.		
16				7/9- 99		
17	McAlester I T 12/15/02					

220

Choctaw By Blood Enrollment Cards 1898-1914

Savanna I.T   **Choctaw Nation**   Choctaw Roll   CASE No.
(Not Including Freedmen)   FIELD No. 4721

	NAME		Relationship to Person	AGE	SEX	BLOOD	TRIBAL ENROLLMENT		
							Year	County	No.
13048	Hill. Nancy A	56	First Named	53	F	1/8	1896	Tobucksy	5364
13049	" Edgar	18	Son	15	M	1/16	"	"	5365
3									
4									
5									
6									
7									
8									
9									
10									
11									
12									
13									
14									
15									
16									
17									

ENROLLMENT
OF NOS. 1 and 2 HEREON
APPROVED BY THE SECRETARY
OF INTERIOR MAR 19 1903

TRIBAL ENROLLMENT OF PARENTS

	Name of Father	Year	County	Name of Mother	Year	County
1	Robt. S. McCarty	Dd	Skullyville	Mary A McCarty		Skullyville
2	Jas. A. Hill	"	Non Cit	No.1		
3						
4						
5						
6						
7						
8						
9						
10						
11						
12						
13						
14						
15						
16					Date of Application for Enrollment.	
17						9/6/99

| RESIDENCE: POST OFFICE: M°Alester I.T. | COUNTY. Choctaw Nation | | | Choctaw Roll (Not Including Freedmen) | CARD NO. FIELD NO. 4722 | |

Dawes' Roll No.	NAME	Relationship to Person	AGE	SEX	BLOOD	TRIBAL ENROLLMENT		
						Year	County	No.
I.W. 479	1 Cartlidge, Edward 39	First Named	36	M	I.W.	1896	Tobucksy	14404
13050	2 " Minnie M 31	Wife	28	F	1/8	"	"	2368
13051	3 " Mary E 12	Dau	9	F	1/16	"	"	2369
13052	4 " Richard 10	Son	7	M	1/16	"	"	2370
13053	5 " Edward Jr 6	"	3	M	1/16	"	"	2371
13054	6 " Margaret J 4	Dau	11mo	F	1/16			
13055	7 " Guy 1	Son	2wks	M	1/16			
	8							
	9							
	10							
	11	ENROLLMENT						
	12	OF NOS. 1 HEREON						
		APPROVED BY THE SECRETARY						
	13	OF INTERIOR SEP 12 1903						
	14							
	15	ENROLLMENT						
	16	OF NOS. 2 3 4 5 6 & 7 HEREON APPROVED BY THE SECRETARY						
	17	OF INTERIOR MAR 19 1903						

TRIBAL ENROLLMENT OF PARENTS

	Name of Father	Year	County	Name of Mother	Year	County
1	Rich⁴ Cartlidge		non-cit	Mary Cartlidge		non-cit
2	Mich'l Gleason			Mary E Gleason	Dd	Gaines
3	Nº1			Nº2		
4	Nº1			Nº2		
5	Nº1			Nº2		
6	Nº1			Nº2		
7	Nº1			Nº2		
8						
9	Nº2 on roll as Minnie Cartledge					
10	All above surnames on roll as Cartledge					
11	Nº5 on roll as Edward Cartledge					
12	Nº7 Enrolled May 24, 1901.					
13	Nº1 was admitted as an intermarried citizen by Dawes					
	Commission in 1896, Choctaw citizenship case #959, as Edward Cartlege[sic]					
14						
15					#1 to 6	
16					Date of Application for Enrollment	
17					9/6/99	

Choctaw By Blood Enrollment Cards 1898-1914

RESIDENCE:
POST OFFICE: Enterprise, I.T.
COUNTY.
Choctaw Nation
Choctaw Roll *(Not Including Freedmen)*
CARD NO.
FIELD NO. 4723

Dawes' Roll No.	NAME		Relationship to Person	AGE	SEX	BLOOD	TRIBAL ENROLLMENT		
							Year	County	No.
13056	1 Riddle, Coleman	31	First Named	29	M	1/2	1896	San[sic] Bois	10672
13057	2 " Nancy	12	Dau	9	F	3/4	"	" "	10690
~~13058~~	~~3 White, Rena~~	~~13~~	~~Niece~~	~~10~~	~~F~~	~~1/2~~	~~1893~~	~~" "~~	~~735~~
	4								
	5								
	6								
	7								
	8								
	9								
	10								
	11								
	12								
	13								
	14								
	15	ENROLLMENT OF NOS. 1 2 & 3 HEREON							
	16	APPROVED BY THE SECRETARY							
	17	OF INTERIOR MAR 9 1903							

TRIBAL ENROLLMENT OF PARENTS

	Name of Father	Year	County	Name of Mother	Year	County
1	Jack Riddle		San[sic] Bois	Hokmer	Dd	San[sic] Bois
2	No.1			Lina Riddle	"	" "
3	~~Jno. White~~	~~Dd~~	~~Non cit~~	~~Fanny White~~	~~"~~	~~" "~~
4						
5						
6						
7	No. 3 is duplicate of No. 1 on Choctaw card #4835 Roll #13373 Enrollment					
8	hereon cancelled under Departmental instructions of June 7, 1905 (I.T.D. 6516-1905)					
9	D.C. #28672-1905					
10	Father of No1 is a Choctaw Freedman on card No 1146					
11	No1 is husband of Nancy Byington } No 3 on page 71- #735- 93- P.R. San[sic] Bois Co on Card #5440 } as Lorena Riddle					
12	For child of No.1 see NB (March 3,1905) #1381					
13						
14						
15						
16					Date of Application for Enrollment.	
17					9/6/99	

Choctaw By Blood Enrollment Cards 1898-1914

COUNTY. **Choctaw Nation**   **Choctaw Roll** *(Not Including Freedmen)*   CARD No. FIELD No. 4724

Dawes' Roll No.	NAME	Relationship to Person First Named	AGE	SEX	BLOOD	TRIBAL ENROLLMENT Year	County	No.
13059	1 Kelton Lizzie S 37	First Named	34	f	1/4	1896	Sans Bois	7420
13060	2 " Russ 8	son	5	m	1/8	1896	" "	7421
	3							
	4							
	5							
	6							
	7							
	8							
	9							
	10							
	11							
	12							
	13							
	14							
	15							
	16							
	17							

ENROLLMENT
OF NOS. 1 and 2 HEREON
APPROVED BY THE SECRETARY
OF INTERIOR   MAR 19 1903

TRIBAL ENROLLMENT OF PARENTS

Name of Father	Year	County	Name of Mother	Year	County
1 Morris Hollins		Cherokee	Lucinda Hollins	Dead	Choctaw
2 Fred Kelton	dead	Non Citizen	No 1		
3					
4					
5					
6					
7					
8	No2 on 1896 roll as Rus Kelton				
9					
10					
11					
12					
13					
14					
15			Date of Application for Enrollment		
16			7/9 - 99		
17					

Choctaw By Blood Enrollment Cards 1898-1914

RESIDENCE:	Sans Bois	COUNTY.			
POST OFFICE:	Sans Bois				

Choctaw Nation

Choctaw Roll (Not Including Freedmen)

CARD NO. FIELD NO. 4725

Dawes' Roll No.	NAME	Relationship to Person First Named	AGE	SEX	BLOOD	TRIBAL ENROLLMENT Year	County	No.
13061	1 McGilberry Turner 29	First Named	26	M	3/4	1896	Sans Bois	8983
I.W. 773	2 " Mamie 32	Wife	32	F	I.W.			
	3							
	4							
	5							
	6							
	7							
	8							
	9							
	10	ENROLLMENT						
	11	OF NOS. ~~2~~ HEREON APPROVED BY THE SECRETARY						
	12	OF INTERIOR MAY -7 1904						
	13							
	14	ENROLLMENT						
	15	OF NOS. ~1~ HEREON APPROVED BY THE SECRETARY						
	16	OF INTERIOR MAR 19 1903						
	17							

TRIBAL ENROLLMENT OF PARENTS

	Name of Father	Year	County	Name of Mother	Year	County
1	Chas McGilberry	Dcd	Sans Bois	Annie McGilberry	dcd	Sans Bois
2	J. M. Coleman		non-citizen	Emma Coleman		non-citz
3						
4						
5						
6						
7						
8	N°1 is now the husband of Mamie McGilberry on Choctaw card #D790. Sept 16 1902					
9	N°2 transferred from Choctaw card #D790. See decision of Feby 27, 1904					
10						
11						
12						
13						
14				Date of Application for Enrollment.		
15						
16						
17						

Choctaw By Blood Enrollment Cards 1898-1914

RESIDENCE: Tobucksy COUNTY.
POST OFFICE: South Canadian

Choctaw Nation

Choctaw Roll (Not Including Freedmen)

CARD NO.
FIELD NO. 4726

Dawes' Roll No.	NAME	Relationship to Person First Named	AGE	SEX	BLOOD	TRIBAL ENROLLMENT		
						Year	County	No.
1	Morgan Frank P	Named	46	M	IW	1896	Tobucksy	14815
2								
3								
4								
5								
6								
7								
8								
9								
10								
11								
12								
13								
15								
16								
17	See Petition #C.118							

DENIED CITIZENSHIP BY THE CHOCTAW AND CHICKASAW CITIZENSHIP COURT

TRIBAL ENROLLMENT OF PARENTS

	Name of Father	Year	County	Name of Mother	Year	County
1	David Morgan	dead	Non Cit	Eleanor Morgan		Non Cit
2						
3						
4	No 1 admitted in 96 Case #380 Appeal taken					
5	Admitted by US Court at So McAlester July 13/97 Case #123					
6	As to residence see his					
7	testimony.					
8	Judgment of U.S. Ct admitting No1 vacated and set aside by Decree of C.C.C.C. Dec' 17 '02					
9	No1 now in C.C.C.C. Case #115					
10	[Without appeal – transferred at Department Feb. 28, 1907]					
11						
12						
13					Date of Application for Enrollment.	
14						
15					Sept 9 - 1899	
16						
17	Lehigh IT 11/1/04					

226

Choctaw By Blood Enrollment Cards 1898-1914

RESIDENCE:	Tobucksy	COUNTY.				Choctaw Roll	CARD No.	
POST OFFICE:	Calvin		Choctaw Nation			(Not Including Freedmen)	FIELD No. 4727	

Dawes' Roll No.	NAME		Relationship to Person	AGE	SEX	BLOOD	TRIBAL ENROLLMENT		
							Year	County	No.
IW1549	1 Jones John W	49	First Named	46	M	IW	1896	Chick Dist	14709
	2								
	3								
	4								
	5								
	6								
	7								
	8								
	9								
	10								
	11								
	12								
	13								
	14								
	15								
	16								
	17								

ENROLLMENT
~1~ HEREON
OF NOS APPROVED BY THE SECRETARY
OF INTERIOR May 28, 1906

TRIBAL ENROLLMENT OF PARENTS

	Name of Father	Year	County	Name of Mother	Year	County
1	Doc Jones		U.S. Citizen	Margaret Jones		U.S. Cit
2						
3						
4			Admitted by Dawes Com.	See Docket		
5						
6			On 1896 roll J. W. Jones			
7	No1 was formerly married to Elsie Collins Choctaw approved roll No 12008					
8	now husband of Josephine Jones, Choctaw approved roll No 14144					
9	No1 is the husband of Josephine Pitchlynn on Choctaw card 7-5601 June 3,1902					
10	Notion to correct entry on original Citizen Docket in Case #1043 so that same shall show No1 to have been admitted as an intermarried citizen filed Oct 18,1902					
11	Certified copy of license and certificate of marriage between No.1 and his former					
12	Choctaw wife filed Oct. 18, 1902					
13	See 1896 citizenship docket Choctaw Case #1043 application granted					
14						
15					Date of Application for Enrollment.	
16					Sept 9 - 1899	
17	Granted. Oct 27, 1905					

227

Choctaw By Blood Enrollment Cards 1898-1914

RESIDENCE: Tobucksy   COUNTY.   **Choctaw Nation**   **Choctaw Roll**   CARD NO.
POST OFFICE: So McAlester   (Not Including Freedmen)   FIELD NO. **4728**

Dawes' Roll No.	NAME		Relationship to Person	AGE	SEX	BLOOD	TRIBAL ENROLLMENT		
							Year	County	No.
15492	1 Boyd, May E	25	First Named	22	f	1/4			
15493	2 Jennings, Georgia D	10	d	7	f	1/8			
15494	3 " Arthur C	8	S	5	M	1/8			
15495	4 " Lilburn L	5	S	2	M	1/8			
15496	5 Boyd, Lillie M	2	Dau	7mo	F	1/8			
	6								
	7	ENROLLMENT							
	8	OF NOS. 1,2,3-4-5 HEREON							
	9	APPROVED BY THE SECRETARY OF INTERIOR May 9, 1904							
	10								
	11	No.2 admitted as Geo. D. Jennings							
	12	Arthur C "							
	13								
	14								
	15								
	16								
	17								

TRIBAL ENROLLMENT OF PARENTS

	Name of Father	Year	County	Name of Mother	Year	County
1	Monk	Dead	Skullyville	Mattie Monk		Choctaw
2	Henry Jennings		U.S. Citizen	No1		
3	" "			No1		
4	" "			No1		
5	Dock Boyd		Non Citizen	No1		
6						
7	Nos. 1,2 &3 Admitted by the Dawes Com Case 219: no appeal					
8						
9	No1 is now the wife of Dock Boyd a non citizen: Oct. 24, 1901					
10	No.5 born March 17, 1901: Enrolled Oct 24, 1901					
11	No1 was divorced from Henry Jennings, Jan 23, 1901: Evidence of divorce filed Dec. 2d 1901. Decree filed Dec. 28, 1901					
12	address of No.1 is now Canadian, I.T. Dec. 28, 1901					
13	Proof of birth No4 Born Aug 18, 1896, proof of birth filed July 24, 1903					
14					#1 to 4 inc.	
15				Date of Application for Enrollment.		
16				Sept 11th 99		
17	P.O. is now Ti. Ind. Ter. 10/20/02					

P.O. Tuskahoma 4/2/04

Choctaw By Blood Enrollment Cards 1898-1914

RESIDENCE:
POST OFFICE: Scipio, I.T.

COUNTY: Oct 15/06 **Choctaw Nation** (See Choctaw Card No. 4622)

Choctaw Roll (Not Including Freedmen)

CARD NO.
FIELD NO. **4729**

Dawes' Roll No.	NAME	Relationship to Person First Named	AGE	SEX	BLOOD	TRIBAL ENROLLMENT		
						Year	County	No.
15986	1 Coleman, Richard S 28	First Named	25	M	1/8	1896	Tobucksy	2311
I.W. 1587	2 " Annie E 30	Wife	27	F	I.W.	1896	"	14388
15987	3 " Winifred 9	Dau	6	"	1/16	1896	Tobucksy	2312
15988	4 " Eva F.E. 6	"	3	"	1/16	"	"	2313
15989	5 " Ida May 3	"	1mo	F	1/16			
15990	6 " Ruth St. Clair 1	"	3wk	F	1/16			
	7							

Enrollment of Nos 1,3,4,5 and 6 granted by decision of
Commission of Aug 8, 1904 (Chairman Bixby dissenting)
Copy of decision forwarded attorney for applicants
and attorneys for Choctaw & Chickasaw nations Aug 8, 1904
Aug 25, 1904. Record forwarded Department Oct 13, 1904:
Case referred to Attorney General Oct 24, 1904: Attorney
General desires brief Nov. 14, 1904: Brief of applicants and
attorneys for Choctaw and Chickasaw Nations forwarded Department.
March 27, 1905: Decision of Commission of Aug. 8, 1904 enrolling
Nos. 1,3,4,5 and 6 affirmed by Secty of Interior

TRIBAL ENROLLMENT OF PARENTS

	Name of Father	Year	County	Name of Mother	Year	County
1	R.B. Coleman		Tobucksy	Eva Coleman		Tobucksy
2	G.E. Aduddell		Non Cit	Frances Aduddell		Non Cit
3	No.1			No.2		
4	" 1		ENROLLMENT OF NOS. ~~2~~ HEREON APPROVED BY THE SECRETARY	" 2		
5	" 1		OF INTERIOR Nov. 26 1906	" 2		
6	" 1			" 2		
7						
8	For children of Nos 1&2 see NB (Apr 26-06) Card #453					
9	March 15, 1906; Department directs enrollment of			Nos 1,3,4,5 and 6 restored to roll by		
10	Nos 1,3,4,5 and 6 as citizens by blood			Departmental authority of February		
11	Enrollment of Nos 1,3,4,5 and 6 cancelled			20, 1909 (File 5-5I)		
12	by order of Department of Feb. 23, 1907			ENROLLMENT OF NOS. 1,3,4,5 and 6 HEREON		
13	No.6 born Nov. 19,1901; Enrolled Dec. 5, 1901			APPROVED BY THE SECRETARY		
14	No.1 on roll as R. St. C. Coleman			OF INTERIOR Jun 16, 1906		
15	" 2 admitted by Dawes Comm #737 as Mrs. Ann Coleman			No.2 { Granted		
16	" 3 on roll as Winfield Coleman.			Sep. 27, 1906		
17	" 4 " " " Ernistine "					
18	See enrollment of Richard B. Coleman			Date of Application for Enrollment.		
19	No.5 enrolled Nov. 2/99			9/11/99		

229

Choctaw By Blood Enrollment Cards 1898-1914

RESIDENCE:	Chick. Nat.	COUNTY.							
POST OFFICE:	Paoli, I.T.		Choctaw Nation			Choctaw Roll (Not Including Freedmen)	CARD No. FIELD No. 4730		

Dawes' Roll No.	NAME	Relationship to Person	AGE	SEX	BLOOD	TRIBAL ENROLLMENT		
						Year	County	No.
I.W. 1031	1 Reel, William E. 28	First Named	25	M	I.W.			
13062	2 " Jennie 23	Wife	20	F	3/8	1896	Chick. Dist.	3081
	3							
	4							
	5							
	6	ENROLLMENT OF NOS. ~~~ 1 ~~~ HEREON APPROVED BY THE SECRETARY OF INTERIOR Oct. 21, 1904						
	7							
	8							
	9							
	10							
	11							
	12							
	13	ENROLLMENT OF NOS. ~~~ 2 ~~~ HEREON APPROVED BY THE SECRETARY OF INTERIOR Mar. 19, 1903						
	14							
	15							
	16							
	17							

TRIBAL ENROLLMENT OF PARENTS						
Name of Father	Year	County	Name of Mother	Year	County	
1 S. A. Reel		non cit	Eliza Reel		non cit	
2 Hugh Campbell		Chick. Dist.	Julia G. Campbell		Chick Dist	
3						
4						
5						
6						
7						
8						
9				See testimony of No. 1		
10						
11						
12						
13						
14	No.2 on 1896 roll as Janie Campbell					
15	No.1 was married to Jennie Campbell - No4 on Choctaw Card #167 August 31, 1899					
16	Marriage license and certificate on file with papers in #4730				Date of Application for Enrollment	
17	See additional testimony of No.1 taken October 20, 1902.					
	Pauls Valley I.T. Oct. 20, 1902					9/11/99

230

Choctaw By Blood Enrollment Cards 1898-1914

RESIDENCE: Tobucksy COUNTY.
POST OFFICE: Scipio

Choctaw Nation

Choctaw Roll
(Not Including Freedmen)

CARD NO.
FIELD NO. **4731**

Dawes' Roll No.	NAME	Relationship to Person First Named	AGE	SEX	BLOOD	TRIBAL ENROLLMENT Year	County	No.
13063	1 Anderson, William [43]	Named	40	M	Full	1896	Tobucksy	124
13064	2 " Margaret [47]	wife	44	f	"	1896	"	125
13065	3 " Luella [4]	d	2	f	"			
13066	4 Smith, Sibbie [16]	neice[sic]	13	f	"	1896	Tobucksy	11283
13067	5 " Jacob [13]	neph	10	M	"	1896	"	11284
13068	6 Anderson, Mamie [1]	Dau	5mo	F	"			
	7							
	8							
	9							
	10							
	11							
	12							
	13							
	14							
	15	ENROLLMENT OF NOS. 1 2 3 4 5 & 6 HEREON						
	16	APPROVED BY THE SECRETARY						
	17	OF INTERIOR Mar. 19 1903						

TRIBAL ENROLLMENT OF PARENTS

	Name of Father	Year	County	Name of Mother	Year	County
1	Daniel Anderson	Dead	Gaines	Nacy[sic] Anderson	dead	Tobucksy
2	Albert Byington	"	Blue	Annie Byington	"	Blue
3	No.1			No.2		
4	Abel Smith	Dead	Tobucksy	Petsy[sic] Smith	dead	Tobucksy
5	" "			" "		
6	No.1			No.4		
7						
8	No.4 on 1896 roll Silvey Smith					
9	No.6 born July 27, 1901: Enrolled Jany 8, 1902					
10	See letter of R. B. Coleman as to parentage of No.6					
	Evidence of birth of No.3 received and filed March 20, 1902.					
11	For child of Nos 1 and 4 see NB (Mar. 3, 1905) #470					
12						
13						
14						
15						
16						
17						

#1 to 6
Date of Application for Enrollment.

Sept. 11th 1899

Choctaw By Blood Enrollment Cards 1898-1914

RESIDENCE:		COUNTY.						
POST OFFICE: Krebs, I.T.		**Choctaw Nation**				Choctaw Roll *(Not Including Freedmen)*	CARD NO. FIELD NO. **4732**	

Dawes' Roll No.	NAME		Relationship to Person	AGE	SEX	BLOOD	TRIBAL ENROLLMENT		
							Year	County	No.
13069	1 Jefferson, Joseph	43	First Named	40	M	Full	1896	Tobucksy	6670
13070	2 " Frances	39	wife	36	F	"	"	"	6671
13071	3 Anderson, Lizzie	20	ward	17	F	"	"	"	141
13072	4 Johnson, Riley	6	"	2	M	"			
	5								
	6								
	7								
	8								
	9								
	10								
	11								
	12								
	13								
	14								
	15	ENROLLMENT OF NOS. 1,2,3 & 4 HEREON APPROVED BY THE SECRETARY OF INTERIOR Mar 19 1903							
	16								
	17								

TRIBAL ENROLLMENT OF PARENTS

	Name of Father	Year	County	Name of Mother	Year	County
1	Isom Jefferson	Dd	Tobucksy	Liza Jefferson		Tobucksy
2	Geo. Waters	"	"	Ellen Waters	Dd	"
3	Mitch Anderson	"	"	Lucinda Anderson		"
4	Danl Johnson		"	No.3		
5						
6						
7						
8						
9						
10						
11						
12						
13						
14						
15						
16					Date of Application for Enrollment	
17					Sept. 11 - 1899	

232

Choctaw By Blood Enrollment Cards 1898-1914

RESIDENCE: Tobucksy   COUNTY. **Choctaw Nation**   **Choctaw Roll**   CARD NO.
POST OFFICE: Krebs, I.T.   *(Not Including Freedmen)*   FIELD NO. 4733

Dawes' Roll No.	NAME		Relationship to Person First Named	AGE	SEX	BLOOD	TRIBAL ENROLLMENT		
							Year	County	No.
13073	1 Johnson, Eliza A	73	First Named	70	F	Full	1896	Tobucksy	667
	2								
	3								
	4								
	5								
	6								
	7								
	8								
	9								
	10								
	11								
	12								
	13								
	14								
	15								
	16								
	17								

ENROLLMENT
OF NOS. 1 HEREON
APPROVED BY THE SECRETARY
OF INTERIOR MAR 19 1903

TRIBAL ENROLLMENT OF PARENTS

	Name of Father	Year	County	Name of Mother	Year	County
1	Chas Sexton	Dd	Tobucksy	Tishahona	Dd	Tobucksy
2						
3						
4						
5						
6						
7	No 1 is duplicate of Eliza A Johnson on Choctaw card #3171. Enrollment hereon					
8	cancelled under Departmental authority of Jan. 21, 1907 (I.T.D. 816-1907) I.D.C. 3178-1907					
9						
10						
11						
12						
13						
14						
15	on roll as Eliza Johnson					
16						
17						

Choctaw By Blood Enrollment Cards 1898-1914

RESIDENCE: Tobucksy COUNTY. **Choctaw Nation** **Choctaw Roll** CARD NO.
POST OFFICE: Krebs *(Not Including Freedmen)* FIELD NO. **4734**

Dawes' Roll No.	NAME	Relationship to Person First Named	AGE	SEX	BLOOD	TRIBAL ENROLLMENT Year	County	No.
13074	1 Ebanowatubbe, Simon 26	Named	23	M	Full	1893	Gaines	316
13075	2 " Bertie 22	wife	19	f	"	1896	Tobucksy	5266
13076	3 Harmby, Wesley 15	wife's bro	12	M	"	1896	"	5293
13077	4 King, John 18	half bro	15	"	"	"	"	7492
13078	5 " Frances 16	" sis	13	F	"	"	"	7494
	6 " Philistine	" bro	5	M	"			
	7							
	8							
	9							
	10							
	11							
	12							
	13							
	14							
	15							
	16							
	17							

ENROLLMENT
OF NOS. 1,2,3,4 & 5 HEREON
APPROVED BY THE SECRETARY
OF INTERIOR Mar. 19, 1903

TRIBAL ENROLLMENT OF PARENTS

	Name of Father	Year	County	Name of Mother	Year	County
1	Ebanowatubbe	Willie	Tobucksy	Losos King	dead	Tobucksy
2	Silas Harmby	Dead	Gaines	Susan Harmby		Tobucksy
3	Do Do			Do Do		
4	Jas. King	Dd	Gaines	Lizzie King	Dd	Gaines
5	" "			" "		
6	" "			" "		
7	No.1 on Gaines Co Pay Roll 1893 P33 #316 as Simon Allen					
8	No.2 " Role[sic] 1896 " Bertie Hurnby[sic]					
9	No.3 " " " Weslly "					
10						
11	No.4 lives with Elissie James 7-2349					
12	No.5 on 1896 roll as Francis King					
13						
14						
15	No.6 is duplicate of Willie Pusley #2 on Choctaw card #3329					
16	Enrollment hereon cancelled December 8, 1906					
17	No.2 P.O. Damon, Okla. 11/26/09					

Date of Application for Enrollment. Sept. 11th

Choctaw By Blood Enrollment Cards 1898-1914

RESIDENCE: Tobucksy   COUNTY. **Choctaw Nation**   **Choctaw Roll**   CARD No.
POST OFFICE: Alderson   *(Not Including Freedmen)*   FIELD No. **4735**

Dawes' Roll No.	NAME		Relationship to Person	AGE	SEX	BLOOD	TRIBAL ENROLLMENT		
							Year	County	No.
13079	1 Carter Nellie	25	First Named	22	f	Full	1893	Tobucksy	226
13080	2 Carney Walton	9	Son	6	M	"	1893	"	225
15590	3 " Isham	(6)	"	4	M	"			
	4								
	5								
	6								
	7								
	8								
	9								
	10								
	11	ENROLLMENT							
	12	OF NOS. ~~~3~~~ HEREON APPROVED BY THE SECRETARY							
	13	OF INTERIOR Sep 22 1904							
	14								
	15	ENROLLMENT							
	16	OF NOS. 1 & 2 HEREON APPROVED BY THE SECRETARY							
	17	OF INTERIOR Mar 19, 1903							

TRIBAL ENROLLMENT OF PARENTS

Name of Father	Year	County	Name of Mother	Year	County
1 Silas Carter	dead	Tobucksy			
2 Aaron Carney		Do	No.1		
3 Aaron Carney		Do	No.1		
4					
5					
6					
7	No.1 on Pay Roll Tobucksy Co 1893 P.22 #226				
8	No.2 " " " " " " P.22 #225				
9					
10	No 3 Born July 24, 1896, proof of birth filed June 22, 1904				
11	For child of No.1 see N.B. (Apr. 26, 06) No. 798				
12	" " " " " " (Mar 3 05) " 356				
13					
14					
15				Date of Application for Enrollment.	
16				Sept. 11 1899	
17					

235

RESIDENCE: Tobucksy   COUNTY. **Choctaw Nation**   **Choctaw Roll**   CARD NO.

POST OFFICE: So M<u>c</u>Alester, I.T.   *(Not Including Freedmen)*   FIELD NO. 4736

Dawes' Roll No.	NAME	Relationship to Person	AGE	SEX	BLOOD	TRIBAL ENROLLMENT		
						Year	County	No.
13081	₁ Carnes, Melina ²⁰	First Named	17	F	Full	1893	Tobucksy	862
15793	₂ " Lizzie ⁵	Dau	4	F	"			
	₃							
	₄							
	₅							
	₆							
	₉							
	₁₀							
	₁₁							
	₁₂							
	₃							
	₄							
	₅							
	₆							
	₇							

ENROLLMENT
OF NOS. 2 HEREON
APPROVED BY THE SECRETARY
OF INTERIOR MAR 15 1905

ENROLLMENT
OF NOS. ~ 1 ~ HEREON
APPROVED BY THE SECRETARY
OF INTERIOR MAR 19 1903

TRIBAL ENROLLMENT OF PARENTS

Name of Father	Year	County	Name of Mother	Year	County
₁ Wesley Anderson	Dd	Chic. residing Choc N. 1ˢᵗ Dist	Jinsie Nail		Tobucksy
₂ Geo. Cann		Tobucksy	No.1		
₃					
₄					
₅					
₆					
₇					
₈					

₉ See testimony taken Jan. 12 & 13, 1905

On p. 102 #862-93-P.R. Tobucksy Co. as Millina Ander

No2 born December 31, 1896. Proof of birth filed January 18, 1905

For child of No1 see NB (Mar 3 '05) Card #357

See Cards 461 and 4737

Date of Application for Enrollment. 9/11

Choctaw By Blood Enrollment Cards 1898-1914

Dawes' Roll No.	NAME		Relationship to Person First Named	AGE	SEX	BLOOD	TRIBAL ENROLLMENT		
							Year	County	No.
13082	1 Nail, Jincy	38	First Named	35	F	Full	1893	Tobucksy	861
13083	2 " Jimmie	19	St. son	16	M	"	1893	"	623
13084	3 Anderson, Mollie	18	Dau	15	F	"	1893	"	863
13085	4 " Gibson	14	"	11	M	"	1893	"	864
15794	5 McCann, Melissa	11	Dau	5	F	"	1893	"	865
	6 Nail, Dock		Son of No.2	1	M	1/2			
	7 No.6 is transferred to Choctaw								
	8 NB card 1520 having been born								
	9 subsequent to Sept 25, 1902								
	10		2/6/06						
	11 ENROLLMENT HEREON								
	12 OF NOS. 5 APPROVED BY THE SECRETARY								
	13 OF INTERIOR Mar. 15 1905								
	14								
	15 ENROLLMENT								
	16 OF NOS. 1, 2, 3 & 4 HEREON APPROVED BY THE SECRETARY								
	17 OF INTERIOR Mar 19, 1903								

TRIBAL ENROLLMENT OF PARENTS

	Name of Father	Year	County	Name of Mother	Year	County
1	Tombi	Dd		Siney Nail	Dd	Tobucksy
2	Alfred Nail		Tobucksy	Winey "		
3	Wesley Anderson	Dd	"	No.1		
4	" "			" 1		
5	Willie McKann[sic]	Dd	Tobucksy	" 1		
6	No.2			Beckie Nail		non Citizen
7						
8	No.6 was born March 4, 1902; application received and No.6 placed					
9	hereon March 28, 1905, under Act of Congress approved March 3, 1905					
10	See testimony taken Jan 12 & 13, 1905					
11	Watch No.5 on this card and No.2 in 4736. Is this a duplication? No.					
12	No 1 On p 102 #861-93 P R Tobucksy Co as Jincy Watkins					
13	" 2 " " 72 #623-93 " " " " Jimmie Nale					
14	" 3 " " 102 #863-93 " " " "					
15	" 4 " " 102 #864-93 " " " "					
16	" 5 " " 102 #865-93 " " " " as Millisie McCann					
	For child of No.2 see NB (April 26,1906) #1209					
	" " " " " " (March 3,1905) #1520 See Cards 461 and 4736				Date of Application for Enrollment	
17						9/11/99

No.2 P.O. Blanco, I.T. 3/27/05

RESIDENCE:	Gaines	COUNTY:		CARD No.
POST OFFICE:	Featherston	**Choctaw Nation**	**Choctaw Roll** (Not Including Freedmen)	FIELD No. 4738

Dawes' Roll No.	NAME		Relationship to Person Named	AGE	SEX	BLOOD	TRIBAL ENROLLMENT		
							Year	County	No.
13086	1 LeFlore James	53	First Named	50	M	1/4	1896	Gaines	7837
I.W.480	2 " Arley M	30	wife	26	f	I.W.	1896	"	14753
13087	3 " James Jr	21	son	18	M	1/8	1896	"	7838
13088	4 " Charley	15	"	12	"	1/8	1896	"	7839
13089	5 " Campbell	13	"	10	"	1/8	1896	"	7840
13090	6 " Ethel	11	d	8	f	1/8	1896	"	7841
13091	7 " Luther	9	d	6	f	1/8	1896	"	7842
13092	8 " Mathias C	6	s	3	M	1/8	1896	"	7843
13093	9 " Lucius C	4	s	1	M	1/8			
12094	10 Eastes, John L	7	G.Son	4	M	1/8	1896	Gaines	3694
13095	11 LeFlore, Mary May	1	Dau	1mo	f	1/8			

12 ENROLLMENT
OF NOS. 2 HEREON
APPROVED BY THE SECRETARY
OF INTERIOR Sep 12 1903
14

15 ENROLLMENT
OF NOS.1,3,4,5,6,7,8,9,10,11 HEREON
APPROVED BY THE SECRETARY
OF INTERIOR Mar 19 1903
17

TRIBAL ENROLLMENT OF PARENTS

	Name of Father	Year	County	Name of Mother	Year	County
1	Adam Laflore[sic]	Dead	Gaines	Sophia Laflore	Dcd	Gaines
2	Jonas Smith	"	Non citizen	Mary Smith	Dead	U.S. Cit
3	No.1			Louisa Leflore	Dead	Non Cit
4	No.1			No.2	"	" "
5	No.1			No.2 Do[sic]		
6	No.1			No.2		
7	No.1			No.2		
8	No.1			No.2		
9	No.1			No.2		
10	Jno Easter[sic]		Non Cit	Carrie Easter	Dead	Gaines
11	No.1			No.2		

12 No.3 on 1896 roll James Leflore
13 No.6 on 1896 ~~Pay Roll~~ Essell Laflore
14 No.8 " " " Christopher "
15 ~~No.10~~ " ~~Jno Lee Easter~~
16 Evidence of parents[sic] marriage to be supplied
No.11 Born Aug 6, 1902; enrolled Sept. 18, 1902
17 For child of Nos 1&2 see NB (Apr 26,1906) Card No.14

Date of Application for Enrollment.
#1 to 10 inc
Sept. 11th
1899

238

Choctaw By Blood Enrollment Cards 1898-1914

| RESIDENCE: | San[sic] Bois | COUNTY. | **Choctaw Nation** | Choctaw Roll | CARD No. |
| POST OFFICE: | Stigler, I.T. | | | (Not Including Freedmen) | FIELD No. 4739 |

Dawes' Roll No.	NAME	Relationship to Person First Named	AGE	SEX	BLOOD	TRIBAL ENROLLMENT Year	County	No.
13006	1 Dwight, Wiley ~~DIED PRIOR TO SEPTEMBER 25, 1902~~	Named	51	F	Full	1893	Sans Bois	26
	2							
	3							
	4							
	5							
	6							
	7							
	8							
	9							
	10							
	11							
	12							
	13							
	14							
	15	ENROLLMENT						
	16	OF NOS. ~~1~~ HEREON APPROVED BY THE SECRETARY						
	17	OF INTERIOR MAR 19 1903						

TRIBAL ENROLLMENT OF PARENTS

	Name of Father	Year	County	Name of Mother	Year	County
1	Chalmon Dwight	Dd	San[sic] Bois	Artie Dwight	Dd	San[sic] Bois
2						
3						
4						
5						
6						
7	No 1 died Sept. 1901; Enrollment cancelled by Department May 2, 1906					
8						
9						
10						
11						
12	On p. 4, #26-93 P.R. San[sic] Bois Co. as Wiley Bell.					
13						
14						
15					Date of Application for Enrollment.	
16						
17						9/11/99

Choctaw By Blood Enrollment Cards 1898-1914

Dawes' Roll No.	NAME		Relationship to Person	AGE	SEX	BLOOD	TRIBAL ENROLLMENT		
							Year	County	No.
13097	1 Folsom, Joseph	42	First Named	39	M	Full	1896	San[sic] Bois	3854
13098	2 " Jincy	53	Wife	50	F	"	"	" "	3855
DEAD.	3 Perry, Jefferson DEAD.		Ward	6	M	"	"	" "	10052
4									
5									
6									
7									
8									
9									
10									
11									
12	No. 3 HEREON DISMISSED UNDER								
13	ORDER OF THE COMMISSION TO THE FIVE CIVILIZED TRIBES OF MARCH 31, 1905.								
14									
15	ENROLLMENT								
16	OF NOS. 1 & 2 HEREON APPROVED BY THE SECRETARY								
17	OF INTERIOR MAR 9 1903								

TRIBAL ENROLLMENT OF PARENTS

	Name of Father	Year	County	Name of Mother	Year	County
1	Tecumseh Folsom	Dd	San[sic] Bois	Mary A Folsom	Dd	San Bois
2	Milton Lntosh[sic]	"	Skullyville	Mollie Lntosh	"	" "
3	Steven Perry		San[sic] Bois	Florence Cass		" "
4						
5						
6						
7						
8	Nº3 Died Jany 20, 1902, proof of death filed Dec. 24, 1902					
9						
10						
11						
12			No.1 on roll as Joseph Folsum			
13			" 2 " " " Jency "			
14						
15						
16					Date of Application for Enrollment.	
17					9/11/99	

Choctaw By Blood Enrollment Cards 1898-1914

						TRIBAL ENROLLMENT		
NAME	Relationship to Person	AGE	SEX	BLOOD	Year	County	No.
1 Courts, Joseph T ³⁰	First Named	27	M	IW			
2 " Grace ²³	wife	20	f	1/8	1896	Tobucksy	8556
3							
4							
5							
6							
7 See his testimony							
8 No2 on 1896 roll Grace Morrison.							
9							
10							

: Tobucksy COUNTY. **Choctaw Nation** Choctaw Roll (Not Including Freedmen)
CE: Krebs
CARD No.
FIELD No. 4741

ENROLLMENT
OF NOS. 1 HEREON
APPROVED BY THE SECRETARY
OF INTERIOR SEP 12 1903

ENROLLMENT
OF NOS. 2 HEREON
APPROVED BY THE SECRETARY
OF INTERIOR MAR 19 1903

TRIBAL ENROLLMENT OF PARENTS

Name of Father	Year	County	Name of Mother	Year	County
1 Joseph Courts		Non Citizen	Louisa Courts		U.S. Cit
2 Jno Morrison	Dead	" "	Lizzie Dodson		Tobucksy
3					
4					
5					
6					
7					
8					
9					
10					
11					
12					
13					
14			Date of Application for Enrollment.		
15			Sept. 11ᵗʰ 1899		
16					
17 P.O. Buck, IT 12/23/02					

241

Choctaw By Blood Enrollment Cards 1898-1914

	San[sic] Bois COUNTY.					Choctaw Roll	CARD NO.	
E:	Iron Bridge, I.T. **Choctaw Nation**					*(Not Including Freedmen)*	FIELD NO. 4742	

NAME	Relationship to Person First Named	AGE	SEX	BLOOD	TRIBAL ENROLLMENT		
					Year	County	No.
McGilberry, Osborn ²⁵		22	M	Full	1896	San Bois	9024
2							
3							
4							
5							
6							
7							
8							
9							
10							
11							
12							
13							
14							
15	ENROLLMENT OF NOS. 1 HEREON						
16	APPROVED BY THE SECRETARY						
17	OF INTERIOR MAR 19 1903						

TRIBAL ENROLLMENT OF PARENTS

Name of Father	Year	County	Name of Mother	Year	County
1 S. McGilberry	Dd	San[sic] Bois	Nellie McGilberry	Dd	San Bois
2					
3					
4					
5					
6					
7					
8					
9					
10					
11					
12					
13					
14					
15					
16					
17			DATE OF APPLICATION FOR ENROLLMENT		9/11/99

Choctaw By Blood Enrollment Cards 1898-1914

RESIDENCE: Gaines COUNTY. POST OFFICE: Wilburton, I.T.

Choctaw Nation

Choctaw Roll (Not Including Freedmen)

CARD No. FIELD No. 4743

Dawes' Roll No.	NAME	Relationship to Person	AGE	SEX	BLOOD	TRIBAL ENROLLMENT		
						Year	County	No.
13101	1 Parker, Johnson 57	First Named	54	M	Full	1896	Gaines	10201
	2							
	3							
	4							
	5							
	6							
	7							
	8							
	9							
	10							
	11							
	12							
	13							
	14							
	15	ENROLLMENT OF NOS. 1 HEREON APPROVED BY THE SECRETARY OF INTERIOR Mar 19 1903						
	16							
	17							

TRIBAL ENROLLMENT OF PARENTS

	Name of Father	Year	County	Name of Mother	Year	County
1	Ontiatabe	Dd	San[sic] Bois	Lila	Dd	Tobucksy
2						
3						
4						
5						
6						
7						
8						
9	*"Died prior to Sept 25, 1902 not entitled to land or money"					
10	See Indian Office letter of August 4, 1911 (No 1238-1911)					
11						
12						
13						
14						
15						
16					Date of Application for Enrollment.	
17						9/11/99

Choctaw By Blood Enrollment Cards 1898-1914

Dawes' Roll No.	NAME	Relationship to Person Named	AGE	SEX	BLOOD	TRIBAL ENROLLMENT Year	County	No.
I.W.482	1 Archibald, Thomas 52	First Named	49	M	I.W.	1896	Tobucksy	14257
13102	2 " Mary A 41	wife	38	f	1/8	1896	"	142
13103	3 " Ella 15	d	12	f	1/16	1896	"	143
13104	4 " Maggie 13	d	10	f	1/16	1896	"	144
13105	5 " David 10	s	7	m	1/16	1896	"	145
13106	6 " Henry 4	s	8mo	m	1/16			
13107	7 Samples Maud R 22	s. Dau	19	f	1/16	1896	Tobucksy	13040
I.W.685	8 " James L 28	Hus of No.7	28	m	I.W.			
	9							
	10	ENROLLMENT OF NOS. 8 APPROVED BY THE SECRETARY OF INTERIOR Mar. 26 1904						
	11							
	12							
	13	ENROLLMENT OF NOS. 1 HEREON APPROVED BY THE SECRETARY OF INTERIOR Sep 12 1903						
	14							
	15							
	16	ENROLLMENT OF NOS. 2,3,4,5,6 & 7 HEREON APPROVED BY THE SECRETARY OF INTERIOR Mar 19, 1903						
	17							

TRIBAL ENROLLMENT OF PARENTS

	Name of Father	Year	County	Name of Mother	Year	County
1	Thos. Archibald		U.S. Citizen	Mary Archibald		U.S. Citizen
2	Edmond Folsom		Skullyville	Ann Folsom		Skullyville
3	No.1			No.2		
4	No.1			No.2		
5	No.1			No.2		
6	No.1			No.2		
7	C Wickett	dead	Tobucksy	No.2		
8	Noah Samples		non citizen	Annie Samples		non citizen
9						
10	No.8 transferred from Choctaw card D 584 January 25, 1904					
11	See decision of January 7, 1904					
12	No.1 admitted by Dawes Com Case #496					
13	No.2 on 1896 roll Mary Archibald					
14	No.7 is now the wife of James L Samples					
15	See Choctaw card #D 584 for husband of No.7.					
16						Date of Application for Enrollment.
17	No12/24/02 P.O. Archibald I.T.					Sept. 11'99

Choctaw By Blood Enrollment Cards 1898-1914

RESIDENCE: **Wade** COUNTY. **Choctaw Nation** **Choctaw Roll** CARD No.
POST OFFICE: Tushkahoma[sic], I.T. *(Not Including Freedmen)* FIELD No. **4745**

Dawes' Roll No.	NAME	Relationship to Person First Named	AGE	SEX	BLOOD	TRIBAL ENROLLMENT		
						Year	County	No.
1	Henderson, Saml		29	M	1/8			
2								
3								
4								
5								
6								
7								
8								
9								
10								
11								
12								
13								
14								
15								
16								
17								

DENIED CITIZENSHIP BY THE CHOCTAW AND CHICKASAW CITIZENSHIP COURT

TRIBAL ENROLLMENT OF PARENTS

	Name of Father	Year	County	Name of Mother	Year	County
1	B. P. Henderson		Jacks Fork	Nancy Henderson	Dd	Jacks Fork
2						
3						
4						
5						
6						
7						

No1 denied in 96 Case #425

No.1 husband of Ida Henderson on Choctaw card #

Applied at So MᶜAlester IT Dec 23, 1902 as Intermarried citizen Choctaw D987

Admitted by U.S. Court at So MᶜAlester, Jan 18-98 - Case No.44
As to residence see his testimony.

Judgement[sic] of U.S. Ct admitting No1 vacated and set aside by Decree of C.C.C. Dec' 17 '02
No1 now in C.C.C.C. Case 112

P.O. Stringtown I.T. 9/6/04

Date of Application for Enrollment.
9/11/99

Choctaw By Blood Enrollment Cards 1898-1914

RESIDENCE: Tobucksy   COUNTY. **Choctaw Nation**   **Choctaw Roll**   CARD NO.
POST OFFICE: McAlester, I.T.   *(Not Including Freedmen)*   FIELD NO. 4746

Dawes' Roll No.	NAME	Relationship to Person	AGE	SEX	BLOOD	TRIBAL ENROLLMENT		
						Year	County	No.
I.W. 1351	1 McEvers, Newton 50	First Named	47	M	I.W.			
	2							
	3							
	4							
	5							
	6							
	7							
	8							
	9							
	10							
	11							
	12							
	13							
	14							
	15							
	16							
	17							

ENROLLMENT
OF NOS. 1 HEREON
APPROVED BY THE SECRETARY
OF INTERIOR   MAR 14 1905

TRIBAL ENROLLMENT OF PARENTS

Name of Father	Year	County	Name of Mother	Year	County
1 Henry McEvers		Non Cit	Kittie A. McEvers		Non Cit
2					
3					
4					
5					
6					
7					
8					
9					
10					
11					
12					
13					
14					
15					
16					
17					

No.1 formerly husband of Priscilla McEvers (formerly Connors), a recognized Choctaw by blood who died in 1884

{ Admitted by Dawes Comm. #398: appeal dismissed.

Date of Application for Enrollment.
9/11/99

246

Choctaw By Blood Enrollment Cards 1898-1914

	RESIDENCE: Chic. Nation	COUNTY.	Choctaw Nation		Choctaw Roll *(Not Including Freedmen)*	CARD No.
	POST OFFICE: Ara, I.T.					FIELD No. 4747

Dawes' Roll No.	NAME		Relationship to Person	AGE	SEX	BLOOD	TRIBAL ENROLLMENT		
							Year	County	No.
I.W. 1032	1 Jones, William J	25	First Named	22	M	I.W.			
13108	2 " Mary Ann	21	Wife	18	F	1/32	1896	Chick. Dist.	11766
13109	3 " Berty Lee	2	Son	4mo	M	1/64			
13110	4 " William Edward	1	Son	3wks	M	1/64			
5									
6									
7	ENROLLMENT OF NOS. ~~~ 1 ~~~ HEREON APPROVED BY THE SECRETARY OF INTERIOR OCT 21 1904								
8									
9									
10									
11	For child of Nos 1&2 see NB (Apr 26-06) Card #478								
12									
13	ENROLLMENT OF NOS. 2 3 & 4 HEREON APPROVED BY THE SECRETARY OF INTERIOR MAR 19 1903								
14									
15									
16									
17									

TRIBAL ENROLLMENT OF PARENTS

	Name of Father	Year	County	Name of Mother	Year	County
1	Edward Jones		Non Cit	Nancy A Jones		Non Cit
2	Thos. G. Spain	1896	Chic. Dist.	Elizab. Spain	1896	Chick. Dist.
3	No.1			No.2		
4	Nº1			Nº2		
5						
6						
7						
8						
9						
10	Nos 2-4 inclusive descendants of Mary M Spain who was admitted by					
11	act of Choctaw Council of Oct. 31, 1877					
12	License Mch 23-99 by Archison Arnouitibby, Judge Pickens Co					
13	Certificate April 13-1899					
14	License to be recorded and filed.					
15	No2 on 1896 roll as Margaret A Spain					
	No.3 Enrolled Sept 4th, 1900					#1&2
16	Nº4 Born Aug. 13, 1902: enrolled Sept 4, 1902					Date of Application for Enrollment.
17	Arthur I.T. 10/28/02					9/11/9

247

Choctaw By Blood Enrollment Cards 1898-1914

RESIDENCE: Sans Bois   COUNTY. **Choctaw Nation**   **Choctaw Roll** *(Not Including Freedmen)*   CARD NO.

POST OFFICE: Stigler   FIELD NO. 4748

	NAME		Relationship to Person First Named	AGE	SEX	BLOOD	TRIBAL ENROLLMENT		
							Year	County	No.
1	Perry, Edmund	22		19	M	Full	1896	Sans Bois	10058
2									
3									
4									
5									
6									
7									
8									
9									
10									
11									
12									
13									
14									
15	ENROLLMENT OF NOS. ~~1~~ HEREON								
16	APPROVED BY THE SECRETARY								
17	OF INTERIOR MAR 19 1903								

TRIBAL ENROLLMENT OF PARENTS

	Name of Father	Year	County	Name of Mother	Year	County
1	Leman Perry	dead	San[sic] Bois	Charlotte Perry	dead	San[sic] Bois
2						
3						
4						
5						
6						
7						
8						
9						
10						
11						
12						
13						
14				Date of Application for Enrollment.		
15				Sept. 11/ 1899		
16						
17						

248

Choctaw By Blood Enrollment Cards 1898-1914

RESIDENCE:	Tobucksy	COUNTY.	**Choctaw Nation**	**Choctaw Roll**	CARD NO.
POST OFFICE:	Mᶜ Alester, I.T.			*(Not Including Freedmen)*	FIELD NO. 4749

Dawes' Roll No.	NAME		Relationship to Person First Named	AGE	SEX	BLOOD	TRIBAL ENROLLMENT		
							Year	County	No.
DEAD.	₁ Amos, Sanders			37	M	Full	1896	Tobucksy	120
13112	₂ " Ann	29	Wife	26	F	"	"	"	121
13113	₃ " John	12	Son	9	M	"	"	"	122
13114	₄ " Eastman	4	"	1	"	"			
	₅								
	₆								
	₇								
	₈								
	₉								
	₁₀								
	₁₁								
	₁₂ No. 1 HEREON DISMISSED UNDER ORDER OF THE COMMISSION TO THE FIVE CIVILIZED TRIBES OF MARCH 31, 1905.								
	₁₃								
	₁₄								
	₁₅ ENROLLMENT OF NOS. 2 3 & 4 HEREON APPROVED BY THE SECRETARY OF INTERIOR MAR 19 1903								
	₁₆								
	₁₇								

TRIBAL ENROLLMENT OF PARENTS

Name of Father	Year	County	Name of Mother	Year	County
₁ James Amos	Dd	Miss	Mahala Amos	Dd	Miss
₂ Tom Barkns[sic]	"	"	Sally Barkns	"	"
₃ No.1			No.2		
₄ " 1			" 2		
₅					
₆					
₇					
₈ For child of No.1 see NB (March 3,1905) Card #379					
₉					
₁₀			No.1 on roll as Sandos Amos		
₁₁			" 2 " " " Annie "		
₁₂ No.1 Died March 15, 1902: Proof of death filed Dec. 30, 1902					
₁₃					
₁₄					
₁₅					
₁₆				Date of Application for Enrollment.	9/
₁₇					

P.O. Carbon IT 11/1/04

Choctaw By Blood Enrollment Cards 1898-1914

RESIDENCE: Tobucksy COUNTY.
POST OFFICE: W[sic] Calvin

Choctaw Nation

Choctaw Roll (Not Including Freedmen)

CARD NO.
FIELD NO. 1750

Dawes' Roll No.	NAME	Relationship to Person Named	AGE	SEX	BLOOD	TRIBAL ENROLLMENT Year	County	No.
13115	1 Joe, Adam ³³	First Named	30	M	Full	1896	Tobucksy	6643
13116	2 " Ellen ⁴³	wife	40	f	Full	1896	"	6644
13117	3 Frazier Salena ⁷	Sister No 2	4	f	Full	1896	"	4014
	4							
	5							
	6							
	7							
	8							
	9							
	10							
	11							
	12							
	13							
	14							
	15							
	16							
	17							

ENROLLMENT
OF NOS. 1 2 & 3 HEREON
APPROVED BY THE SECRETARY
OF INTERIOR MAR 19 1903

TRIBAL ENROLLMENT OF PARENTS

	Name of Father	Year	County	Name of Mother	Year	County
1	Joe Frabbe[sic]	dead	Skullyville			
2	Mack Durant	"	San[sic] Bois	X Anderson		Atoka
3	Emziar[sic] Frazier		Tobucksy	X Mrs. Anderson		Atoka
4						
5						
6						
7						
8						
9						
10			No3 on 1896 roll as Serena Frazier	X Mrs Anderson wife		
11				of Wᵐ Anderson of		
12				Atoka Co		
13						
14						
15				Date of Application for Enrollment.		
16				Sept. 11/ 1899		
17						

250

Choctaw By Blood Enrollment Cards 1898-1914

RESIDENCE: Tobucksy COUNTY. **Choctaw Nation** **Choctaw Roll** CARD No.
POST OFFICE: McAlester, I.T. *(Not Including Freedmen)* FIELD No. 4751

Dawes' Roll No.	NAME		Relationship to Person First Named	AGE	SEX	BLOOD	TRIBAL ENROLLMENT		
							Year	County	No.
13118	1 Hancock, Lewis	36	First Named	33	M	Full	1896	Tobucksy	5325
13119	2 " Betsy	33	Wife	30	F	"	"	"	5326
13120	3 " Cornelia	13	Dau	10	F	"	"	"	5327
13121	4 " Simon M	10	Son	7	M	"	"	"	5328
	5								
	6								
	7								
	8								
	9								
	10								
	11								
	12								
	13								
	14								
	15								
	16								
	17								

ENROLLMENT
OF NOS. 1 2 3 & 4 HEREON
APPROVED BY THE SECRETARY
OF INTERIOR Mar 19, 1903

TRIBAL ENROLLMENT OF PARENTS

	Name of Father	Year	County	Name of Mother	Year	County
1	Simon Hancock	Dd	San[sic] Bois	Maggie Hancock	Dd	Tobucksy
2	William Joel	"	Sugar Loaf	Manda Joel	"	Sugar Loaf
3	No.1			No.2		
4	" 1			" 2		
5						
6						
7						
8						
9						
10						
11						
12						
13						
14						
15						
16						
17						Date of Application for Enrollment 9/11/99

RESIDENCE: Sans Bois COUNTY. **Choctaw Nation** **Choctaw Roll** CARD NO.
POST OFFICE: Stigler (Not Including Freedmen) FIELD NO. 4752

Dawes' Roll No.	NAME	Relationship to Person First Named	AGE	SEX	BLOOD	TRIBAL ENROLLMENT		
						Year	County	No.
VOID 1	James Sissie	Named	23	f	Full	1893	Tobucksy	839
VOID 2	Nail Amanda ⁴	D	2	f				
3								
4								
5								
6								
7								
8								
9								
10								
11								
12								
13								
14								
15								
16								
17								

CANCELLED

Record transferred to Choc. Card 4851

TRIBAL ENROLLMENT OF PARENTS

	Name of Father	Year	County	Name of Mother	Year	County
1	Melvin James	Dead	Gaines	[Illegible] Williams		Gaines
2	Dick Nail		San[sic] Bois	No 1		
3						
4						
5						
6						

No1 on Tobucksy Co PR 1893 P 100 No 839
No.2 Died Oct 7, 1902: Proof of death filed Dec 30, 1902.
Correct given name of N°1 is Salina. She was the wife of
Richard Nail on Choc. Card #2844 in 1896. In 1899
they were separated but are now living together
Name of N°1 is also on Choctaw card #4851. See testimony
of Richard Nail Dec. 22, 1902

Enrollment of N°1 on this card cancelled as N°1 is a duplicate
enrollment of N°1 on Choc. Card #4851 Feb 3, 1903
See testimony of Richard Nail of Dec 22, 1903
N°2 hereon transferred to Choc Card #4851 with
its mother, Feb 3, 1903

Sept 12/ 1899
Date of Application for Enrollment.

252

Choctaw By Blood Enrollment Cards 1898-1914

RESIDENCE: Chickasaw Dist.   COUNTY. **Choctaw Nation**   **Choctaw Roll**   CARD No.

POST OFFICE: Marlow   *(Not Including Freedmen)*   FIELD No. 4753

Dawes' Roll No.	NAME	Relationship to Person First Named	AGE	SEX	BLOOD	TRIBAL ENROLLMENT		
						Year	County	No.
DP 1/28/03	1 Brummett Wilburn	Named	76	M	IW			
	2							
	3							
	4							
	5							
	6							
	7							
	8							
	9							
	10							
	11							
	12							
	13							
	14							
	15							
	16							
	17							

DISMISSED FEB 4 1907

TRIBAL ENROLLMENT OF PARENTS

	Name of Father	Year	County	Name of Mother	Year	County
1	John Brummett	Dead	US Cit	Elizabeth Brummett	dead	US Cit
2						
3						
4						
5						
6	Admitted by Dawes Com #630					
7	See letter of Taylor Percival filed March 17,1903					
8						
9						
10	No1 died about September 19, 1902; Proof of death filed February 4, 1907					
11						
12						
13						
14						
15					Date of Application for Enrollment.	
16						
17					Sept 12/ 1899	

Choctaw By Blood Enrollment Cards 1898-1914

Dawes' Roll No.	NAME		Relationship to Person First Named	AGE	SEX	BLOOD	TRIBAL ENROLLMENT		
							Year	County	No.
13124	1 Durant James	36	First Named	33	m	full	1896	Atoka	3590
13125	2 " Susan	31	wife	28	f	"	1896	"	3591
	3 " Dixon		s	1	m	"			
	4								
	5								
	6								
	7								
	8								
	9								
	10								
	11								
	12								
	13								
	14								
	15								
	16								
	17								

RESIDENCE: Blue
POST OFFICE: Caddo
COUNTY. Choctaw Nation
Choctaw Roll (Not Including Freedmen)
CARD NO.
FIELD NO. 4754

#3 DISMISSED JAN 31 1907

ENROLLMENT OF NOS. 1 and 2 HEREON APPROVED BY THE SECRETARY OF INTERIOR MAR 19 1903

TRIBAL ENROLLMENT OF PARENTS

	Name of Father	Year	County	Name of Mother	Year	County
1	Esias Pisachabe	Dead	Atoka			
2						
3	No1		No2[sic]			
4						
5						
6						
7	Testimony as to the birth of No3 to be supplied					
8						
9	For children of No2 see NB (Apr 26-06) Card #379					
10						
11	No3 died in the winter of 1900. Proof of death filed January 28, 1907					
12	No1 Died prior to Sept 25, 1902 not entitled to land or money					
13	See copy of Indian Office letter of Aug 4,1908 (Land 45887-1908)				Date of Application for Enrollment.	
14						
15					Sept 12th 1899	
16						
17	No2 now Susan Shadkey P O Boswell Okla					

RESIDENCE:	Cherokee Nation COUNTY.	**Choctaw Nation**		Choctaw Roll		CARD NO.	
POST OFFICE:	Nowata			(Not Including Freedmen)		FIELD NO. 4755	

Dawes' Roll No.	NAME	Relationship to Person First Named	AGE	SEX	BLOOD	TRIBAL ENROLLMENT		
						Year	County	No.
DP	1 Poe Georgia C	Named	33	f	1/8	1896	Tobucksy	939
DP	2 Bryce Czarina V	d	14	f	1/16	1896	"	940
DP	3 " Charles M	Son	12	m	1/16	1896	"	941
DP	4 " Annie L	d	10	f	1/16	1896	"	942
DP	5 " Walter J	Son	5	m	1/16	1896	"	944
	6							
#1-2-3-4-5- DISMISSED								
	8	JAN 26 1905						
	9 No1 on 1896 roll Geo C Bryce							
	10 No2 " " " C M A "							
	3 " " " Charles M "							
	11 4 " " " Annie L "							
	12 5 " " " Jordan "							
	13 Nº2 on Cherokee Card #4989 as Czarina V M'Caffree							
	14							
	15 Nos 1,3,4 and 5 selected allotment of lands in the Cherokee Nation May 3'04 See letter of Dec 17 '04							
	16							
	17							

TRIBAL ENROLLMENT OF PARENTS

Name of Father	Year	County	Name of Mother	Year	County
1 Jno P Rogers	Dead	Jackforks[sic]	Mary E Rogers		Chickasaw Dist
2 W.P. Bryce		Non Citizen	No1		
3 Do		" "	No1		
4 Do		" "	No1		
5 Do		" "	No1		
6					
7		Enrollment of Nº1 on Cherokee Card 4988 Approved by Secy of Int 12/5/02			
8		" Nº2,3,4&5 on Cherokee Card 4989 " " " " 12/5/02			
9		See letter of Cherokee Enrollment Division 12/16/02 filed this date, 12/16/02			
10			No 1-2&3 admitted to citizenship in		
11			Cherokee Nation Apl 12th 1888.		
12			Certificate of admission exhibited.		
13			All above enrolled in the Cherokee		
			Nation & No1 elects for herself &		
14			children to be enrolled & take		
15			allotment with the in the		
16 Date of Application for Enrollment.			Cherokees[sic] Nation(?)		
17 Sept 12 - 1899	No.2 Ramona IT 1/12/05				

255

Choctaw By Blood Enrollment Cards 1898-1914

RESIDENCE: Tobucksy   COUNTY. **Choctaw Nation**   **Choctaw Roll** CARD NO.
POST OFFICE: McAlester   *(Not Including Freedmen)* FIELD NO. 4756

Dawes' Roll No.	NAME		Relationship to Person Named	AGE	SEX	BLOOD	TRIBAL ENROLLMENT		
							Year	County	No.
I.W.575	1 Hill David	45	First Named	32	M	IW	1896	Tobucksy	14612
13126	2 " Nellie B	24	Wife	21	f	1/16	1896	"	5343
13127	3 " J B	5	Son	2	m	1/32			
13128	4 " Harry F	3	Son	1/3yr	"	1/32			
13129	5 " Mable Luceil[sic]	2	Dau	1mo	F	1/32			
13130	6 " Houston E	1	Son	4mo	m	1/32			
	7								
	8								
	9	ENROLLMENT							
	10	OF NOS. ~~~~1~~~~ HEREON APPROVED BY THE SECRETARY							
	11	OF INTERIOR FEB -8 1904							
	12								
	13	ENROLLMENT							
	14	OF NOS. 2 3 4 5 & 6 HEREON APPROVED BY THE SECRETARY							
	15	OF INTERIOR MAR 19 1903							
	16								
	17								

TRIBAL ENROLLMENT OF PARENTS

	Name of Father	Year	County	Name of Mother	Year	County
1	JB Hill	dead	Non Cit	Catherine Hill	Dead	Non Cit
2	Frank Morgan		Tobucksy	Essima Morgan	"	Choctaw
3	No 1			No 2		
4	No1			No2		
5	No.1			No.2		
6	No.1			No.2		
7						
8	Admitted by Dawes Com Case (#1312?) - Error					
9	No.1 admitted as a intermarried citizen: case 1370,					
10	No2 on 1896 roll Nellie B Hill					
11	No.5 Enrolled Oct 26th, 1900					
12	No.6 Born Dec. 2, 1901: Enrolled April 4, 1902					
13	See additional testimony of No.1, taken Oct 15, 1902					
14	See affidavit of N⁰1 as to residence at time of his marriage to N⁰2 filed July 11, 1903					
15	For child of Nos 1&2 see NB (Apr 26'06) #1172 " " " " " " (Mar 3'05) #380				Date of Application for Enrollment.	
16	P.O. Naples I.T.				Sept 12/ 1899	
17	[Illegible] Okla					

256

Choctaw By Blood Enrollment Cards 1898-1914

RESIDENCE: Gaines   COUNTY. **Choctaw Nation**   **Choctaw Roll** *(Not Including Freedmen)*   CARD NO.

POST OFFICE: Wilberton[sic]   FIELD NO. **4757**

Dawes' Roll No.	NAME	Relationship to Person First Named	AGE	SEX	BLOOD	TRIBAL ENROLLMENT Year	County	No.
13131	1 Christie Isham 48	First Named	45	m	Full	1896	Gaines	2294
13132	2 " Edward 11	son	8	m	"	1896	"	2296
13133	3 " Andrew 7	"	4	"	"	1896	"	2297
13134	4 DIED PRIOR TO SEPTEMBER 25, 1902 Dora	d	1/2	f	"			
	5							
	6							
	7							
	8							
	9							
	10							
	11							
	12							
	13							
	14							
	15							
	16							
	17							

ENROLLMENT
OF NOS. 1 2 3 & 4
APPROVED BY THE SECRETARY HEREON
OF INTERIOR   Mar 19 1903

TRIBAL ENROLLMENT OF PARENTS

	Name of Father	Year	County	Name of Mother	Year	County
1	Alex Christie	Dead	Kiamitia			Towson
2	No.1			Lucinda Christie	Dead	Gaines
3	No.1			Do Do		
4	No.1			Do Do		
5						
6						
7						
8	No.4 died March 7, 1901: Enrollment cancelled by Department July 8, 1904					
9						
10						
11						
12						
13						
14						
15						Date of Application for Enrollment.
16				Date of Application for Enrollment.		Sept 12/ 1899
17						

RESIDENCE: Tobucksy COUNTY. **Choctaw Nation** Choctaw Roll CARD No.
POST OFFICE: Kiowa, I.T. (Not Including Freedmen) FIELD No. **4758**

Dawes' Roll No.	NAME	Relationship to Person Named	AGE	SEX	BLOOD	TRIBAL ENROLLMENT		
						Year	County	No.
13135	₁ Kemp, Stanton	³¹ First Named	28	M	Full	1896	Tobucksy	2356
15497	₂ Noel, Jennie	¹⁹ Step Dau	16	F	"	1896	"	9608
15498	₃ Kemp, Bennett	⁸ Son	8	M	"	1896	"	2358
15499	₄ " Sinie	⁷ Dau	7	F	"	1896	"	2359
15591	₅ " Lena	① Dau	3	F	"			
	6							
	7							
	8	ENROLLMENT						
	9	OF NOS. 2-3-4 HEREON APPROVED BY THE SECRETARY						
	10	OF INTERIOR May 9 1904						
	11							
	12	For child of Nos 1 and 2 see NB (March 3,1905) #1294						
	13	ENROLLMENT		ENROLLMENT				
	14	OF NOS. ~~~ 1 ~~~ HEREON		OF NOS. ~~ 5 ~~ HEREON				
	15	APPROVED BY THE SECRETARY OF INTERIOR Mar. 9 1903		APPROVED BY THE SECRETARY OF INTERIOR Sep 22 1904				
	16							
	17							

TRIBAL ENROLLMENT OF PARENTS

	Name of Father	Year	County	Name of Mother	Year	County
₁	Bennett Kemp		Tobucksy	Siney Kemp		Tobucksy
₂	No.1			Celie Kemp	dead	"
₃	No.1			" "		"
₄	No.1			" "		"
₅	No.1			No.2		
₆						
₇	No.5 Born Sept 26-1901. Application first received April 4,1902 and returned for					
₈	information relative to mother. Additional affidavits filed and No.5 enrolled July 19, 1904.					
₉	No.3 on 1896 Choctaw roll as Bennett Campbell					
₁₀	No.4 on 1896 " " " Sinie "					
₁₁	Nos 3 and 4 transferred from Choctaw Card #D 924.					
₁₂	No 1 On P 54 - #484 - 93 - P R Tobucksy Co as Stanton Kemp					
₁₃	" 2 " " " 487 " " " " " Jimmie Noel					
₁₄						
₁₅	No 1 on 1896 roll as Stanton Campbell					
₁₆	No 2 " 1896 " " Jennie Noel					
₁₇	See testimony of Isom Perkins as to No.2.					

Date of Application for Enrollment. 9/12/99

Blanco I.T. April 13' "04

Choctaw By Blood Enrollment Cards 1898-1914

RESIDENCE:
POST OFFICE: Bokchito, I.T. COUNTY. **Choctaw Nation** **Choctaw Roll** CARD NO.
(Not Including Freedmen) FIELD NO. **4759**

Dawes' Roll No.	NAME	Relationship to Person	AGE	SEX	BLOOD	TRIBAL ENROLLMENT		
						Year	County	No.
I.W. 1033	1 Landerdale, Thomas J ⁴³	First Named	40	M	I.W.			
13136	2 " Eliza ⁴³	wife	40	F	Full	1896	Blue	1598
13137	3 Beams, Ephraim W ¹³	Son	10	M	3/4	"	"	1602
13138	4 Landerdale, William T ²	Son	4mo	M	1/2			
	5							
	6							
	7							
	8							
	9							
	10							
	11							
	12							
	13							
	14							
	15							
	16							
	17							

ENROLLMENT
OF NOS. ~~~ 1 ~~~ HEREON
APPROVED BY THE SECRETARY
OF INTERIOR Oct 21 1904

ENROLLMENT
OF NOS. 2, 3 and 4 HEREON
APPROVED BY THE SECRETARY
OF INTERIOR Mar 19 1903

TRIBAL ENROLLMENT OF PARENTS

	Name of Father	Year	County	Name of Mother	Year	County
1	Eph. Landerdale		Non Cit	Sarah Landerdale		Non Cit
2	Saml Houston	Dd	Blue	Eliz Houston	Dd	Blue
3	Calvin Beams	"	"	No.2		
4	No.1			No.2		
5						
6						
7						
8						
9	Affidavit of No.2 as to marriage to two men prior to her marriage					
10	with No.1 and stating date of death of each husband, filed July 10, 1903.					
11	No.4 Enrolled July 6, 1901.					
12	See 3853					
13	No.2 on 1896 roll as Eliza Beams					
14						
15	See Choctaw Card No. 3684 for Calvin					
16	P.O. Wade I.T. 12/10/02	S Beams, and Choctaw Card No 3775 for				Date of Application for Enrollment.
17	P.O. Jackson, Oct 21, 1903	Julius J and Arthur G Beams, the other children of No.2				9/12/99

259

Choctaw By Blood Enrollment Cards 1898-1914

RESIDENCE: Tobucksy   COUNTY. **Choctaw Nation**   **Choctaw Roll**   CARD No.
POST OFFICE: McAlester, I.T.   *(Not Including Freedmen)*   FIELD No. 4760

Dawes' Roll No.		NAME	Relationship to Person	AGE	SEX	BLOOD	TRIBAL ENROLLMENT		
							Year	County	No.
DEAD.	1	Thompson, John P	First Named	40	M	Full	1896	Tobucksy	12017
DEAD.	2	" Catherine DEAD	Wife	33	F	"	"	"	12018
13139	3	" Lucinda 13	Dau	10	F	"	"	"	12019
	4								
	5								
	6								
	7								
	8								
	9								
	10	No.1 and 2 HEREON DISMISSED UNDER							
	11	ORDER OF THE COMMISSION TO THE FIVE							
	12	CIVILIZED TRIBES OF MARCH 31, 1905.							
	13								
	14	ENROLLMENT							
	15	OF NOS. ~ 3 ~~ HEREON APPROVED BY THE SECRETARY							
	16	OF INTERIOR MAR 19 1903							
	17								

TRIBAL ENROLLMENT OF PARENTS

	Name of Father	Year	County	Name of Mother	Year	County
1	Saml. Thompson	Dd	San[sic] Bois	Maggie Thompson	Dd	Tobucksy
2	Jas A no li tub be	"	Tobucksy	Lucinda	"	"
3	No.1			No.2		
4						
5						
6						
7	No.2 Died November 25, 1900. Evidence of death filed March 21, 1901.					
8	No.1 Died November 27, 1900. Evidence of death filed March 21, 1901.					
9						
10						
11						
12	On roll as J. P. Thompson.					
13						
14						
15					Date of Application for Enrollment.	
16						
17					9/12/99	

Choctaw By Blood Enrollment Cards 1898-1914

RESIDENCE: Jacks Fork   COUNTY. **Choctaw Nation**   **Choctaw Roll**   CARD NO.

POST OFFICE: Antlers   *(Not Including Freedmen)*   FIELD NO. 4761

Dawes' Roll No.	NAME	Relationship to Person First Named	AGE	SEX	BLOOD	TRIBAL ENROLLMENT		
						Year	County	No.
I.W. 483	1 Arnote Andrew J ³⁷	First Named	34	m	IW			
13140	2 " Annie T ³⁰	Wife	27	f	1/8	1896	Jack Fork	9472
13141	3 MᶜCulic Vivian M ⁹	S Dau	6	f	1/16	1896	" "	9473
13142	4 Arnote William T ²	Son	1mo	M	1/16			
13143	5 " Dorothy V ¹	Dau	3wks	F	1/16			
	6							
	7							
	8							
	9							
	10							
	11	ENROLLMENT						
	12	OF NOS. 1 HEREON APPROVED BY THE SECRETARY						
	13	OF INTERIOR SEP 12 1903						
	14	ENROLLMENT						
	15	OF NOS. 2 3 4 and 5 HEREON						
	16	APPROVED BY THE SECRETARY OF INTERIOR MAR 19 1903						
	17							

TRIBAL ENROLLMENT OF PARENTS

	Name of Father	Year	County	Name of Mother	Year	County
1	Wᵐ Arnate[sic]		Non Cit	Eliza Arnate		Non Cit
2	Geo Taaffe	Dead	Non Cit	Fudorua Taaffe		
3	Robt P MᶜCulic			No2		
4	No.1			No2		
5	Nº1			Nº2		
6						
7						
8						
9	Nº2 on 1896 roll as Annie T MᶜCulic					
10	No4 Enrolled April 27, 1901					
11	Nº5 Born Aug. 15, 1902: enrolled Sept. 4, 1902					
	For child of Nos 1&2 see NB (March 3,1905) #1044					
12						
13						
14						
15						
16					Date of Application for Enrollment.	
17						

Choctaw By Blood Enrollment Cards 1898-1914

RESIDENCE:	Tobucksy	COUNTY.							
POST OFFICE:	South Canadian								

Choctaw Nation

Choctaw Roll
(Not Including Freedmen)   FIELD NO. 4762

Dawes' Roll No.	NAME	Relationship to Person First Named	AGE	SEX	BLOOD	TRIBAL ENROLLMENT		
						Year	County	No.
DEAD 1	McDuff Andrew J		71	M	IW	1896	Tobucksy	4864
2								
3								
4								
5								
6								
7								
8								
9								
10								
11								
12								
13								
14								
15								
16								
17								

No._____ HEREON DISMISSED UNDER
ORDER OF THE COMMISSION TO THE FIVE
CIVILIZED TRIBES OF MARCH 31, 1905.

TRIBAL ENROLLMENT OF PARENTS

	Name of Father	Year	County	Name of Mother	Year	County
1	Wm F McDuff	Dead	Non Cit	Christian McDuff		Non Cit
2						
3						
4						
5						
6						
7	Admitted by the Dawes Com					
8	Case 1308 as A J McDuff					
9						
10	No1 Died about the middle of April 1901. See sworn statement					
11	of Will T Walker County Clerk Tobucksey[sic] Co C.N. filed herein May 18, 1901					
12						
13						
14						
15					Date of Application for Enrollment.	
16						
17					Sept 14- 1899	

CANCELLED

Applicant died prior to1 ratification of Choctaw-Chickasaw agreement Sept. 25, 1902

Choctaw By Blood Enrollment Cards 1898-1914

Choctaw Nation

Choctaw Roll *(Not Including Freedmen)*

CARD No. FIELD No. 4763

Dawes' Roll No.	NAME	Relationship to Person First Named	AGE	SEX	BLOOD	TRIBAL ENROLLMENT Year	County	No.
13144	1 Jennings Richard P ⁴⁹	First Named	46	M	1/2	1896	Gaines	6619
DEAD	2 " Rosco DEAD	Son	4	M	1/4	"		
15769	3 Jennings, Noah ¹⁷	Son	17	M	1/4	1896	Gaines	6621
15770	4 " Martha J ¹³	Dau	13	F	1/4	1896	"	6622
	5							
	6							
	7	ENROLLMENT						
	8	OF NOS. 3 and 4 HEREON APPROVED BY THE SECRETARY						
	9	OF INTERIOR DEC 28 1904						
	10	No. 2 HEREON DISMISSED UNDER ORDER OF THE COMMISSION TO THE FIVE						
	11	CIVILIZED TRIBES OF MARCH 31, 1905.						
	12	Nos 3 and 4 originally listed for enrollment						
	13	Sept 14, 1899 on Choctaw card #D-492 transferred						
	14	to this card Dec. 15,1904. See decision of Nov 28,1904						
	15	ENROLLMENT						
	16	OF NOS. ~~~1~~~ HEREON APPROVED BY THE SECRETARY						
	17	OF INTERIOR MAR 19 1903						

TRIBAL ENROLLMENT OF PARENTS

	Name of Father	Year	County	Name of Mother	Year	County
1	Noah Jennings	Dead	Skullyville	Martha Jennings	Dead	Skullyville
2	No.1			Annie M Jennings	Dead	Non Cit
3	No.1			Lizzie Jennings		
4	No.1			" "		
5			3/30/23 See Old Creek Card 1197			
6	No1 On roll Richard R Jennings					
7						
8	Evidence of parents[sic] marriage to					
9	be supplied					
10						
11	Wife, Lizzie Jennings and two children of No.1 are on Chickasaw card #1786					
12	Lizzie Jennings, wife of No.1 and 3 children					
13	on Choctaw card D.492 3/7, 1900					
	No.2 died in the fall of 1899. See testimony of Richard P Jennings					
14	No.1 is the legal guardian of the two Kanawa			Date of Application for Enrollment.		
15	children on Chickasaw card #1648			Sept 14ᵗʰ 99		
16	No.3 on 1893 Choctaw Pay Roll Gaines Co Page 28 No. 260					
	No.4 " " " " " " " 28 No. 261					
17	For child of No3 see NB (Apr 26-06) #1275					

Choctaw By Blood Enrollment Cards 1898-1914

RESIDENCE: Tobucksy COUNTY.
POST OFFICE: ~~So~~ Canadian

Choctaw Nation

Choctaw Roll
(Not Including Freedmen)

CARD NO.
FIELD NO. **4764**

Dawes' Roll No.	NAME		Relationship to Person Named	AGE	SEX	BLOOD	TRIBAL ENROLLMENT		
							Year	County	No.
13145	1 Martin, Sillen	47	First Named	44	F	1/2	1893	P.R. Gaines	400
13146	2 " Gertrude	19	D	16	F	1/4	1893	Kiamitia	103
13147	3 " Edmund	16	S	13	M	1/4	1893	"	104
13148	4 " Tandy N	8	S	5	"	1/4			
15927	5 " Oscar	13	Son	13	M	1/4			
	6	ENROLLMENT							
	7	OF NOS. Five HEREON APPROVED BY THE SECRETARY							
	8	OF INTERIOR Aug 23, 1905							
	9	No.2 on 1894 Cherokee Roll #1112 Illinois							
	10	No.3 " 1894 " " #1113 "							
	11	No.4 " 1894 " " #1115 "							
		No.2 on 1896 " " #1255 "							
	12	No.3 " " " " #1256 "							
	13	No.4 " " " " #1258 "							
	14								
	15	ENROLLMENT							
	16	OF NOS. 1 2 3 & 4 HEREON APPROVED BY THE SECRETARY							
	17	OF INTERIOR Mar. 9, 1903							

TRIBAL ENROLLMENT OF PARENTS

	Name of Father	Year	County	Name of Mother	Year	County
1	Edmund F Krebs	Dead	Gaines	Pomelia Krebs	Dead	Skullyville
2	Lewis Martin		a Cherokee	No.1		
3	Do Do		"	No.1		
4	Do Do		"	No.1		
5	Lewis J Martin		"	No.1		
6	No2 on P. 120 No 103 Kimatia[sic] Co P.R.					
7	No3 " " " " 104 " " " "					
8	Lewis A Martin- father of Nos 2,3,4 is a Cherokee citizen and enrolled on Cherokee card #2227 with one child named Oscar by same mother.					
9	No4 Born Feb 9, 1894. Proof of birth received and filed Dec. 24, 1902					
10						
11	All on Cherokee roll, but No1 is a Choctaw					
12						
13	See about this. See testimony of Lewis A Martin					
14	Application was made for enrollment of No5 at Canadian I.T. in					
15	Sept, 1899: Name placed on this card April 7, 1905.				#1 to 4	
16					Date of Application for Enrollment.	
17					Sept 14/99	

Choctaw By Blood Enrollment Cards 1898-1914

Dawes' Roll No.	NAME	Relationship to Person First Named	AGE	SEX	BLOOD	TRIBAL ENROLLMENT Year	County	No.
13149	1 Robinson, Lourena L 38	Named	35	F	3/4	1896	Blue	10916
13150	2 " Coleman 19	Son	16	M	3/4	"	"	10917
13151	3 " Carrie A 17	Dau	14	F	3/4	"	"	10918
13152	4 " Nannie B 15	"	12	F	3/4	"	"	10919
13153	5 " Ella L 12	"	9	F	3/4	"	"	10920
13154	6 " McKee F 7	Son	4	M	3/4	"	"	10921
	7							
	8							
	9							
	10							
	11							
	12							
	13							
	14							
	15	ENROLLMENT OF NOS. 1 2 3 4 5 & 6 HEREON						
	16	APPROVED BY THE SECRETARY						
	17	OF INTERIOR MAR 9 1903						

TRIBAL ENROLLMENT OF PARENTS

	Name of Father	Year	County	Name of Mother	Year	County
1	Watson Daney	Dd	Red River	Nancy Daney	1896	Blue
2	M F Robinson	"	Blue	No.1		
3	"	"	"	" 1		
4	"	"	"	" 1		
5	"	"	"	" 1		
6	"	"	"	" 1		
7						
8						
9						
10						
11	For child of No.1 see NB (March 3, 1905) #1241					
12						
13				No.1 on roll as L. L. Roberson		
14				" 2 " " " Coleman D "		
15				" 3 " " " Carrie A "		
16				" 4 " " " Nannie B "		
17				" 5 " " " Ella L "		
				" 6 " " " M F "		

Date of Application for Enrollment.

9/14/99

265

RESIDENCE: Tobucksy   COUNTY.
POST OFFICE: Choate, I.T.   **Choctaw Nation**

Choctaw Roll (*Not Including Freedmen*)

CARD NO.
FIELD NO. **4766**

Dawes' Roll No.	NAME	Relationship to Person First Named	AGE	SEX	BLOOD	TRIBAL ENROLLMENT Year	County	No.
13155	1 Pearson, Robert T 41	First Named	38	M	1/4	1896	Tobucksy	10269
I.W. 576	2 " Amelia E 33	Wife	30	F	I.W.	"	"	14933
13156	3 " Walter R 14	Son	11	M	1/8	"	"	10270
13157	4 " Laura B 11	Dau	8	F	1/8	"	"	10271
13158	5 " Hazel F 10	"	7	F	1/8	"	"	10272
13159	6 " Paul E 7	Son	4	M	1/8	"	"	10273
DEAD.	7 " William F 2	Son	2mo	M	1/8			
13160	8 " James C 1	Son	6mo	M	1/8			
	9							
	10							

ENROLLMENT
OF NOS. 1 3 4 5 6 & 8 HEREON
APPROVED BY THE SECRETARY
OF INTERIOR MAR 19 1903

ENROLLMENT
OF NOS. 2 HEREON
APPROVED BY THE SECRETARY
OF INTERIOR Feb -8 1904

No.7 Died Sept 29,1900: Proof of death filed Dec 30,1902
Nº8 Born Sept 12,1901: enrolled March 19, 1902
Certified copy of certificate of marriage between
Nºˢ 1 and 2 filed Jany. 3, 1903

TRIBAL ENROLLMENT OF PARENTS

	Name of Father	Year	County	Name of Mother	Year	County
1	Robert Pearson	Dd	Chic. Cit	Eliz. Pearson	Dd	Chic. Nat.
2	Heffner	"	Non Cit	Sarah J Heffner	"	Non Cit
3	No.1			No.2		
4	" 1			" 2		
5	" 1			" 2		
6	" 1			" 2		
7	No.1			No.2		
8	Nº2			Nº2		

No. 7 HEREON DISMISSED UNDER ORDER OF THE COMMISSION TO THE FIVE CIVILIZED TRIBES OF MARCH 31, 1905.

For child of Nos1&2 see NB (Mar3 05) #632

No.1 on roll as Robt T Piercen
" 2 " " " Emeline E Pearson
" 3 " " " Walter R Piercen
" 4 " " " Laura V "
" 5 " " " Hazel T "
" 6 " " " Ernest P "

No.7 Enrolled Aug. 24, 1900

Cert of Mar. of R.T. Pearson and A.E. Heifner [sic] Oct 16-87
PO Indianola IT 4/1/05 presented; same is in due form and satisfactory but not in condition to be filed.

Date of Application for Enrollment 9/14/9

Choctaw By Blood Enrollment Cards 1898-1914

RESIDENCE: Tobucksy COUNTY.
POST OFFICE: South Canadian

Choctaw Nation

Choctaw
(Not Including Freedmen) FIELD NO. 4767

	NAME		Relationship to Person First Named	AGE	SEX	BLOOD	TRIBAL ENROLLMENT		
							Year	County	No.
1	Haight Nancy B	22		19	f	1/2	1896	Jackson	4842
2	Gardner Critten A	7	son	4	m	1/2	1896	"	4843
3	" Winnie J	4	d	1	f	1/2			
4	Haight, Dora Viola	1	Dau	16mo	F	1/4			
5									
6									
7									
8									
9									
10									
11									
12									
13									
14									
15	ENROLLMENT OF NOS. 1 2 3 & 4 HEREON								
16	APPROVED BY THE SECRETARY OF INTERIOR MAR 19 1903								
17									

TRIBAL ENROLLMENT OF PARENTS

	Name of Father	Year	County	Name of Mother	Year	County
1	Edmund Gardner		Kiamitia	Jane Gardner	Dead	Jackson
2	R Gardner		Jackson	No1		
3	Do Do		Do	No1		
4	Albert Haight		noncitizen	N°1		
5						
6						
7						
8						
9	No1 on 1896 roll Nancy Gardner					
10	No2 " " " Critte W "					
11	N°4 Born April 10, 1901: enrolled Aug 21, 1902					
12						
13						
14						
15					#1 to 3	
16					Date of Application for Enrollment.	
17					Sept 19th 1899	

267

RESIDENCE:	Tobucksy	COUNTY.	**Choctaw Nation**			Choctaw Roll		CARD NO.	
POST OFFICE:	South Canadian					*(Not Including Freedmen)*		FIELD NO. 4768	

Dawes' Roll No.	NAME	Relationship to Person	AGE	SEX	BLOOD	TRIBAL ENROLLMENT		
						Year	County	No.
13165 ₁	Walker, William T ²⁵	First Named	22	M	1/8	1896	Tobucksy	13030
13166 ₂	" Elsie Louise ²	Dau	3m	F	1/16			
₃								
₄								
₅								
₆								
₇	ENROLLMENT OF NOS. 1 and 2 HEREON							
₈	APPROVED BY THE SECRETARY							
₉	OF INTERIOR MAR 19 1903							
₁₀	N⁰1 is now the husband of Ada Hamilton on							
₁₁	Choctaw card #4588 June 3, 1902							
₁₂								
₁₃	See also Choctaw cards							
₁₄	D.215, #4770 and #2395							
₁₅	★ ✗ See Old Creek Card No 2472 for No.1							
₁₆	No.2 Enrolled January 23, 1901							
₁₇								

	TRIBAL ENROLLMENT OF PARENTS					
	Name of Father	Year	County	Name of Mother	Year	County
₁	Geo W Walker	Dead	Tobucksy	Sallie Walker		Tobucksy
₂	No1			Elsie Walker	dead	non-citizen
₃						
₄						
₅						
₆						
₇	On roll Wᵐ L. Walker					
₈						
₉	As to parents[sic] marriage see enrollment					
₁₀	of Sallie Walker Mother					
₁₁	Certificate of marriage dated Sept 10ᵗʰ 99					
₁₂				No1 is husband of Elsie Walker on Choctaw		
₁₃	Also claims Cherokee			Card #D-401. She died October 23, 1900.		
₁₄	No.1 is also on Creek census card #2472. Not on final Creek Roll					
₁₅	It is stated on the above card that G.W. Walker			Sept 14, 1899		
₁₆	father of No.1 is a Creek citizen			Date of Application for Enrollment.		
₁₇	No.1 is on 1895 Creek pay roll as W.T. Walker					

Choctaw By Blood Enrollment Cards 1898-1914

RESIDENCE: Tobucksy
POST OFFICE: South Canadian
COUNTY. **Choctaw Nation**
Choctaw Roll (Not Including Freedmen)
CARD No.
FIELD No. 4769

Dawes' Roll No.	NAME	Relationship to Person	AGE	SEX	BLOOD	TRIBAL ENROLLMENT Year	County	No.
13167	1 Turner Robert F 48	First Named	45	M	1/8	1896	Tobucksy	12023
13168	2 " Olga T 46	Wife	43	f	1/4	1896	"	12024
13169	3 Manners, Eva 23	d	20	f	3/16	1896	"	12026
13170	4 Turner, Leona 21	d	18	f	3/16	1896	"	12027
13171	5 " James 17	S	14	M	3/16	1896	"	12028
13172	6 " Benjamin 15	S	12	"	3/16	1896	"	12029
13173	7 " Apuckshunnebbe 10	S	7	"	3/16	1896	"	12030
13174	8 " Nora F 8	D	3	f	3/16	1896	"	12031
DEAD.	9 Manners, Cynthia Olga 1	Grand Dau	2wks	F	3/32			
I.W. 774	10 " Thomas Edgar	Hus of Nº3	29	M	I.W.			
	11		No1 on roll Robt F Turner					
	ENROLLMENT OF NOS ~~~~ 10 ~~~~ HEREON APPROVED BY THE SECRETARY OF INTERIOR MAY -7 1904		No2 " " Alger G "					
	13		No7 " " Apukshanubbe Turner					
	14		No8 " " Nova F Turner					
	ENROLLMENT OF NOS. 1 2 3 4 5 6 7 & 8 HEREON APPROVED BY THE SECRETARY OF INTERIOR MAR 19 1903		No.3 is now the wife of T.E. Manners a non-citizen. Evidence of marriage filed May 13, 1901.					
	17 T.E. Manners appears on Choc Card D 633 12/20/02							

TRIBAL ENROLLMENT OF PARENTS

	Name of Father	Year	County	Name of Mother	Year	County
1	R F Turner	dead	Non Cit	Ada E Turner	dead	Tobucksy
2	Jas Standly	"	" "	Margaret Standly	"	Non Cit
3	No1			No2		
4	No1			No2		
5	No1			No2		
6	No1			No2		
7	No1			No2	No. 9 HEREON DISMISSED UNDER	
8	No1			No2	ORDER OF THE COMMISSION TO THE FIVE CIVILIZED TRIBES OF MARCH 31, 1905.	
9	T.E. Manners		non-citizen	Nº3		
10	W.B. Manners		" "	Cynthia Manners		non-citz
11	No2 admitted by act of Choctaw Council of Oct, 1874					
12	Nº10 transferred from Choctaw card #D633. See					
13	decision of Feby 29, 1904.					
14	#2 As to parents[sic] marriage see enrollment of					
15	brother J.S. Standly				Date of Application for Enrollment.	
16	Nº9 Born Feby 10, 1902; enrolled Feby 21, 1902				Sept 14th 1899	
17	No.9 Died Aug 19, 1902: Proof of death filed Dec 30/1902					

Choctaw By Blood Enrollment Cards 1898-1914

RESIDENCE: Tobucksy COUNTY.
POST OFFICE: So Canadian, I.T.

Choctaw Nation

Choctaw Roll *(Not Including Freedmen)*

CARD NO.
FIELD NO. 4770

Dawes' Roll No.	NAME	Relationship to Person Named	AGE	SEX	BLOOD	TRIBAL ENROLLMENT		
						Year	County	No.
I.W.577	1 Walker, Sallie 45	First Named	42	F	I.W.	1896	Tobucksy	15162
13175	2 " Cora L R 22	Dau	19	F	1/8	"	"	13031
13176	3 " Arthur L 19	Son	16	M	1/8	"	"	13032
	4							
	5							
	6							
	7							
	8	ENROLLMENT						
	9	OF NOS. ~~~ 1 ~~~ HEREON						
		APPROVED BY THE SECRETARY						
	10	OF INTERIOR FEB -8 1904						
	11							
	12	ENROLLMENT						
	13	OF NOS. 2 & 3 HEREON						
		APPROVED BY THE SECRETARY						
	14	OF INTERIOR MAR 19 1903						
	15	See Choctaw cards						
	16	#2395, #4768 and D.215						
	17							

TRIBAL ENROLLMENT OF PARENTS

Name of Father	Year	County	Name of Mother	Year	County
1 Jake Fatterling		Non Cit	Jane Fatterling		Non Cit
2 G. W. Walker	Dd	Tobucksy	No.1		
3 " " "	"	"	No.1		
4					
5					
6					
7					
8 No.2 and 3 are also on Creek census card #2473					
9 It is stated on the above card that G.W. Walker					
father of these children is a Creek citizen.					
10 Nos 2 and 3 are on the 1890 and 1895 rolls of the					
11 Not on final Creek Roll					
12 3/23/23 See Old Creek Census Card No. 2473 for No.2&3					
13					
14 No.1 admitted by Dawes Comm. #512 as Mrs. Sallie Walker.					
15 " 2 on roll as Cora R. S. Walker.					
16 As to marriage see testimony of No.1 and of					
Cynthia [Illegible]					9/14/99
17 Nos 2 and 3 also claim Cherokee				Date of Application for Enrollment 9/14/99

270

Choctaw By Blood Enrollment Cards 1898-1914

RESIDENCE: Tobucksy COUNTY.
POST OFFICE: So Canadian, I.T.
Choctaw Nation
Choctaw Roll (Not Including Freedmen)
CARD NO.
FIELD NO. 4771

Dawes' Roll No.	NAME		Relationship to Person	AGE	SEX	BLOOD	TRIBAL ENROLLMENT		
							Year	County	No.
13177	1 Smart, Annie	26	First Named	23	F	1/32	1896	Tobucksy	11290
13178	2 " Hazel	8	Dau	5	F	1/64	"	"	11291
13179	3 " Herbert	5	Son	2	M	1/64			
13180	4 " Leroy	3	Son	3mo	M	1/64			
13181	5 " Claud	1	Son	2mo	M	1/64			
	6								
	7								
	8								
	9								
	10								
	11								
	12								
	13								
	14								
	15	ENROLLMENT OF NOS. 1 2 3 4 & 5 HEREON APPROVED BY THE SECRETARY OF INTERIOR MAR 19 1903								
	16								
	17								

TRIBAL ENROLLMENT OF PARENTS

	Name of Father	Year	County	Name of Mother	Year	County
1	Jim Marrs	Dd	Tobucksy	Liza A Marrs		Tobucksy
2	James Smart		Non Cit	No.1		
3	" "		" "	" 1		
4	" "		" "	No.1		
5	" "		" "	No.1		
6						
7						
8						
9						
10	No4 enrolled Dec 18/99. Affidavit					
11	irregular and returned for correction.					
12	~~No3 Affidavit irregular and returned for correction.~~					
13	Affidavits of birth of both Nos 3 and 4					
14	returned corrected and filed Feby 20, 1900					
15	~~No.5 Born August 31, 1901 and enrolled October 29, 1901~~					Date of Application for Enrollment.
16	For child of No.1 see NB (Apr 26-06) No. 561					
17	" " " " " " (Mar 3'05) #384					9/14/99

P.O. Crowder IT 3/17/05

271

RESIDENCE:		COUNTY.								
POST OFFICE: So Canadian, I.T.		**Choctaw Nation**				**Choctaw Roll** *(Not Including Freedmen)*		CARD NO. FIELD NO. 4772		

Dawes' Roll No.	NAME	Relationship to Person	AGE	SEX	BLOOD	TRIBAL ENROLLMENT		
						Year	County	No.
I.W.578	1 Crowder, William E (41)	First Named	38	M	I.W.	1896	Tobucksy	14393
13182	2 " Juanita H 30	Wife	27	F	1/16	1896	Tobucksy	2332
13183	3 " Robert S 8	Son	5	M	1/32			2333
13184	4 " Edwin McC 1	Son	1mo	M	1/32			
	5							
	6							
	7							
	8							
	9							
	10	ENROLLMENT OF NOS. ~~~ 1 ~~~ HEREON						
	11	APPROVED BY THE SECRETARY						
	12	OF INTERIOR FEB 8 1904						
	13							
	14	ENROLLMENT OF NOS. 2 3 & 4 HEREON						
	15	APPROVED BY THE SECRETARY						
	16	OF INTERIOR MAR 19 1903						
	17							

TRIBAL ENROLLMENT OF PARENTS

	Name of Father	Year	County	Name of Mother	Year	County
1	M. C. Crowder		Non Cit	Rosa E Crowder		Non Cit
2	Aaron Harlan	Dd		Sarah A Harlan		Tobucksy
3	No.1			No.2		
4	Nº1			Nº2		
5						
6						
7	No 1 admitted by Dawes Commission as an intermarried					
8	citizen, Choctaw Case #724. No appeal					
9	Nº4 Born Aug 5, 1902. Enrolled Aug. 30, 1902					
10						
11						
12						
13				No.2 on roll as Inanita[sic] Crowder		
14				" 3 " " " R. "		
15				No1 on 1896 " " Wm E. "		
16					Date of Application for Enrollment.	
17	P.O. Juanita, I.T.				9/14/99	

Choctaw By Blood Enrollment Cards 1898-1914

RESIDENCE: Tobucksy COUNTY. **Choctaw Nation** **Choctaw Roll** CARD No.
POST OFFICE: South Canadian *(Not Including Freedmen)* FIELD No. 4773

Dawes' Roll No.	NAME		Relationship to Person	AGE	SEX	BLOOD	TRIBAL ENROLLMENT		
							Year	County	No.
13185	1 Turner Robert S	24	First Named	21	m	1/16	1896	Tobucksy	12025
I.W. 579	2 " Lena	23	W	19	f	IW			
	3								
	4								
	5								
	6								
	7								
	8								
	9								
	10								
	11								
	12	ENROLLMENT OF NOS. ~~1~~ HEREON APPROVED BY THE SECRETARY OF INTERIOR MAR 19 1903				ENROLLMENT OF NOS. ~~2~~ HEREON APPROVED BY THE SECRETARY OF INTERIOR FEB -8 1904			
	13								
	14								
	15								
	16								
	17								

TRIBAL ENROLLMENT OF PARENTS

	Name of Father	Year	County	Name of Mother	Year	County
1	Robt F Turner		Tobucksy	Olga T Turner		Tobucksy
2	J G Terrell		Non Cit	Ella Terrell		Non cit
3						
4						
5						
6	No1 on roll Standly Turner					
7						
8	No1 mother Olga T admitted by act					
9	of Choctaw Council as Olga T Standly in same act with J S Standly. No1 born					
10	since then					
11						
12	For child of Nos 1&2 see NB (March 3,1905) #690					
13						
14						
15						
16				Date of Application for Enrollment. 9/14/99		
17	P.O. Indianola I.T. 12/22/02					

Choctaw By Blood Enrollment Cards 1898-1914

RESIDENCE: Tobucksy COUNTY.
POST OFFICE: ~~South~~ Canadian **Choctaw Nation**
Choctaw Roll *(Not Including Freedmen)*
CARD NO.
FIELD NO. 4774

Dawes' Roll No.	NAME	Relationship to Person First Named	AGE	SEX	BLOOD	TRIBAL ENROLLMENT Year	County	No.
DEAD	1 ~~Dodson Isaac P~~		52	m	IW	1896	Tobucksy	14461
13186	2 " Elizabeth 43	w	40	f	1/8	1896	"	3291
13187	3 Morrison Hannibal E 25	Step son	22	m	1/16	1896	"	8566
13188	4 Dodson Ella W 16	d	13	f	1/16	1896	"	3292
	5							
	6							
	7							
	8							
	9							
	10							
	11							

No. 1 HEREON DISMISSED UNDER ORDER OF THE COMMISSION TO THE FIVE CIVILIZED TRIBES OF MARCH 31, 1905.

ENROLLMENT OF NOS. 2 3 & 4 HEREON APPROVED BY THE SECRETARY OF INTERIOR MAR 9 1903

TRIBAL ENROLLMENT OF PARENTS

Name of Father	Year	County	Name of Mother	Year	County
1 ~~W^m W Dodson~~	~~dead~~	~~non citizen~~	~~Adeline Dodson~~	~~dead~~	~~non-citizen~~
2 Dave Harkins	Dead	Kiamitia	Isabelle Harkins	Dead	Kimatia[sic]
3 Jno Morrison	"	Non Cit	No2		
4 No1			No2		
5					
6					
7					
8					
9	No3 on roll Hannibol[sic] S Morrison				
10	No4 " " Emma M Dodson				
11	For information relative to parents of No1 see letter filed				
12	~~Died Feby 20, 1902 proof of death filed June 27, 1904~~				
	For child of No3 see NB (Apr 26-06) Card #324				
13					
14					
15	Date of Application for Enrollment. Sept 14th 1899				
16					
17					

274

Choctaw By Blood Enrollment Cards 1898-1914

RESIDENCE: Tobucksy   COUNTY. **Choctaw Nation**   **Choctaw Roll** CARD NO.
POST OFFICE: St Louis, I.T.   *(Not Including Freedmen)* FIELD NO. **4775**

Dawes' Roll No.	NAME		Relationship to Person First Named	AGE	SEX	BLOOD	TRIBAL ENROLLMENT Year	County	No.
13189	1 Gibson, Cillin	51	First Named	48	F	1/4	1896	Gaines	6615
13190	2 " Thenton	24	Son	21	M	1/8	1896	"	6616
13191	3 " Samuel	22	"	19	"	1/8	1896	"	6617
13192	4 " Emily	14	Dau	11	F	1/8	1896	"	6618
13192	5 " Charlotte Susan	1	G.Dau	6mo	F	1/16			
I.W. 1352	6 " Sallie	18	Wife of No 2	18	F	I.W.			
	7								
	8 For child of No4 see NB (Apr 26-06) Card #351								
	9 " " " Nos2&6 " (Mar -05) " #1269								
	10 ENROLLMENT								
	11 OF NOS. 6 HEREON								
	12 APPROVED BY THE SECRETARY OF INTERIOR Mar. 14, 1905								
	13 ENROLLMENT								
	14 OF NOS. 1 2 3 4 & 5 HEREON APPROVED BY THE SECRETARY								
	15 OF INTERIOR Mar. 19, 1903								
	16 No6 originally listed for enrollment on Choctaw card D-985 Dec. 24, 1902 ·								
	17 transferred to this card Jan. 29, 1905. See decision of Jan. 13, 1905.								

TRIBAL ENROLLMENT OF PARENTS

	Name of Father	Year	County	Name of Mother	Year	County
1	Ed. Brookings	Dd		Charlotte Brookings	Dd	San[sic] Bois
2	John Gibson		Creek Indian	No1		
3	" "		" "	No1		
4	" "		" "	No1		
5	No2			Sallie Gibson		White Woman
6	Charlie Minyard		Non Citizen	Laura Minyard		Non Citizen
7						
8	No1 on 1896 roll as Sillin Jipson					
9	For child of No3 see NB (Apr 26-06) Card #673					
10	Surnames on 1896 roll is Jipson					
11	Nos 2,3 and 4 also on Choctaw rejected card #R.102. Choctaw Card					
12	#R.102 cancelled and testimony transferred to Choctaw #4775 March 23, 1901.					
13	Nos 2 and 6 were married Dec. 2, 1900. On P.35, #354-93 P.R. San[sic] Bois Co No.2 is now husband of Sallie Gibson Choctaw Card #D985. Evidence of					
14	marriage filed Dec 24,1902. Now on file in 7D-985 #2,3&4 All but No1 enrolled					
15	No.5 Born July 24, 1902. Enrolled Dec. 24, 1902					
16	P.O. Russelville[sic] I.T.			Date of Application for Enrollment.	Nov.	13/99
	No6 PO Featherston IT 5/24/05					9/14/99

Choctaw By Blood Enrollment Cards 1898-1914

Choctaw Nation

Choctaw Roll *(Not Including Freedmen)*   CARD NO.

FIELD NO. **4776**

Dawes' Roll No.	NAME	Relationship to Person	AGE	SEX	BLOOD	TRIBAL ENROLLMENT Year	County	No.
13194	1 Smith, Hervey R 69	First Named	66	M	1/8	1896	Sans Bois	11092
I.W. 580	2 " Elizabeth J 65	Wife	61	F	I.W.	1896	" "	15014
13195	3 " Elmore 23	Son	20	W	1/16	1896	" "	11093
13196	4 Thrasher, Ellen 16	Ward	13	F	1/8	1896	" "	11819
13197	5 Thrasher, Benjamin 1	Son of No.4	2mo	M	1/16			
I.W. 933	6 Smith, Essie 21	Wife of No.3	21	F	I.W.			
	7					(application for #6 on D-716-May 5, 1902)		
	8 No6 transferred from Choctaw card D-716 June 12-1904 See decision of May 27-1904							
	9		No.1 on roll H.R. Smith.					

ENROLLMENT
OF NOS. ~~~2~~~ HEREON
APPROVED BY THE SECRETARY
OF INTERIOR Feb 8, 1904

ENROLLMENT
OF NOS. 1 3 4 & 5 HEREON
APPROVED BY THE SECRETARY
OF INTERIOR Mar 19, 1903

TRIBAL ENROLLMENT OF PARENTS

	Name of Father	Year	County	Name of Mother	Year	County
1	Freeman J Smith	Dead	Non Cit	Eliza Smith	Dead	Choctaw
2	Thos Thrasher	"	" "	Eliza Thrasher		Non Cit
3	No.1			No.2		
4	Enoch Tucker	Dead	Non Cit	Rhoda Tucker	Dead	San[sic] Bois
5	H.D. Thrasher		Non-Citizen	No.4		
6	J.D. Hightower		" "	Ophelia Hightower	Dead	Non Citizen
7						
8	No2 admitted by Dawes Com #791					
9	as Mrs E. J. Smith			For child of No3 see NB (Apr 26-1906) #1169		
10	No 1&3 admitted by Act of Choctaw			" " " " " (Mar 3-05) #674		
11	Council #28. Not as H.R. Smith & No3 as Elmo Smith. Act approved Oct 26-1889			ENROLLMENT OF NOS. 6 HEREON APPROVED BY THE SECRETARY		
12	No3 is now the husband of Essie Smith on			OF INTERIOR Aug 3, 1904		
13	Choctaw Card #D716 May 5, 1902					
14	No4 is now the wife of H.D. Thrasher-non-citizen, evidence of marriage requested Aug.			For child of No4 see NB (Apr 26-1906) #133		
15	25,1902. Filed Sept 27, 1902			Date of Application for Enrollment.	1 to 4	
16	No5 Born June 3,1902, enrolled Aug. 25, 1902			Sept. 14th 1899		
17	No3 PO Cowlington IT					

4/28/04

276

Choctaw By Blood Enrollment Cards 1898-1914

RESIDENCE: Tobucksy	COUNTY.	**Choctaw Nation**	**Choctaw Roll** (Not Including Freedmen)	CARD NO.
POST OFFICE: Choate				FIELD NO. 477

Dawes' Roll No.	NAME		Relationship to Person First Named	AGE	SEX	BLOOD	TRIBAL ENROLLMENT		
							Year	County	No.
13198	1 Choate William F	32	First Named	29	m	1/2	1893	Tobucksy	182
I.W. 581	2 " Mary E	33	wife	30	f	IW	1896	Tobucksy	14403
13199	3 " Edgar E	10	son	7	m	1/4	1896	"	2375
13200	4 " George R	7	"	4	"	1/4	1896	"	2376
13201	5 " Lydia E	1	Dau	1/2	F	1/4			
	6								
	7								
	8								
	9								
	10								
	11	ENROLLMENT OF NOS. ~~~ 2 ~~~ HEREON APPROVED BY THE SECRETARY OF INTERIOR FEB 8 1904							
	12								
	13								
	14								
	15	ENROLLMENT OF NOS. 1 3 4 & 5 HEREON APPROVED BY THE SECRETARY OF INTERIOR MAR 19 1903							
	16								
	17								

TRIBAL ENROLLMENT OF PARENTS

Name of Father	Year	County	Name of Mother	Year	County
1 Geo W Choate		Tobucksy	Eliza Choate		Tobucksy
2 Rudolph Piepgrass	dead	noncitizen	Augusta Piepgrass	dead	noncitizen
3 No1			No2		
4 No1			No 2		
5 No 1			No 2		
6					
7 No1 on Tobucksy Co 1893 PR Page 18 - #182 as W F Choate					
8 No.5 born July 14, 1901: Enrolled Jan. 2, 1902					
9 No3 on roll Tuskahoma Choate No4 " " Geo B "					
10					
11 Certificate of marriage of Wᵐ F Chote[sic] & May[sic] E Piepgrass dated Sept 2,					
12 1891 in due form & satisfactory exhibited			Certified copy of certificate of marriage between Nᵒˢ 1 and 2 received and filed		
13 but not in condition to be filed.			Feby 25, 1903		
14 Names of parents of No2 supplied June 22, 1901 See letter of No1 on file					
15					#1 to 4
16					Date of Application for Enrollment.
17					Sept 14ᵗʰ 1899

PO Indianola IT 3/24/05

Choctaw By Blood Enrollment Cards 1898-1914

RESIDENCE: Tobucksy COUNTY. **Choctaw Nation** **Choctaw Roll** CARD NO.
POST OFFICE: Choate (Not Including Freedmen) FIELD NO. 4778

Dawes' Roll No.	NAME	Relationship to Person	AGE	SEX	BLOOD	TRIBAL ENROLLMENT		
						Year	County	No.
13202	1 Choate Geo W 62	First Named	59	m	1/2	1896	Tobucksy	2344
13203	2 " Eliza 62	wife	59	f	1/2	1896	"	2345
	3							
	4							
	5							
	6							
	7							
	8							
	9							
	10							
	11							
	12							
	13							
	14							
	15	ENROLLMENT OF NOS. 1 and 2 HEREON						
	16	APPROVED BY THE SECRETARY						
	17	OF INTERIOR MAR 19 1903						

TRIBAL ENROLLMENT OF PARENTS

Name of Father	Year	County	Name of Mother	Year	County
1 Jas Choate	Dead	Tobucksy	Winnie Choate	Dead	Tobucksy
2 Simon Wade	"	Wade	Jinsey Wade	"	Wade
3					
4					
5					
6					
7		No 1 on roll Geo. W Choate			
8					
9					
10					
11					
12					
13					
14		Date of Application for Enrollment.			
15					
16		Sept 14th 1899			
17					

278

Choctaw By Blood Enrollment Cards 1898-1914

RESIDENCE: Tobucksy   COUNTY. **Choctaw Nation**   **Choctaw Roll** *(Not Including Freedmen)*   CARD NO.
POST OFFICE: Indianola, I.T.   FIELD NO. 4779

Dawes' Roll No.	NAME	Relationship to Person Named	AGE	SEX	BLOOD	TRIBAL ENROLLMENT		
						Year	County	No.
1	Marrs, Thomas	First Named	27	M	1/8			
2								
3								
4								
5								
6								
7								
8								
9								
10								
11								
12								
13								
14								
15								
16								
17								

DENIED CITIZENSHIP BY THE CHOCTAW AND CHICKASAW CITIZENSHIP COURT

TRIBAL ENROLLMENT OF PARENTS

	Name of Father	Year	County	Name of Mother	Year	County
1	J. R. Marrs		Tobucksy	Jane Marrs		Tobucksy
2						
3						
4						
5						
6						
7						
8						
9	No1 denied by C.C.C.C. March 28 '04					
	No1 denied in 96 Case #28					
10	Admitted by U.S. Court at So M°A Jan. 19-98 Case #88					
11	As to residence see his testimony.					
12						
13	No1 now in C.C.C. Case #109					
14						
15					Date of Application	
16					for Enrollment.	
17					9/14/99	

Choctaw By Blood Enrollment Cards 1898-1914

RESIDENCE:	Tobucksy	COUNTY.							CARD NO.	
POST OFFICE:	Choate, I.T.		**Choctaw Nation**			Choctaw Roll *(Not Including Freedmen)*			FIELD NO. 4780	

Dawes' Roll No.	NAME		Relationship to Person	AGE	SEX	BLOOD	TRIBAL ENROLLMENT		
							Year	County	No.
I.W. 582	1 York, Wallace	34	First Named	31	M	I.W.	1896	Tobucksy	15209
DEAD.	2 " Alice J	29	Wife	26	F	1/2	"	"	14221
13204	3 " Clinton J	9	Son	6	M	1/4	"	"	14222
13205	4 " Myrtle A	7	Dau	4	F	1/4	"	"	14223
DEAD.	5 " Mabel	3	"	10ds	F	1/4			
13206	6 " Mary Allice	1	Dau	2mo	F	1/4			
	7								
	8								
	9								
	10	ENROLLMENT OF NOS. ____ 1 ____ HEREON							
	11	APPROVED BY THE SECRETARY OF INTERIOR FEB -8 1904							
	12								
	13	No. 2 and 5 HEREON DISMISSED UNDER ORDER OF THE COMMISSION TO THE FIVE							
	14	CIVILIZED TRIBES OF MARCH 31, 1905.							
	15	ENROLLMENT							
	16	OF NOS. 3 4 & 6 HEREON APPROVED BY THE SECRETARY							
	17	OF INTERIOR MAR 9 1903							

TRIBAL ENROLLMENT OF PARENTS

Name of Father	Year	County	Name of Mother	Year	County
1 Jno. H York		Non Cit	Amanda York		Non Cit
2 Geo. Choate		Tobucksy	Eliza Choate		Tobucksy
3 No.1			No.2		
4 " 1			" 2		
5 " 1			" 2		
6 No.1			No.2		
7					
8					
9					
10					
11					
12			No.1 Admitted by Dawes Com. #951		
13			No.2 on roll as Alice York		
14	No6 born Nov. 21, 1901: Enrolled Jany. 18, 1902		" 3 " " Clinton "		
	Nos 3&4 admitted by Dawes Com in 1896 Case #951		" 4 " " Myrtle "		
15	No.2 Died March 11, 1902: Proof of death filed Dec 30,1902				
16	No.5 " Nov. 1, 1899 : " " " " " 30, 1902		Date of Application		
17			for Enrollment. 9/14/99		

280

Choctaw By Blood Enrollment Cards 1898-1914

RESIDENCE: Tobucksy   COUNTY: **Choctaw Nation**   **Choctaw Roll**   CARD NO.
POST OFFICE: South Canadian   (Not Including Freedmen)   FIELD NO. 4781

Dawes' Roll No.	NAME	Relationship to Person	AGE	SEX	BLOOD	TRIBAL ENROLLMENT		
						Year	County	No.
13207	1 Smith Freeman R ³⁴	First Named	31	m	1/16	1896	Tobucksy	11285
	2							
	3							
	4							
	5							
	6							
	7							
	8							
	9							
	10							
	11							
	12							
	13							
	14							
	15							
	16							
	17							

ENROLLMENT
OF NOS. 1 HEREON
APPROVED BY THE SECRETARY
OF INTERIOR   MAR 19 1903

TRIBAL ENROLLMENT OF PARENTS

	Name of Father	Year	County	Name of Mother	Year	County
1	Smith, H R		Tobucksy	E J Smith		Tobucksy
2						
3						
4						
5						
6			On roll Freeman Smith			
7			Admitted by act of Choctaw			
8			Council #28, Oct 26, 1886 as Freeman			
9			Smith			
10						
11						
12			See Choctaw card #D.494			
13			For child of No.1 see NB (Mar 3 '05) #383			
14						
15						
16				Date of Application for Enrollment.		
17				Sept 14ᵗʰ 1899		

Choctaw By Blood Enrollment Cards 1898-1914

RESIDENCE: San[sic] Bois   COUNTY. **Chocta**   **Choctaw Roll**   CARD NO.

POST OFFICE: Brooken   (Not Including Freedmen)   FIELD NO. 4782

Dawes' Roll No.	NAME	Relationship to Person First Named	AGE	SEX	BLOOD	TRIBAL ENROLLMENT		
						Year	County	No.
1	Neal Susan	Named	33	f	1/2	1896	San[s] Bois	9537
2	" La	S	3	m	1/4	1896	" "	9538
3	" Green	S	1	"	"			
4								
5								
6								
7								
8								
9								
10								
11								
12								
13								
14								
15								
16								
17								

CANCELLED

Cancelled December 7th, 1900 Choctaw

and transferred to Choctaw W. Neal Tams Bixby

Card N3.3156 Acting Chairman

TRIBAL ENROLLMENT OF PARENTS

	Name of Father	Year	County	Name of Mother	Year	County
1	Wm Walker	dead	San Bois	Louisa Neal	dead	Atoka
2	J.W. Neal	1W	"	Noi		
3	" " "			Noi		
4						
5						
6						
7						
8						
9						
10						
11						
12						
13						
14						
15					Date of Application for Enrollment.	
16						
17					Sept 14th 1899	

282

Choctaw By Blood Enrollment Cards 1898-1914

RESIDENCE: Sans Bois   COUNTY. **Choctaw Nation**   **Choctaw Roll**   CARD No.

POST OFFICE: Whitefield   *(Not Including Freedmen)*   FIELD No. 4783

Dawes' Roll No.	NAME	Relationship to Person	AGE	SEX	BLOOD	TRIBAL ENROLLMENT		
						Year	County	No.
13208	1 Franklin Nicholas ²⁶	First Named	23	M	Full	1896	Sans Bois	3843
	2							
	3							
	4							
	5							
	6							
	7							
	8							
	9							
	10							
	11							
	12							
	13							
	14							
	15	ENROLLMENT						
	16	OF NOS. ~~~~ 1 ~~~~ HEREON APPROVED BY THE SECRETARY						
	17	OF INTERIOR MAR 19 1903						

TRIBAL ENROLLMENT OF PARENTS

	Name of Father	Year	County	Name of Mother	Year	County
1	Wᵐ Franklin	Dead	San[sic] Bois	Sissy Franklin	Dead	San Bois
2						
3						
4						
5						
6						
7						
8						
9						
10						
11						
12						
13						
14					Date of Application for Enrollment.	
15						
16					Sept 14ᵗʰ 1899	
17						

Choctaw By Blood Enrollment Cards 1898-1914

RESIDENCE:		COUNTY.				Choctaw Roll	CARD NO.	
POST OFFICE:		**Choctaw Nation**				*(Not Including Freedmen)*	FIELD NO. 4784	

Dawes' Roll No.	NAME	Relationship to Person	AGE	SEX	BLOOD	TRIBAL ENROLLMENT		
						Year	County	No.
✓✓	1 Marrs, John	First Named	25	M	1/8			
Ø	2 " Nelly May	Dau	1mo	F	1/16			
	3							
	4							
	5							
	6							
No.2	7 DISMISSED MAY 27 1904							
	8							
	9							
	10							
	11							
No.1	12 DENIED CITIZENSHIP BY THE CHOCTAW AND							
	13 CHICKASAW CITIZENSHIP COURT Mar 28 '04							
	14							
	15							
	16							
	17							

TRIBAL ENROLLMENT OF PARENTS

Name of Father	Year	County	Name of Mother	Year	County
1 J.R. Marrs		Tobucksy	Jane Marrs		Tobucksy
2 No.1			Minnie Marrs		intermarried
3					
4					
5					
6					
7					
8 No.2 born Jany. 6, 1902: Enrolled Jany. 21st, 1902					
9 No1 Denied by C.C.C.C. Mar 28 '04					
10 No2 Dismissed					
11					
12 No1 denied in 96 Case #28					
13 Admitted by U.S. Court at So McA, Jan. 29-98- Case #88					
14 As to residence see his testimony					
15 No.1 is now the husband of Minnie Marrs on Choctaw card #D.630					
16 Evidence of marriage filed in #D.630 May 14, 1901.					
Judgement[s] of U.S. Cad mitting No1 vacated and set aside by Decree of Choctaw Chickasaw Citizenship Court De[c] 17 '02					
17 No1 now in C.C.C.C. Case #109				Date of Application for Enrollment.	9/14/99

284

Choctaw By Blood Enrollment Cards 1898-1914

RESIDENCE: Tobucksy
POST OFFICE: Thurman, I.T.

COUNTY. **Choctaw Nation**

Choctaw Roll
(Not Including Freedmen)

CARD NO.
FIELD NO. 4785

Dawes' Roll No.	NAME	Relationship to Person First Named	AGE	SEX	BLOOD	TRIBAL ENROLLMENT		
						Year	County	No.
1	Cargill, John B	Named	58	M	I.W.	1896	Gaines	14387
2								
3	DISMISSED							
4								
5	FEB 4- 1907							
6								
7								
8								
9								
10								
11								
12								
13								
14								
15								
16								
17								

TRIBAL ENROLLMENT OF PARENTS

	Name of Father	Year	County	Name of Mother	Year	County
1	J. R. Cargill		Non Cit	Marily Cargill		Non Cit
2						
3						
4						
5						
6						
7						
8						
9						
10						
11						
12			Admitted by Dawes Com. #732 as John B. Corgill			
13			On 96 roll as J.C. Cargal. No appeal			
14						
15						
16						
17					Date of Application for Enrollment	9/14/99

Choctaw By Blood Enrollment Cards 1898-1914

RESIDENCE: Tobucksy COUNTY. **Choctaw Nation** **Choctaw Roll** CARD No.
POST OFFICE: South Canadian (Not Including Freedmen) FIELD No. **4786**

Dawes' Roll No.	NAME	Relationship to Person Named	AGE	SEX	BLOOD	TRIBAL ENROLLMENT Year	County	No.
13209	1 Jones, Lou 27	First Named	24	F	1/8	1896	Tobucksy	6647
13210	2 " , Andrew 12	Son	9	M	1/16	1893	"	441
13211	3 " , Nina 10	D	7	F	1/16	1896	Tobucksy	6666
13212	4 " , Eva 4	D	1	F	1/16			
13213	5 " , Harry Dewitt 1	Son	2mo	M	1/16			
I.W. 686	6 " , James A 29	Hus	29	M	I.W.	1896	Tobucksy	14691
	7		No1 on Tobucksy Co P.R. P. 49 #440					
	8		No2 " " " " " " #441 as Andy					
	9		No3 " " " " " " 49 No 442					
	10							
	11							
	12	ENROLLMENT						
	13	OF NOS. 6 HEREON APPROVED BY THE SECRETARY						
	14	OF INTERIOR Mar 26, 1904						
	15	ENROLLMENT						
	16	OF NOS. 1 2 3 4 & 5 HEREON APPROVED BY THE SECRETARY						
	17	OF INTERIOR Mar 19, 1903						

TRIBAL ENROLLMENT OF PARENTS

	Name of Father	Year	County	Name of Mother	Year	County
1	Walker Russell	Cherokee		Viney Jones	Dead	San[sic] Bois
2	Jas. A. Jones	IW		No1		
3	" " "	"		No1		
4	" " "	"		No1		
5	" " "	"		No1		
6	R. A. Jones		Non Citizen	Maggie Jones		Non Citizen
7						
8						
9						
10						
11	No3 on 1896 roll as Nannie Jones,			For children of Nos. 1&6 see NB (March 3, 1905 #812		
12	No1 " 1896 " " Lone					
13	No5 Enrolled May 21, 1901.					
14	Husband of No1 & Father of Nos 2,3,4 & 5 on Choctaw D496.					
15	No6 transferred from Choctaw Card D496 January 23, 1904			#1 to 4 inc		
16	]See decision of January 6, 1904			Date of Application for Enrollment. Sept 14th 1899		
17	PO Fitzhugh I T					

286

Choctaw By Blood Enrollment Cards 1898-1914

					Choctaw Roll	CARD NO.	
RESIDENCE: Tobucksy		Choctaw Nation			(Not Including Freedmen)	FIELD NO. 4787	
POST OFFICE: Stuart							

NAME	Relationship to Person First Named	AGE	SEX	BLOOD	Year	TRIBAL ENROLLMENT County	No.
1 Newton, Eobert	56	56	M	I.W.			
2 " Katie 50	Wife	47	F	1/2	1896	Tobucksy	9609
3 " Robert 26	S	23	M	1/4	1896	"	9610
4 Bowers, Susan 24	D	21	F	1/4	1896	"	9611
5 Newton, Joseph 22	S	19	M	1/4	1896	"	9612
6 " Lucinda 20	D	17	F	1/4	1896	"	9613
7 " Mada 14	D	11	F	1/4	1896	"	9614
8 " Ernest 12	S	9	M	1/4	1896	"	9615
9 " Bessie 9	D	6	F	1/4	1896	"	9616
10 " Claude V 4	S	1	M	1/4			
11 Bowers, Rubie 1	Gr.Dau	7wks	F	1/8			
12							
13 Feb 6, 1905; Decision of Commissioner of Jany 19, 1905 denying No.1 affirmed by [illegible...]							
14							
15 ENROLLMENT							
16 OF NOS. 2345678910&11 HEREON APPROVED BY THE SECRETARY							
17 OF INTERIOR MAR 19 1903							

TRIBAL ENROLLMENT OF PARENTS

	Name of Father	Year	County	Name of Mother	Year	County
1	Wm Newton	Dead	non-cit	Eveline Newton	Dead	non-cit
2	Jas. Trayhern	Dead	Skullyville	Sarah Trayhern	Dead	Skullyville
3	Nº1			Nº2		
4	Nº1			Nº2		
5	Nº1			Nº2		
6	Nº1			Nº2		
7	Nº1			Nº2		
8	Nº1			Nº2		
9	Nº1			Nº2		
10	Nº1			Nº2		
11	Ray Bowers		noncitizen	Nº4		
12	Nº7 on roll Mattie Newton.					
13	Nº4 is now the wife of Ray Bowers non-citizen. Evidence of marriage requested Sept 10,1902. Received and filed Sept. 17,1902 As to marriage see his testimony and that of Sillen Martin.					
14	Nº11 Born Aug 25, 1902, enrolled Sept 10, 1902					
15	For child of No.4 see NB (March 3,1905) Card #595					
16	" " " No.6 " " " #1229					
17	No 4 PO Tuttle 4/2/05			Date of Application for Enrollment.	Sept. 14th, 99	#1 to 10

287

Choctaw By Blood Enrollment Cards 1898-1914

RESIDENCE: San[sic] Bois   COUNTY. **Choctaw Nation**   **Choctaw Roll**   CARD NO.
POST OFFICE: Featherstone   *(Not Including Freedmen)*   FIELD NO. 4788

Dawes' Roll No.	NAME	Relationship to Person First Named	AGE	SEX	BLOOD	TRIBAL ENROLLMENT		
						Year	County	No.
13224	1 Franklin Houston ²⁸		25	M	Full	1896	San[sic] Bois	3904
	2							
	3							
	4							
	5							
	6							
	7							
	8							
	9							
	10							
	11							
	12							
	13							
	14							
	15	ENROLLMENT						
	16	OF NOS. ~~~ 1 ~~~ HEREON APPROVED BY THE SECRETARY						
	17	OF INTERIOR MAR 19 1903						

TRIBAL ENROLLMENT OF PARENTS

Name of Father	Year	County	Name of Mother	Year	County
1 Wᵐ Franklin	dead	San[sic] Bois	Sissy Franklin	Dead	San[sic] Bois
2					
3					
4					
5					
6					
7					
8					
9					
10					
11					
12					
13					
14					
15			Date of Application for Enrollment.		
16			Sept 14, 1899		
17					

288

Choctaw By Blood Enrollment Cards 1898-1914

RESIDENCE:	Tobucksy	COUNTY.								

RESIDENCE: Tobucksy COUNTY. **Choctaw Nation** **Choctaw Roll** (Not Including Freedmen) CARD NO.
POST OFFICE: South Canadian FIELD NO. 4789

Dawes' Roll No.	NAME	Relationship to Person	AGE	SEX	BLOOD	TRIBAL ENROLLMENT		
						Year	County	No.
13225	1 McDuff Charles J ⁴⁵	First Named	42	M	1/8	1896	Tobucksy	9199
	2							
	3							
	4							
	5							
	6							
	7							
	8							
	9							
	10							
	11							
	12							
	13							
	14							
	15	ENROLLMENT OF NOS. ~~1~~ HEREON APPROVED BY THE SECRETARY OF INTERIOR MAR 19 1903						
	16							
	17							

TRIBAL ENROLLMENT OF PARENTS

	Name of Father	Year	County	Name of Mother	Year	County
1	A J McDuff		Tobucksy	Minerva McDuff	dead	Tobucksy
2						
3						
4						
5						
6						
7						
8						
9	No 1 Died Nov 2, 1902· Proof of death filed Dec. 30, 1902					
10						
11						
12						
13						
14						
15						
16					Date of Application for Enrollment.	
17					Sept 14 99	

Choctaw By Blood Enrollment Cards 1898-1914

RESIDENCE: Tobucksy COUNTY.
POST OFFICE: Indianola, I.T.

Choctaw Nation

Choctaw Roll
(Not Including Freedmen)

CARD No.
FIELD No. 1790

Dawes' Roll No.	NAME	Relationship to Person First Named	AGE	SEX	BLOOD	TRIBAL ENROLLMENT Year	County	No.
I.W. 583	1 Hightower, Benjamin F	First Named	62	M	IW	1896	Tobucksy	14613
13226	2 " Madora E	wife	47	F	1/8	1896	"	5386
132276	3 " Mary A	Dau	25	"	1/16	1896	"	5387
	4							
	5	ENROLLMENT OF NOS. 2&3 HEREON APPROVED BY THE SECRETARY OF INTERIOR MAR 19 1903						
	6							
	7							
	8							
	9	ENROLLMENT OF NOS. ~~One~~ HEREON APPROVED BY THE SECRETARY OF INTERIOR FEB -8 1904						
	10							
	11							
P CERTIFICATE NO 2&3 24 1903	12							
	13							
	14							
	15							
SHIP CERTIFICATE OR NO One N 21 1904	16							
	17							

TRIBAL ENROLLMENT OF PARENTS

	Name of Father	Year	County	Name of Mother	Year	County
1	Wm Hightower	Dead	Non-Citizen	Elizabeth A Hightower	Dead	Non-Cit
2	R F Turner	"	" "	Ada E. Turner	"	Tobucksy
3	No.1			No.2		
4						
5						
6						
7			Admitted by Dawes Com #1414 as B. F. Hightower			
8			No1 On Roll as Benj Hightower			
9			No2 " " " Madord "			
10						
11						
12						
13						
14						
15						
16						
17					Sept 14 1899	

Choctaw By Blood Enrollment Cards 1898-1914

RESIDENCE: Tobucksy   COUNTY.
POST OFFICE: South Canadian   **Choctaw Nation**

Choctaw Roll *(Not Including Freedmen)*

CARD NO.
FIELD NO. 4791

Dawes' Roll No.	NAME		Relationship to Person First Named	AGE	SEX	BLOOD	TRIBAL ENROLLMENT Year	County	No.
13228	1 Toole John O	50		47	m	1/8	1896	Tobucksy	12032
I.W. 584	2 " Etta E	40	wife	44	f	IW	1896	"	15096
13229	3 " Mary A	15	D	12	f	1/16	1896	"	12033
	4								
	5								
	6								
	7								
	8 ENROLLMENT OF NOS. ~~~~ 2 ~~~~ HEREON								
	9 APPROVED BY THE SECRETARY								
	10 OF INTERIOR FEB -8 1904								
	11								
	12								
	13								
	14								
	15 ENROLLMENT OF NOS. 1 & 3 HEREON								
	16 APPROVED BY THE SECRETARY								
	17 OF INTERIOR MAR 19 1903								

TRIBAL ENROLLMENT OF PARENTS

Name of Father	Year	County	Name of Mother	Year	County
1 Alfred Toole	Dead	Tobucksy	Belinda Toole	Dead	Tobucksy
2 W. L. Wynne	"	Non Cit			Non Citizen
3 No1			No2		
4					
5					
6					
7	No1 on roll 1896 Jno O Toole				
8					
9					
10	See if No2 was admitted by the Dawes Com Application was				
11	made - Case 1388				
12	Docket shows No2 was denied by Dawes Commission in 1896				
13	Choctaw case #1388, no appeal				
14	The above denial shown by Docket entry in this case. Endorsement on original application shows: "Admit Etta Toole as an intermarried citizen."				
15					
16			Date of Application for Enrollment.	Sept 14th 1899	
17					

Choctaw By Blood Enrollment Cards 1898-1914

RESIDENCE: Tobucksy COUNTY. **Choctaw Nation** *4792* **Choctaw Roll** CAR
POST OFFICE: So Canadian, I.T. *(Not Including Freedmen)* FIEL

Dawes' Roll No.	NAME	Relationship to Person First Named	AGE	SEX	BLOOD	TRIBAL ENROLLMENT		
						Year	County	No.
13230	1 Russell, William M ²⁸	First Named	25	M	1/8	1896	Tobucksy	10759
I.W. 1352	2 " Mattie M ³²	Wife	27	F	I.W.	"	"	14968
13231	3 " Maggie M ⁸	Dau	5	F	1/16	"	"	10760
13232	4 " Lula Myrtle ⁴	"	14ᵐᵒ	F	1/16			
13233	5 " Betha Violce ²	Dau	5mo	F	1/16			
13234	6 " Lola Orin ¹	Dau	2wks	F	1/16			
	7							
	8	No2 restored to roll by Departmental authority of January 19,1909 (File 5-51)						
	9	Enrollment of No2 cancelled by order of Department March 4, 1907						
	10							
	11	ENROLLMENT						
	12	OF NOS. 2 HEREON APPROVED BY THE SECRETARY						
	13	OF INTERIOR MAR 14 1905						
	14	ENROLLMENT						
	15	OF NOS. 1 3 4 5 & 6 HEREON APPROVED BY THE SECRETARY						
	16	OF INTERIOR MAR 19 1903						
	17							

TRIBAL ENROLLMENT OF PARENTS

	Name of Father	Year	County	Name of Mother	Year	County
1	Walker Russell		Cher. Nat.	Viney Russell	Dd	Tobucksy
2	Andy Jones		Non Cit	Maggie Jones		Non Cit
3	No.1			No.2		
4	" 1			" 2		
5	No.1			No.2		
6	N⁰1			N⁰2		
7						
8	Dec 6/99 No2 see Dawes Commission					
9	record 1896, Case 1116, N⁰2 Denied in this case. No appeal.					
	No.5 Enrolled December 3rd, 1900					
	N⁰6 Born May 25, 1902: enrolled June 7, 1902					
	N⁰5 Died Oct 4. 1902; proof of death filed Nov. 12, 1902					
	No2 Decree of divorce from former hus -			No1 on roll as Wᵐ M Russell		
	band filed Dec 8, 1902			" 2 " " Mattie "		
				" 3 " " Maggie "		

For child of Nos 1&2 see NB (Apr 26 '06) Card #170

Date of Application for Enrollment.

hugh I.T. 9/14/

292

Choctaw By Blood Enrollment Cards 1898-1914

RESIDENCE: **Tobucksy** COUNTY.
POST OFFICE: **So Canadian, I.T.** **Choctaw Nation** **Choctaw Roll** CARD
(Not Including Freedmen) FIELD NO. **4793**

Dawes' Roll No.		NAME		Relationship to Person	AGE	SEX	BLOOD	TRIBAL ENROLLMENT		
								Year	County	No.
13235	1	Moncrief, George	21	First Named	18	M	1/16	1896	Tobucksy	8561
	2									
	3									
	4									
	5									
	6									
	7									
	8									
	9									
	10									
	11									
	12									
	13									
	14									
	15									
	16									
	17									

ENROLLMENT
OF NOS. ~~1~~ HEREON
APPROVED BY THE SECRETARY
OF INTERIOR **MAR 9 1903**

TRIBAL ENROLLMENT OF PARENTS

	Name of Father	Year	County	Name of Mother	Year	County
1	Geo. W. Moncrief	Dd	Tobucksy	Alice Moncrief		Tobucksy
2						
3						
4						
5						
6						
7						
8						
9						
10						
11						
12						
13		As to parents[sic] marriage see testimony of Benjamin F Hightower					
14						
15						
16						Date of Application for Enrollment.
17						9/14/99

RESIDENCE: Tobucksy COUNTY.
POST OFFICE: So Canadian, I.T.

Choctaw Nation

Choctaw Roll
(Not Including Freedmen)

CARD No.

FIELD No. 4794

Dawes' Roll No.	NAME		Relationship to Person First Named	AGE	SEX	BLOOD	TRIBAL ENROLLMENT		
							Year	County	No.
I.W. 687	1 Fulton, James D.	27	First Named	24	M	I.W.			
13236	2 " Leona S	23	Wife	20	F	1/16	1896	Atoka	11634
13237	3 " Alice Maurine	2	dau	1mo	F	1/32			
13238	4 " Norma E	1	Dau	2wks	F	1/32			
5									
6									
7									
8									
9									
10									
11									
12									
13									
14									
15									
16									
17									

ENROLLMENT OF NOS. 1 HEREON APPROVED BY THE SECRETARY OF INTERIOR MAR 26 1904

ENROLLMENT OF NOS. 2 3 & 4 HEREON APPROVED BY THE SECRETARY OF INTERIOR MAR 19 1903

TRIBAL ENROLLMENT OF PARENTS

	Name of Father	Year	County	Name of Mother	Year	County
1	D. W. Fulton		Non Cit	Betty Fulton		Non Cit
2	J.S. Standley		Atoka	Alice Standley		Atoka
3	No.1			No.2		
4	N⁰1			N⁰2		
5						
6						
7						
8						
9						
10						
11						
12						
13						
14						
15						
16						
17						

Nos 2 to 4 inclusive descendants of J S Standley who was admitted
by act of Choctaw Council of Oct 1874
For child of Nos 1&2, see NB (Apr 26, 1906) Card No. 134.

No.2 on roll as Loney S Standley. As to parents [sic]
marriage see enrollment of Joseph G Ralls, and
Butler S Smizer.
No.3 Enrolled May 24, 1900
N⁰4 Born Aug. 30, 1902; enrolled Sept. 15, 1902

#1&2
Date of Application
for Enrollment.

9/14/9

Choctaw By Blood Enrollment Cards 1898-1914

RESIDENCE: Tobucksy COUNTY.
POST OFFICE: South Canadian

Choctaw Nation

Choctaw Roll
(Not Including Freedmen)

CARD No.
FIELD No. 4795

Dawes' Roll No.		NAME		Relationship to Person	AGE	SEX	BLOOD	TRIBAL ENROLLMENT		
								Year	County	No.
13239	1	Toole Joseph Y	41	First Named	38	M	1/8	1896	Tobucksy	12035
I.W. 585	2	" Nellie M	26	wife	23	f	IW	1896	"	15099
13240	3	" May Elizabeth		Dau	3m	F	1/16			
13241	4	" Helen	1	Dau	6das	F	1/16			
	5									
	6									
	7									
	8									
	9									
	10									
	11	ENROLLMENT								
	12	OF NOS. ~~~ 2 ~~~ HEREON								
	13	APPROVED BY THE SECRETARY OF INTERIOR FEB -8 1904								
	14									
	15	ENROLLMENT								
	16	OF NOS. 1 3 & 4 HEREON APPROVED BY THE SECRETARY								
	17	OF INTERIOR MAR 19 1903								

TRIBAL ENROLLMENT OF PARENTS

	Name of Father	Year	County	Name of Mother	Year	County
1	Alfred Toole	Dead	Tobucksy	Belinda Toole	Ded	Tobucksy
2	S. A. Cope		Non Cit	May Cope	"	Non Cit
3	No 1			No 2		
4	N⁰1			N⁰2		
5						
6						
7						
8		No3 Enrolled February 21, 1901				
9		N⁰4 Born Sept. 24, 1902. Enrolled Sept. 30, 1902				
10		For child of Nos 1&2, see NB (Apr. 26, 1906) Card No 132.				
11						
12						
13						
14						
15					#1 and 2	
16				Date of Application for Enrollment.	Sept 14th 1899	
17						

295

Choctaw By Blood Enrollment Cards 1898-1914

RESIDENCE: Tobucksy	COUNTY:			CARD NO.
POST OFFICE: Choate	**Choctaw Nation**		**Choctaw Roll** (Not Including Freedmen)	FIELD NO. 4796

Dawes' Roll No.	NAME	Relationship to Person	AGE	SEX	BLOOD	TRIBAL ENROLLMENT		
						Year	County	No.
DEAD	1 Choate Nelson	First Named	32	m	1/2	1896	Tobucksy	2346
I.W. 1034	2 DeLaughter, Ada 27	wife	24	f	IW	1896	"	14396
	3							
	4							
	5 Take no further action relative to enrollment of No 2							
	6 Protest of Attys for Choctaw and Chickasaw Nations							
	7 Jan 2 '04							
	8							
	9 ENROLLMENT							
	10 OF NOS. ~~~ 2 ~~~ HEREON APPROVED BY THE SECRETARY							
	11 OF INTERIOR OCT 21 1904							
	12							
	13 No. 1 HEREON DISMISSED UNDER ORDER OF THE COMMISSION TO THE FIVE							
	14 CIVILIZED TRIBES OF MARCH 31, 1905.							
	15							
	16							
	17							

TRIBAL ENROLLMENT OF PARENTS

	Name of Father	Year	County	Name of Mother	Year	County
1	Dave Choate	dead		Frances Choate	dead	
2	B F Clark	"	Non Cit	H D Clark		Non Cit
3						
4						
5						
6	No2 on roll Ada Choat					
7						
8						
9						
10						
11	Certificate of license filed					
12						
13	No.1 Died November 6,1899. Evidence of death filed March 21, 1901					
14	N°2 is now the wife of J.A. DeLaughter, non-citizen. See her testi-					
15	mony of Dec. 22, 1902					
16					Date of Application for Enrollment.	
17					Sept 14- 1899	

Choctaw By Blood Enrollment Cards 1898-1914

RESIDENCE: Tobucksy COUNTY. **Choctaw Nation** **Choctaw Roll** CARD NO.
POST OFFICE: South Canadian *(Not Including Freedmen)* FIELD NO. 4797

Dawes' Roll No.	NAME	Relationship to Person	AGE	SEX	BLOOD	TRIBAL ENROLLMENT		
						Year	County	No.
13242	1 Moncrief Byron 29	First Named	26	M	1/16	1893	Tobucksy	371
	2							
	3							
	4							
	5							
	6							
	7							
	8							
	9							
	10							
	11							
	12							
	13							
	14							
	15	ENROLLMENT OF NOS. 1 HEREON						
	16	APPROVED BY THE SECRETARY						
	17	OF INTERIOR MAR 9 1903						

TRIBAL ENROLLMENT OF PARENTS

	Name of Father	Year	County	Name of Mother	Year	County
1	Geo W Moncrief	Dead	Tobucksy	May J Moncrief	dead	Non Cit
2						
3						
4						
5						
6						
7	On p 41 No 371-1893 PR Tobucksy Co					
8						
9	As to parents[sic] marriage see enroll-					
10	ment of brother Cap R Moncrief					
11						
12						
13						
14						
15				Date of Application for Enrollment.		
16						
17				Sept 14 99		

297

Choctaw By Blood Enrollment Cards 1898-1914

		POST OFFICE:								
RESIDENCE:	Tobucksy COUNTY.	**Choctaw Nation**				**Choctaw Roll** (Not Including Freedmen)	CARD NO. FIELD NO. 4798			
	South Canadian									

	NAME		Relationship to Person Named	AGE	SEX	BLOOD	TRIBAL ENROLLMENT		
							Year	County	No.
9580 1	Young Madison C	37	First Named	34	m	IW	1896	Tobucksy	15208
13243 2	" Emma	25	wife	22	f	1/16	1896	"	14212
13244 3	" Vivian	6	D	2	f	1/32			
13245 4	" Lois	1	Dau	9mo	F	1/32			
5									
6									
7									
8									
9									
10									
11									
12	ENROLLMENT OF NOS. 1 HEREON APPROVED BY THE SECRETARY								
13									
14	OF INTERIOR FEB 8 1904								
15	ENROLLMENT OF NOS. 2 3 & 4 HEREON APPROVED BY THE SECRETARY								
16									
17	OF INTERIOR MAR 9 1903								

TRIBAL ENROLLMENT OF PARENTS

	Name of Father	Year	County	Name of Mother	Year	County
1	Jas M Young	dead	Non Cit	Catherine Young	Dead	Non Cit
2	John Morrison	Dead	Non-Citizen	Elizabeth Morrison		Tobucksy
3	No1			No2		
4	Nº1			Nº2		
5						
6						
7						
8	License filed.					
9						
10	No.1 admitted as an intermarried citizen by					
11	Dawes Commission in 1896; Choctaw Case #240: No appeal					
12	Nº4 Born June 15, 1901; enrolled March 20, 1902					
13						
14	For child of Nos 1&2 see NB (Apr 26 '06) Card #1191.					
15						
16						
17				Date of Application for Enrollment.		Sept 14 99

Choctaw By Blood Enrollment Cards 1898-1914

RESIDENCE: San[sic] Bois COUNTY. **Choctaw Nation**   Choctaw Roll   CARD No.
POST OFFICE: Enterprise   *(Not Including Freedmen)*   FIELD No. 4799

Dawes' Roll No.		NAME	Relationship to Person	AGE	SEX	BLOOD	TRIBAL ENROLLMENT		
							Year	County	No.
13246	1	Southard Lottie L DIED PRIOR TO SEPTEMBER 25 2092	First Named	17	f	1/4	1896	San[sic] Bois	10698
	2								
	3								
	4								
	5								
	6								
	7								
	8								
	9								
	10								
	11								
	12								
	13								
	14								
	15	ENROLLMENT OF NOS. 1 HEREON							
	16	APPROVED BY THE SECRETARY							
	17	OF INTERIOR MAR 19 1903							

TRIBAL ENROLLMENT OF PARENTS

	Name of Father	Year	County	Name of Mother	Year	County
1	C M Randall		Non Cit	Lucinda Randall	Dead	San[sic] Bois
2						
3						
4						
5						
6						
7						
8			On roll Lottie Randall			
9		No.1 died in 1900	Enrollment cancelled by Department [illegible]			
10						
11						
12						
13						
14						
15						
16					Date of Application for Enrollment.	
17					Sept 14. 1899	

299

Choctaw By Blood Enrollment Cards 1898-1914

RESIDENCE: San[sic] Bois   COUNTY. **Choctaw Nation**   **Choctaw Roll** _(Not Including Freedmen)_   CARD NO.
POST OFFICE: Enterprise   FIELD NO. **4800**

Dawes' Roll No.	NAME	Relationship to Person	AGE	SEX	BLOOD	TRIBAL ENROLLMENT		
						Year	County	No.
15928	1 Randall, Grover _17_	First Named	13	M	1/4	1896	San[sic] Bois	10679
	2							
	3							
	4							
	5							
	6							
	7							
	8							
	9							
	10							
	11							
	12							
	13							
	14							
	15	ENROLLMENT OF NOS. One HEREON						
	16	APPROVED BY THE SECRETARY						
	17	OF INTERIOR Aug 23, 1905						

TRIBAL ENROLLMENT OF PARENTS

Name of Father	Year	County	Name of Mother	Year	County
1 C. M. Randall		Non Cit	Lucinda Randall	Dead	San[sic] Bois
2					
3					
4					

DISMISSED Action of Commission of September 23, 1904 dismissing No1 rescinded and No1 granted 6/6/05.
Sep 23, 1904

No1 restored to roll by Departmental authority of January 19, 1909 (File 5-51)
Enrollment of No1 cancelled by order of Department March 4, 1907
No.1 admitted by Dawes Com: in '96 Case #667
No.1 was admitted by U.S. Court, Central District, Ind. Ter.
So. McAlester I.T. September 8, 1897; Court Case #20 Charles M Randall et al
No appeal to C.C.C.C.

Date of Application for Enrollment.
Sept 14th 1899

16 PO c/o Co. G - US Army
17   Ft. Leavenworth Kan.